THE STANCE OF ATLAS

THE STANCE OF ATLAS:

An Examination of the Philosophy of Ayn Rand

by

PETER F. ERICKSON

HERAKLES PRESS, INC.
PORTLAND, OREGON, U.S.A.

HERACLES PRESS
Portland, Oregon

Printed in the United States of America

Publisher's Cataloging-in-Publication

Erickson, Peter F.
      The stance of Atlas: an examination of the philosophy of Ayn Rand/by Peter F. Erickson.
        p. cm.
      Includes bibliographical references(p.) and index.
      ISBN: 0-9654183-0-8

      1. Rand, Ayn. 2. Objectivism (Philosophy)
      3. Philosophy--History   I. Title

      B945.R234E75 1997   191
                             QB197-570

Typeface 11 pt. Palatino
Cover design by Bruce DeRoos
Book design and layout by DIMI PRESS

To Those Who Love Truth

ACKNOWLEDGMENTS

Eight people receive special mention. The first is my mother. The second is my late father, Arthur M. Erickson, who died in 1960. The third is the late Willmoore Kendall, Associate Professor of Political Science at Yale University. I met him while he was Visiting Professor in Political Theory at Stanford University. Since I was among a small group of students who published a debate on Christian pacifism in which he had participated, he mentioned my name and even included it in the index for his: **The Conservative Affirmation**. His name is placed here, not only because of that, but because he made me conscious of how crucial the struggle against Marxism and its allies was and still is for the preservation of the West. The fourth is the late Leo Strauss, Professor of Political Science at University of Chicago, under whom I had once studied as a graduate student. He pointed out both the absurdity of the fact-value distinction as ordinarily conceived, exposed the pretensions of behavioristic political science, pointed out that everything should be considered first on its own level before it is encompassed into some "unifying" hypothesis, and proved that much could still be learned from books which antedated the industrial revolution. The fifth is the late Ayn Rand, who affirmed more frankly than any other prominent intellectual in this century that philosophical truth is not only conceivable but also obtainable; she also presented the first complete defense of human liberty which I have ever witnessed. I think she was the century's greatest novelist. We never met. The sixth is Dean Turner, Professor Emeritus of Philosophy at the University of Northern Colorado. It was he and his co-author, the scientist and engineer, Richard Hazelett, who showed me the fallacious nature of much of what passes for truth in modern physics. He encouraged me when I told him of my work.

The seventh is the late Arthur O. Lovejoy, Professor Emeritus of Philosophy at Johns Hopkins University. He refuted the root of the Randian theory of "context" decades before it was written. The eighth is the late John Cook Wilson, Professor of Logic at Oxford University, who passed away decades before I was born. Notice of my intellectual debt to him will appear in the text.

Next, it is only proper to thank the following publishers and authors for allowing me to quote "with permission" from their works. Such permission is not required under the "fair use" provision of the Federal copyright law, 17USC8107, which allows quotation for critical or scholarly work. However, they are to be thanked for the graciousness which they have extended to me. (Page numbers and year of publication appear in their appropriate position in the endnotes):

*By permission of Crown Publishers, Inc., from **Relativity: The Special and The General Theory** by Albert Einstein, Translated by Robert W. Larson; by permission of Doubleday, a division of Bantam Doubleday Dell Publishing Group inc., from **The Passion Of Ayn Rand**; by permission of W. H. Freeman And Company, from **The Animal Mind** by James L. and Grant Gould; by permission of International Publishers, from **Ludwig Feuerbach and the Outcome of Classical German Philosophy** by Frederick Engels, ed. by C. P. Dutt; by permission of **The Journal Of The Optical Society Of America**, from "Derivation of the Mass-Energy Relation" by Herbert E. Ives; by permission of Charles H. Kerr Company, from **Anti-Dühring: Herr Eugen Dühring's Revolution in Science** by Friedrich Engels; by permission of National Review, from "A Tribute To Barry Goldwater," by William F. Buckley, a L. P. recording; by permission of Open Court Trade & Academic books, from **The Revolt Against Dualism** by Arthur O. Lovejoy; by permission of Oxford University Press, from **An Introduction To Logic** by H. W.B. Joseph; also, from **The Nature Of Truth: An Essay** by Harold Joachim; finally, from **Statement and Inference: With Other Philosophical Papers** by John Cook Wilson; by permission of Pacific Press, from **The***

AUTHOR'S PREFACE

The Stance of Atlas: An Examination Of The Philoso-phy Of Ayn Rand is told in the form of a dialogue, consisting of four characters. This is a departure from the modern prac-tice of the extended essay. It is a return to a more ancient way. The dialogues of Plato are still widely read, although they were composed more than 400 years before the time of Christ. It is reported that Aristotle's dialogues, now lost, were greatly admired. Much of what remains began as dictations to his students. At the beginning of the modern era, Giordano Bruno and Galileo wrote in that mode. It was widely prac-ticed even into the 18th century.

This brings up the question as to why it is being applied in this book on Ayn Rand. In truth, it did not have to be. Not a single point made in **The Stance of Atlas** could not have been made in a work written in the discursive form. In fact, the book was first written that way. It was only months after the second draft had been completed that the decision was made to compose a dialogue instead. With the exception of the tenth chapter (which is completely new), the sequence of themes is similar, any changes being only corrections or improvements.

Why then? There are three reasons. The first is that this book moves beyond mere criticism of Ayn Rand. Her an-swer to the problem of universals, for instance, is not sim-ply refuted, but a new and better one is put in its place, a solution that incorporates some of the points which she her-self had made. Although, as has been admitted above, such points can also be shown in the common form, it is particu-larly striking when presented through the dialogue.

The second reason concerns the form of Ayn Rand's most famous works. She was herself the author of two of the most celebrated philosophical novels in world literature. Novels like hers show ideas (including their conflict) through the action of their characters, exhibiting them more memorably than would a treatise with its categories and subcategories. The dialogue shows the *conflict* of ideas even more directly (including partial acceptance of some point of a refuted teaching) without in any way implying acceptance of a dialectical metaphysics.

Third, employing the form of a dialogue is in a sense a tribute to the author of those great novels, since it too has its *personae*, albeit on a much reduced scale.

Peter F. Erickson
April, 1997

TABLE OF CONTENTS

TITLE PAGE iii

DEDICATION v

ACKNOWLEDGMENTS viii

AUTHOR'S PREFACE xi

TABLE OF CONTENTS xiii

DAY I. TO AMERICA WITH LOVE 1

DAY II. AYN RAND'S PHILOSOPHY OF OBJECTIVISM 7

DAY III. PERCEPTION 25

DAY IV. FORMS OF PERCEPTION vs. *PERCEPTION* 41

DAY V. THE CONCEPTUAL LEVEL OF CONSCIOUSNESS 71

DAY VI. DEFINITIONS AND UNIVERSALS 101

DAY VII. AXIOMS 131

DAY VIII. TIME AND SPACE 173

DAY IX. AYN RAND AND V. I. LENIN 199

DAY X. FACTS AND UNIVERSALS 221

DAY XI. THE RATIONAL BASE OF ETHICS 247

DAY XII. FREE WILL 271

DAY XIII. MONEY 289

DAY XIV. CONCLUSION 307

ENDNOTES 319

BIBLIOGRAPHY...345

INDEX 353

ORDER FORM 363

DAY I

TO AMERICA WITH LOVE

*T**he movement of the sky is very much in evidence. It is Portland, Oregon in February. Three adults in their thirties are inside a restaurant, drinking various non-alcoholic beverages. Outside the wind and the rain are tearing at banners proclaiming an important game for the city's famous basketball team. The three barely know each other. They are Dr. Stanford, a history professor at a nearby college, Miss Doxa, an intense young woman lawyer, and Penelope, a much prettier young woman and also a millionairess through inheritance.*

Stanford: It has been called the "American Century." During this period, more technological achievements have been made by Americans than that of any other country, besides which the achievements of our countrymen in the nineteenth century—such as, the telegraph, the telephone, the electric light, the gyrocompass, and the Pullman passenger railroad carriage—seem almost quaint by comparison. Yet, at American's center, there is a spiritual vacuum. Outside of science and technology, the intellectual Protestantism which gave the country its birth and beginnings has not had much influence since the twenties. In its place has come liberalism and conservatism. The liberals measure their progress by the degree and extent they have changed the institutions set up by the country's founders. The conservatives, who have been in retreat most of the time, have done little more than protest the excesses of their rival. As long ago as 1960, William F. Buckley, Jr. admitted in a speech that the "conservative spirit of America" was "a wasting battery, perhaps...."[1]

Doxa: That is how it is with the old America championed by the conservatives. But there is a solution. It was provided by Ayn Rand. Arriving in America in 1925, she brought with her a love for her new country that was uniquely her own. After living here a while, she espied what you people call, "spiritual emptiness." This, she has filled with a philosophy of unbreached rationality. In 1991, only nine years after her death, a survey of Americans made by the Library of Congress as to which books have had the greatest influence on the respondents' lives, shows that her novel, *Atlas Shrugged*,[2] was exceeded only by the *Bible*.

Penelope: That was a very interesting book, but I liked the *The Fountainhead* more. What sort of life did she lead?

Doxa: A life of intense work. She began in Hollywood as a script writer. In the next decade, she wrote a successful Broadway play which was later made into a movie and published a novel protesting conditions in Soviet Russia. She composed a novelette which was, in a way, a forerunner of Orwell. In 1943 came that book which you liked so much. Out of this was made a successful movie starring Gary Cooper and Patricia O'Neill. But it was with the publication of "*Atlas*" in 1957 that her fame started growing by leaps and bounds. Although most of the book reviews were hostile, it sold to an ever greater audience through word of mouth.

Stanford: Yes, I know. It combined intense intellectuality with a romantic idealism, all set in a plot of high adventure—in a word, it had "splendour."

Doxa: So you have read it.

Stanford: Yes. But please go on.

Doxa: By the mid sixties, Ayn Rand was easily one of the most famous women in America. In 1964 came the best selling collection of essays, *The Virtue Of Selfishness*. There, she took on the hoary equation of self-interest with harm to others, affirming that a "'selfless,' 'disinterested' love is a contradiction in terms: it means that one is indifferent to that which one values."[3]

Then, throughout 1966 and 1967 came her philosophical masterpiece, *Introduction To the Objectivist Epistemology*, the most widely read work of philosophy written during the second half of the century. The dominant American philosophies, pragmatism and behaviorism, were served notice.

Penelope: Did she write any more novels?

Doxa: No, her last novel was unfinished. But she did write articles for her publications; several were put in book form. The most famous is *Capitalism: the Unknown Ideal*, which included a piece by the then unknown, Alan Greenspan, now Chairman of the Federal Reserve Board.

Ayn Rand died in 1982. Of the famous American intellectuals who reached international fame in the sixties, only she still has a following.

Stanford: There is also still a great interest in Buckminster Fuller. But tell us, why this fame?

Doxa: *Back in the late 1950's, when most of America's conservatives were arguing that the welfare state and foreign aid were noble but impractical ideals, she was emphatically stating that such programs were not only potentially ruinous but also immoral.* Yet, since she was also emphatically against racism, she could not be so easily dismissed.

At a time when standard fiction was drawing industrialists as villains, she depicted them as heroes. In her biggest novel, the creators of wealth, the capitalists, were dishonored by the very society which they had made great. Then these creators, led by the greatest of all, John Galt, the inventor of a motor capable of transforming static into moving or dynamic electricity, withdraws his power from the earth and persuades the other creators to join him in a great strike. As a result, the ungrateful collectivists and the masses who followed them are reduced to impotent poverty. Then the heroes return to reclaim and redeem the dishonored earth.

Penelope: This reminds me of the Bible where God withdraws his favor to the children of Jacob for their sins, allowing first Assyria and then Babylon to reduce them and take them into captivity.

Doxa: Her theme was more original than that!
She expressed herself clearly and with almost never failing eloquence, while her competitors either simply emoted or wrote in virtually untranslatable academese. Whereas establishment literati proclaimed vulgar street-talk to be emblematic of a special kind of wisdom, she insisted on identifying her premises and defining her terms.
Her main competition in the field of ideas were the philosophers hired by Academia. Most of them denied that the mind could know reality. In America, the great majority of these professors could be classified as belonging to one or more of the following schools of thought: The oldest one, pragmatism, taught that men could never know whether or not an idea was true, only whether it was consistent with the evidence. The second one, known under various names, but commonly dubbed, "positivism," or "behaviorism," taught that men could know only the facts disclosed by the scientific method....

Stanford: ...at least, provisionally....

Doxa: ...but never would be able to prove that any set of values were better than any other in any absolute sense. The third, existentialism, was more literate than the first two, but denied that either facts or values could be objective. Then there was a fourth school which affirmed that science was objective and that men could learn how to act. Its name was *Marxism.*

College students who expected more of reason were profoundly disappointed. "Is that all there is?" they asked. "Is there no place for values, for heroes?" Along came Ayn Rand who promised moral absolutes, a new ethics based on reason, and a theory of knowledge which would carry humanity toward a new Atlantis.

Stanford: But with those promises, she introduced atheism into the American right. Atheism is more common on the Left.

Penelope: Yes, I know how that is. Disbelieving the *Bible*, their faith weakened by the loud chorus of professional scientists proclaiming some form of the theory of evolution, their bodies packed with hormones designed to carry them through a lifetime, yielding to fleeting flights of imagination....

Stanford: But they were conscious that some moral code is necessary, that it cannot be simply a question of one choice of life being as arbitrary as the other, or that the rules of a civilized people are no better than those of a cannibalistic society; surely, they reasoned, there must be some standards discoverable to reason which can be communicated to one's fellows—standards which can bring peace to a situation which threatens to be resolved only by anarchy or despotism. A. R.'s words carry hope. We will not have to face old age and its problems for a long time. In the meantime, maybe modern science will be able to extend human life greatly. Continue, please....

Doxa: *Many of us women admire her because she has triumphed in the field of ideas, an arena in which men are usually the winners.* Yet, she never expressed any of the envy which has become so much a part of Women's Lib.

Although she had never made the explicit claim, I see in her philosophy a way in which capitalism and freedom can be reconciled with Einstein's revolution in physics.

Today, the passion is more subdued than it was. But her books still sell very well.

Stanford: Notwithstanding the undeniable influence of her books, there has been no great cultural Renaissance. *Atlas Shrugged* was published by a major house almost forty years ago. Where are the beautiful music, the sonorous sculpture, the magnificent plays inspired by that genius? I know of no discoveries made in the natural sciences using her epistemology. John Galt was depicted as the greatest inventor of all time. A. R.'s biographer, Barbara Brandon, lists several pages of distinguished people who claim to have been influenced to one degree or another by her.[4] But there is no evidence in their success of something missing in others who have also gone as far in life.

Doxa: Miss Rand's ideas have encountered such tremendous opposition. They are against the traditions of the last two thousand years.

Stanford: I see what you mean. This might be like the American standard of living, which has been in decline since 1973 or 1974, depending on whose figures are being used. Yet, beginning in the late 1970's there came the personal computer and the many improvements which it engendered. In times past, such startling advances have produced enormous wealth. This time, however, the revolution in technology has so far proved unable to stop the decline of U.S. living standards.

Doxa: Ayn Rand's philosophy can save the West. In fact, I think it will. Let us meet again, and I will show how this can be done.

The Others: All right.

DAY II

AYN RAND'S PHILOSOPHY OF OBJECTIVISM

*T*he scene is as before. The three acquaintances are once again at the same table at the same restaurant. Outside, the wind is blowing. The rivers have reached flood stage, but the mayor has announced that sandbags will be able to contain the water. Each of the three has done some homework. In front of **Miss Doxa** is a notepad and some opened books. In front of **Dr. Nolan Stanford** and **Penelope,** also, are some sheets of paper with writing on them.

Doxa: Many, when they hear of Ayn Rand, are reminded of Frederick Nietzsche. Like Nietzsche, she criticized altruism. The late 19th century German philosopher blamed Christianity for the weakness that he saw in European culture.

Penelope: Quite true. And, hardly any automobiles existed while Nietzsche was living—electrification was only beginning, and the aviators were balloonists and glider pilots—yet, few would think today that the post-Christian Europe is stronger than the one he knew. At the present time, the culture of the Western part of Europe seems to be a copy of the America set against monuments of the dead past.

Doxa: Intellectually careless people sometimes refer to Ayn Rand as a warmed-over Nietzsche. But this is false. Nietzsche taught that millions should be sacrificed for the superman. She, on the other hand, says that "the *rational* interests of men do not clash—that there is no conflict of interests among men who do not desire the unearned, who do not make sacrifices nor accept them, who deal with one another as *traders*, giving value for value."[1]

Let us begin by considering some of the things which Ayn Rand has to say about value.

She defines "Value" as "that which one acts to gain and/ or keep."[2]

In terms of this definition, all living creatures have values; it is not necessary that an organism be conscious; an oak tree must have air and water to survive; these things (plus the materials of the soil) are values to the plant, even though it does not, as far as we know, have the slightest kind of a nervous system. All that is required to be a value is that it be sought for or give satisfaction.

This is a departure from the common understanding, which presumes that there be an evaluator and that this evaluator be conscious. In place of that, she puts the beneficiary; the plant benefits from water, sunlight, and minerals in the soil. If the roots grow without desire and the leaves spread open, destitute of any germ of awareness, the actions involved are still value oriented. A being without consciousness can still have values, can still act to keep or take something. The proper questions are: of value to whom? *and* for what purpose?[3]

Rand is well known for her opposition to sacrifice. By that, she means "the surrender of a greater value for the sake of a lesser one or of a nonvalue."[4] Trade is clearly not a sacrifice, since, presumably what one acquires is thought to be worth more to oneself than what is being exchanged for it. Giving away money need not be a sacrifice, providing that the object of largess is worth more to the giver than is the gift; going broke in order to pay the medical bills of a beloved child would not be a sacrifice; destroying one's savings in order to pay for the rent of a bum whom one would not care to have as a guest in one's house would certainly be sacrificial.

Penelope: Standing by itself, however, this definition is insufficient. If all that was required to avoid being sacrificial is that the value given up be more important to one than what it was being used for, then practically nobody does anything sacrificial. The widow in the New Testament who gave her last mite to the temple would not have been making a sacrifice, for she hoped for a greater reward. Then there is the woman who recently proposed before an audience of the rich and famous in San Francisco that the world's population be shorted by twenty five percent; it might be argued that in terms of Rand's definition, she would not be sacrificing anybody, for she valued her intended victims less than she did a reduced population.

Doxa: Obviously, the term "value" means something more to Ayn Rand than simply what anyone would want to get or keep. The values would have to be rational. She would not regard the religious woman as rational; the second, she would have regarded as a potential tyrant as well. She holds that all definition is contextual and it is only within this context that it has full meaning. (Later on we shall study exactly what that means.)

Ayn Rand's meaning becomes clear from her solution to the famed fact-value distinction, which has had widespread acceptance in the twentieth century; this is the idea that neither facts nor values could be derived from each other. This fact-value distinction is frequently associated with ethical relativism; and for good reason: if there were no basis in reality for preferring one set of values over another, then cannibalism would be as acceptable as civilization; no reason would exist for choosing a life of reason over any other. Each would depend upon a groundless choice which was not rationally verifiable.

Ayn Rand's solution is to hold that the concept of "value" depends upon that of "life." An inanimate object like a cut diamond has no values of it own, regardless of how beautiful it might appear to us. The rock does not need to undertake any action to keep itself in existence. It just exists. Yet, even an amoeba has to generate action in order to sustain itself. As she puts it, "Metaphysically, *life* is the only phenomenon that is an end in itself: a value gained and kept by a constant process of action. Epistemologically, the concept of 'value' is genetically dependent upon and derived from the antecedent concept of 'life.' To speak of 'value' as apart from 'life' is worse than a contradiction in terms."[5]

Other authors have come close to offering this as the solution to the fact-value distinction, but Ayn Rand is the first to announce it emphatically and without qualification.

The concept "value," she contends, "presupposes an entity capable of acting to achieve a goal in the face of an alternative. Where no alternative exists, no goals and no values are possible."[6] And the principal alternative, the one in terms of which all the others coalesce, is that between existence and non-existence. Mortality underlies all values. For Ayn Rand, the clash between life and death sets the context for all evaluation; since all values point to life as the base, any code of values must hold life as the *summum bonum*, the highest good.

Stanford: She did not mean simply the health and pleasure of the physical body, did she?

Doxa: "Human life" does not mean mere biological existence, on top of which the other values are added like ornaments on a Christmas tree. If these other values are rational, they are supposed to be as fully integrated into this life as the brain and nervous system are to the physical body. To cut off a rational concept would be as much as dismemberment as the loss of some body part. There is to be no breach in rationality, whatsoever. In a fully rational person, the whole man is alive.

Neither does Ayn Rand hold human life to be the basis in the sense merely of the physical body plus the rudiments of reason. That is the case with a baby, almost a pure potentiality. The baby's life is an end unto itself; and so is the fully developed potentiality of a John Galt or a Howard Roark to themselves, individually.

"*Value* is that which one acts to gain and/or keep—*virtue* is the act by which one gains and/or keeps it. The three cardinal values of the Objectivist ethics—the three values which, together, are the means to and the realization of one's ultimate value, one's own life—are: Reason, Purpose, Self-esteem, with their three corresponding virtues: Rationality, Productiveness, Pride."[7]

Stanford: But, if life were the basis on which value is to be determined, then John Galt, the main hero in *Atlas Shrugged*, had contradicted himself when he said that he would commit suicide if his heroine, Dagny Taggart, were to be destroyed by his enemies. If life were the basis and he were still alive, then he should go on, anyway like a man who had lost his house, taking the loss in his stride.

Doxa: You are wrong! John Galt perfected the three virtues, Rationality, Productiveness, and Pride. And this particular catastrophe—the loss of his greatest value, a value greater to him than his invention, greater than his plan to save the world— would be of such magnitude that the writer who created this figure concluded that Galt could not continue as he was. Knowing this, Galt would have ended his life while he still had it. Dagny Taggart, for her part, even before she had met him, while he was nearby, although she did not know his identity, thought of a "man who existed only in her knowledge of her capacity for an emotion she had never felt, but would have given her life to experience."[8] By human life, Rand does not mean mere biological maintenance, but the full potentiality of human development. In the case of John Galt, it would be the life of this fully realized man that would be at stake, not simply someone who can still eat, but is in a constant state of mourning for his highest.

Stanford: Well, of course, we must be alive to have values, but that does not mean that values as such all derived from the idea of *life*.

Doxa: Objectivism does not hold that life is necessary as a condition for having values. What it teaches is that all values rest ultimately on survival—in the case of man, on the decision to survive.

Stanford: The notion that all values are rooted in the preference of existence over non-existence has some plausibility; one could argue that even the ideal of pursuing truth for its own sake is rooted in the notion that knowing the real state of affairs is good for survival. But let us consider her own case.

Doxa: Ayn Rand offers as evidence for her thesis the supposition of "an immortal, indestructible robot, an entity which moves and acts, but which cannot be affected by anything, which cannot be changed in any respect, which cannot be damaged, injured or destroyed. Such an entity would not be able to have any values; it would have nothing to gain or to lose; it could not regard anything as *for* or *against* it, as serving or threatening its welfare, as fulfilling or frustrating its interests."[9]

Penelope: I noticed that Rand did not say whether the robot is alive or not. If it is not, then the example is beside the point; values can only be for a being which acts to get them; an automobile without fuel cannot move, but, while it is running, it does not act to obtain more fuel. One may agree that no creature can have values without being alive; but what is needed is to show that all human values originate from human life, or to put it differently, that everything a rational man desires is rooted, ultimately in the desire to live.

If the robot is alive but unconscious, then the matter is moot. One could argue that since it needs no food and would suffer nothing from bad weather or from a fall off of a cliff, it could have no values. But its designer might have put certain unconscious urges in it which would cause it to want to travel and at the same time to prefer to live on higher ground rather than lower. Hence, as it traveled about, it would stay in the hills, crossing valleys very quickly in order to get to the next ridge. These values would be analogous to those of plants and unconscious animals, but not rooted in the need to keep living. (Remember, it was Rand and not I who chose this thought experiment.)

Stanford: Suppose that the creature is conscious! Then, it might still be motivated to go in the direction of pleasure even though it could feel no pain. A. R. herself volunteers the information that some children are born without the ability to feel pain; she states that they die soon because they receive no warning of danger from their body—they might walk into a blazing fireplace.[10] Such being the case with certain humans, we may suppose the indestructible robot can at least feel pleasure. A. R. would be the first to admit that pleasure is not simply the absence of pain, but is a positive thing. Pleasures are what they are felt to be. The creature would move in the direction which brings it pleasure. That would be its value. Why could this robot not have been constructed as a male? Could there not also be a female indestructible robot?

Doxa: Leonard Peikoff, Ayn Rand's intellectual heir, takes up the case of this robot having a conceptual faculty. He asks whether abstract knowledge can be a value to it. Why would it need to have any? It doesn't need knowledge in order to accomplish any of its aims. The robot aims at nothing.[11]

Dr. Peikoff asks whether the robot could place a value on money. What would it need to buy? It doesn't need an airplane ticket or a mansion with servants. Quite simply, it has no use for any of that.[12]

Neither has it any need to value friends. Friends are those with whom one shares values. If one has no values, then one can have no friends.[13]

Penelope: But this begs the question, doesn't it? The answer to Mr. Peikoff's first point is that while this creature you have imagined does not have any goals built upon survival needs, it might still be curious. Neither you nor the people whom you quote have, to my knowledge, shown that curiosity is impossible unless there is some danger to one's life or pleasure at stake. This possibility being open, then the creature can make up its own ends.

As for his second point that the creature would have no use for money: Perhaps the indestructible being —I can no longer say "robot"—was in a hurry to drive to the ocean so that he could walk on the ocean floor across to Europe. The creature wanted to get there in time for the observation of an eclipse of the sun or moon which it could not see as well from the Americas. Or, going back to my previous illustration, perhaps it wanted to see the stars and begin a deep study of rocketry and astronomy.

As for Peikoff's point that this indestructible being could have no friends because there was no one like it to share any values with: Friends do not have to share all the same values or even be equals; the well-known friendship between men and dogs comes to mind. Suppose some little bird who used to flutter around him was torn apart by a wolf. Wouldn't he miss it, inasmuch as this little friend had died before its time? Granted that the creature could not die, why would he have to feel nothing when he saw a human being whom he liked being destroyed in war? Even if he concluded that there were plenty where that came from, one thinks that he would first experience the absence and the desire to fill it.

Rand's thought experiment does not prove her case. It is too easy to give this, perhaps, impossible creature disconfirming attributes.

Stanford: But simply by drawing alternative scenarios for an indestructible robot does not prove A.R. wrong, either.

Penelope: To return to the original question. Are all human values rooted in the fear of fatality? I think not. In life, we find ourselves enjoying things without thought of losing it or of its stopping—simply the enjoyment of it. This is not merely because we have forgotten the base. Do babies smile because they know they will die? If they do, then *tabula rasa*, as understood by the Objectivists, would have to be false. Let us look beyond this. I have no direct knowledge of what they actually feel. I can only sense that they are smiling because they perceive pleasure, and that this pleasure is not rooted in a sense of what the existentialist calls "finitude," but simply in that which they are experiencing. If a little kid never had thought of death—if, for all he knew, he would be live forever—he would still play catch and climb the jungle gym and romp through the fields with the dog. At the minimum, he would feel the pleasures which come from the exercise of his limbs. (I dimly recall being told by my parents that someday I will die—and being somewhat surprised.)

Stanford: Even those values most connected to self-preservation can be separated from their base. The pleasure of food is certainly tied to it; it allows us to want the material which sustains life. But many people, especially children, eat even when they are not hungry, when they sense nothing life-sustaining in it. They eat for pleasure, even when they know that it may make them fat and weak; therefore, less likely to live. Sexual pleasure exists in order to get men to procreate. Yet, this pleasure can easily be separated from this origin. Rand herself radically separated the two. She taught that sex was the highest form of celebration. But if a person was not born with that ability to feel that particular kind of pleasure, would he or she necessarily die? Of course not. They would simply pick another pleasure. Does it follow that the pleasure is sought simply as an escape from death? No. People do it because it is fun, not because they feel mortal.

Doxa: Just because we can separate pleasure from considerations of survival does not mean that to do this would be rational. Dangerous narcotics can make people feel happy for a short period of time. In a fully rational human being, pleasure alone is not the final standard.

Stanford: Inseparability is not proof of identity, either. The fact that life requires values and values require life does not mean that all values are deduced from the fact of *human* life. Being alive is not the same thing as possessing the concept, "life." It is because of reflections about desires, thoughts, and the like that we are able to form this concept. Later on, we may append a theory about values to our concept of life, but that is not our original understanding of it.

Penelope: An alternative hypothesis to Rand's is that man was made by God; that the Creator impressed life on dust and brought it together from without. Some of the values, then, would reflect the One that made us.

Stanford: Obviously, the issue cannot be resolved on the basis of the information here. To answer it and other questions of a similar nature, one would have to make a study of man and particularly of the nature of human knowledge.

Doxa: And with that, the floor returns to me! Ayn Rand did indeed make a profound study of this and related questions. This is the second great difference between Ayn Rand and Friedrich Nietzsche; the latter was a pronounced irrationalist. She, on the other hand, more than any other philosopher of note in the twentieth century, was an advocate of reason.

Ayn Rand wanted to call her philosophy, "existentialism," but that term had already been appropriated by another school of thought. So she took her second choice and called it, "Objectivism."[14]

Objectivism teaches that there are only two kinds of philosophy: those that are based on the primacy of existence and those based on the primacy of consciousness.[15]

Primacy of existence philosophy teaches that reality exists outside of consciousness and that the function of the latter is to be aware of the former, not to create it.

Primacy of consciousness philosophy, by contrast, teaches that external reality—or better, our idea of it—is a construction of the mind. Her prime examples of this school are Plato and Kant. The first held that the existence which we perceive through our senses is only a shadow version of real existence, which consists of pure ideas. The second claimed that we have no knowledge of things-in-themselves, only of the impressions which they produce upon us, and that reason cannot move outside of the phenomena created by this shadow world.

Ayn Rand is the most modern and most advanced of the first school. This primacy of existence school, she holds, was founded by Aristotle. "No matter what remnants of Platonism did exist in Aristotle's system, his incomparable achievement lay in the fact that he defined the *basic* principles of a rational view of existence and of man's consciousness: that there is only *one* reality, the one which man perceives—that it exists as an *objective* absolute (which means: independently of the consciousness, the wishes or the feelings of any perceiver)—that the task of man's consciousness is to *perceive*, not to create, reality—that abstractions are man's method of integrating his sensory material—that man's mind is his only tool of knowledge—that A is A."[16]

Ayn Rand teaches that all knowledge comes initially from the senses; that man is not equipped at birth with any innate ideas to guide him. Every concept from the most rudimentary to the most recondite owes its origin to the senses.

Concepts are made from the material supplied by the senses. She has an original theory on the nature of perception and how concepts are obtained from them. She offers a solution to the problem of universals, the problem which exists when, for instance, we ask: How can the manness of man be explained if all that exists are individual men who differ in every thing from age, height, color of eyes, skin, etc., and are divided by sex? She also provides answers for other questions of great interest to thoughtful people. She examines the relationship between concepts and mathematics. In her account of the nature of definition, she saw how the specific contents of a concept can change with the growing fund of knowledge, how even its essence can be altered and yet the concept as a whole remains the same. At our next meeting, her philosophy will be discussed in detail.

All concepts come ultimately from experience, she says, but there are some which are so basic that they cannot be denied without contradiction. These are the axiomatic concepts. The three primary ones are "existence," "identity," and "consciousness." If someone tried to deny any of these, he would be using them in the very act of denial—in effect, digging at the intellectual ground on which he was standing. For instance, a person who tried to deny that there was such a thing as consciousness would have to try to convince the mind of the person with whom he was arguing that he was not conscious, a contradiction. A person who attacked the law of identity, namely that A is A, would have to use logic in the act of attempting to defeat it. A person who denied that existence exists would have to show that existence did not exist.

Ayn Rand's eloquent summary of her position on axioms: "Existence exists—and the act of grasping that statement implies two corollary axioms: that something exists which one perceives and that one exists possessing consciousness, consciousness being the faculty of perceiving that which exists."[17] Her philosophy has great subtlety, and those who try to refute it must be careful that they understand it. An example from a recent critic should suffice to make this plain: One of Ayn Rand's doctrine's was that the meaning of a word is to be determined by its referents—for example, that the meaning of the concept "red" is all the instances in which that color appears, past, present, and future. Berkeley Professor Wallace Matson answered: "This can be only a partial account of meaning. For if the meaning of concept C is all its units, i.e., all the particulars subsumed, then if there are no such particulars, the concept must be without meaning. So *ghost, witch, dodo, centaur,* and so on are meaningless."[18]

Actually, Objectivism has little problem with any of them. An Objectivist could define a "dodo" as an extinct bird with certain characteristics which lived on the island of Mauritius; since the Objectivist concepts refer to all the instances that ever were or ever will be, as well as those of the present time, a bird that no longer exists would be included. Likewise, the Objectivist could define a witch as a mythological woman who was supposed to have magical powers which were usually reserved for sinister purposes. To the Objectivist, the witches referred to by Matson would be such as The Wicked Witch Of The West in *Wizard Of Oz,* the three witches in Shakespeare's play, *Macbeth,* and the evil Queen who in the form of an ugly old woman gave the poisoned apple to Snow White.

Ayn Rand lays great interest on the distinction between metaphysics and epistemology. Metaphysics is concerned with the ultimate nature of reality; epistemology with how men come to know. Except for basic questions where the two fields cross, as in the distinction between external reality and consciousness or the nature of reason, Objectivism prefers to defer metaphysical concerns to the special sciences. There is, for instance, no Objectivist theory on the atom or even an Objectivist definition of matter.

One of the most famous quarrels in metaphysics consists of the conflict between the materialists and idealists. The first taught that everything, including mind, was derived from matter. The latter, of which Hegel is the most famous modern example, taught that nature derives from concepts. The Objectivists, although they disagree emphatically with the idealists, do not embrace the position of the materialists. They say that it is dogmatic to assert that everything is derived from one sort of existence. The issue, they aver, can only be settled by the natural sciences, not by armchair thinkers.

Materialists are *monists* in that they hold that all the complex phenomena of the world, including the highest concepts of the most brilliant men, are ultimately derived from matter. So are idealists, except they hold that matter is a product of mind. The Objectivists, however, are not dualists, either. As Leonard Peikoff, her intellectual heir puts it: "A philosophy that rejects the monism of idealism or materialism does not thereby become 'dualist.' This term is associated with a Platonic or Cartesian metaphysics; it suggests the belief in two realities, in the mind-body opposition, and in the soul's independence of the body—all of which Ayn Rand denies."[19]

Penelope: I think that Objectivism, although it may not wish to make a stand, is, in fact, monist. Between dualism and monism, there cannot be any middle ground for a comprehensive school of philosophy. There is either one basic principle in existence or more than one; there can't be a fraction of one. The law of the excluded middle, A or non-A, forbids any other conclusion. Objectivism may claim a certain empirical modesty by deferring it to the natural sciences, but when this philosophy is examined in depth, it is monistic materialism in all but name.

Doxa: Objectivism takes no position on the ultimate constitution of matter; instead, it holds that all such questions must be answered not by some philosophical Guru, pontificating on what the scientists are going to find, but on the actual discoveries of those whose business it is to uncover the nature of reality.

Ayn Rand thinks that science can someday answer these questions, but until it does, philosophy must not try to dictate a conclusion.

Stanford: Final knowledge is possible? How could that be, given our own smallness and the infinite ocean of facts which lies beyond us?

Doxa: There is no need to feel "a stranger and afraid." Ayn Rand has shown that there is no actual infinity; that it is only a matter of potential. Stated briefly, her position is the following: taking numbers as an example, starting with "1", you can count as high as you wish. But any number you come to, however great—even a "google," which means "1" with a hundred zeros after it—is finite. Regardless of how immense the number of atoms or whatever the smallest unit of matter or energy may be, that number is finite. Like Einstein, she believed that the universe is finite but unbounded. And like that physicist, she also denied the intrinsic existence of space and time. This and much more will be discussed in its place.

Penelope: Rand asserted that the one philosopher from whom she took her bearings was Aristotle. But this does not appear to be true. Mention has already been made of Nietzsche. His critique of altruism was world famous even before she was born. Less well known is that the same emphasis on the objectivity of external reality, in words very similar to hers, were made by the Marxist-Leninists. In the words of Vladimir Lenin: "Once you deny objective reality, given to us in sensation, you have already lost every one of your weapons against fideism, for you have slipped into agnosticism or subjectivism—and that is all fideism wants. If the perceptual world is objective reality, then the door is closed to every other 'reality' or quasi-reality...."[20]

The Marxist-Leninists are materialists, but of a special type. Gustave Wetter, in his study of Dialectical Materialism, the official philosophy of the former Soviet Union, has shown that the dialectical materialists sometimes define "matter" as that which is disclosed by the senses—a purely materialistic conception. On the other hand, they sometimes use a realistic conception, namely, that matter is all that exists, including thought, feeling, and the rest that is within the domain of consciousness.[21] Their realistic formulation of matter is very similar to what Rand calls "existence."

Doxa: One must not allow superficial similarities to obscure real differences. Ayn Rand distinguishes between matter and thought; but unlike the dialectical-materialists, she does not dogmatically make mind a variety of matter. Consciousness, for her, is simply the faculty that perceives existence. It is not necessarily reducible to the same thing as that which is perceived as existing outside of it.

Penelope: I still say that there is within Objectivism an unwillingness to declare an unambiguous monism, together with a dislike of dualism.

Stanford: Questions like that can only be answered definitively when the philosophy is in full view.

Penelope: Rand admitted to having been educated under the Soviets; she left that country in the 1920's, when Marxism-Leninism was still in its enthusiastic stage. In college, she undoubtedly came across the words of Lenin and Marx and Engels. Here is something which Engels wrote: "Those who asserted the primacy of spirit to nature and, therefore, in the last instance, assumed world creation in some form or other ... comprised the camp of idealism. The others, who regarded Nature as primary, belong to the various schools of materialism."[22] In these words are adumbrated the distinction between the primacy of existence and the primacy of consciousness.

Doxa: A parallelism or two does not mean that she got this distinction from Engels or from one of his followers. The difference between the two primacies is fundamental to philosophy, and that the mere fact that she agreed with the

Marxist on this one issue merely indicates a common dislike of idealism.

Ayn Rand was a great anti-Communist. During the late 1940's, when the patriots were trying to kick the Marxist-Leninists and their ilk out of the U.S. Government and expose their hidden role in American culture, she testified before the House Committee Of Un-American Activities in favor of the congressional investigations that were going on.[23]

Despite some superficial similarities, Ayn Rand's disagreement with Marx and his successors could not have been greater. She held off the rush to the Left. Having some points like atheism and the rejection of Christian ethics in common has made this easier.

Her differences with them remain immense. She chose pure capitalism; she denies that the state had any right to determine what men should believe. While they are determinists who hold that man's actions resulted from the state of the universe, she holds that man possesses volition. The Marxist-Leninists assert that matter is internally contradictory; she denies that any contradictions could ever exist in reality. While they believe that the universe is infinite, she holds it to be finite.

Rand's metaphysics and epistemology provide intelligibility for her more famous advocacy of selfishness. They are the ultimate premises for her magnificent novels. Like her fiction, they are a work of genius. Studying them will enable us to learn not only about the thoughts of one of the century's most influential thinkers, but of the greatest. It will show us what must still be done to bring about the triumph of man's rights.

Stanford: In our next discussion, I propose that we begin with a study of A.R.'s theory of knowledge, since it is out of small bits that the great cathedrals of knowledge are built.

Doxa: You are right. We shall begin next time with a discussion of sensations and percepts as fundamental to the development of concepts.

Penelope: I would like to bring a friend who is quite versatile in philosophy.

Stanford: That might be fair! I incline toward Objectivism. You appear to disagree with much of it. The four of us might result in a balanced discussion.

Doxa: Is this person obstreperous?

Penelope: Mr. Philosophus is very polite.

Doxa: Is he an advocate of Analytical philosophy, Existentialism, or some other modern form of irrationality?

Penelope: No.

Doxa: Very well! He is accepted provisionally. But it is to be understood that it is to be a discussion of Objectivism only and not a debate with some rival upstart or will o' the wisp.

Penelope: I understand.

Stanford: So be it!

DAY III

PERCEPTION

*T*he scene is once more at the same restaurant. Present *are* **Miss Doxa, Dr. Stanford,** and **Penelope,** *as before. Also present is a certain* **Mr. Philosophus,** *a distinguished looking gentleman of indeterminate age. Introductions have already been made. Outside, there is heavy rain. The river is starting to go down from its crest. There has been some flooding, but not as much as was expected in the down town area.*

Doxa: Ayn Rand is the most intellectual of novelists, the most novel of 20th century intellectuals. Objectivism is like a cloud through which one can see that there is a sun; in contrast to it, most of the philosophy written in this century is pitch darkness, relieved only occasionally by flashes of intelligence.

According to Ayn Rand, consciousness is in its beginning a *tabula rasa*, a blank slate; all the content of thought, however recondite in its final stages, begins with the senses.[1] This is the initial awareness produced by the action of an external object, such as light rays on the eye, a change in air pressure on the ear, or the contact of the swaying branch of a tree on one's bare arm. This state of awareness cannot be reduced to any form of consciousness that is simpler.[2]

But sensations, although they are the first stage in awareness, are not "the base of all of man's knowledge."[3] She doubts that men can remember them or experience a single sensation in isolation.[4] Even a slight contact with a tree branch as one is passing by must be experienced through the nervous system.

The true basis of consciousness, Ayn Rand affirms, is the *percept*. This, she defines as "a group of sensations automatically retained and integrated by the brain of a living organism. It is in the form of percepts that man grasps the evidence of his senses and apprehends reality. When we speak of 'direct perception' or 'direct awareness,' we mean the perceptual level."[5] They are the given, the basis of cognition. It is only much later, after one has learned to speculate about these things, that one can realize that percepts originated from sensations.

Sensations point to percepts. And it is through these percepts that the world is experienced in terms of entities, of earth, sky and sea, instead of patches of color, noise, unintelligible pleasures or pain, and the like. Percepts are the self-evident basis. When one has a percept of a tree standing alone on a meadow, the only evidence there is for the existence of that tree is that one has perceived it. Satellite pictures would provide no better proof, for, in the long run, verification of the photo would depend on the human eye. Laboratory samples of bark from the tree would provide no greater grasp of reality; they too would depend on the human perceptive system for their verification. One cannot manufacture a real tree out of supposition.

Concepts are formed out of percepts. It through the hierarchical development of concepts that the great towers of the intellect take their rise. Just as percepts integrate sensations into entities and their actions, so concepts immensely extend the scope of human intelligence. Ayn Rand says that "without abstract ideas you would not be able to deal with concrete particular, real-life problems. You would be in the position of a new-born infant, to whom every object is a unique, unprecedented phenomenon. The difference between his mental state and yours lies in the number of conceptual integrations your mind has performed."[6]

This is a brief summary of her position on this question. Perceptions are the cognitive basis of all consciousness, although they are preceded in time by sensations. Percepts enable us to see entities and their actions. But if that was the only level to which our consciousness had reached, we would have to treat each and every object as a new thing: we would be able to perceive a tree as that object rising from the ground with the thick brown base and the green leaves and the fruits (if it had any), but not that it was a tree of a general type.

Penelope: The distinction between percepts and sensations is not unique with Rand; neither is the insistence of the great difference between the realm of percepts and that of concepts.

Doxa: True, but what is typically Randian about it is the insistence that percepts are self evident. Her handling of the conceptual stage is unique.

The most fundamental concept, she affirms, is "existence." An existent is anything that exists, whether it be an object, an action of that object, or one of its attributes.

The concept of "existent" goes through three stages: the first stage is only implicit. The child is aware that there are existents, although he is too young to form that word or its synonyms. At this stage, the child is aware of "entities." The second and closely related stage is when he is able to distinguish certain things that stand out in his consciousness from the background of his awareness; this stage, Ayn Rand calls "identity." The third and final stage is when the child is able to grasp the similarities among two or more existents and separate them mentally from their background—which means that the child is able to transform the implicit concept "entity" into "units."[7]

The concept "unit" refers to man's ability to regard two or more existents which are similar in some respect as a part of a group.[8] For instance, the child might see how certain shades of color which he will someday characterize as "pink," "carmine," and "ruby" belong together in contradistinction to what he will later call "blue" and "yellow." The first three resemble each other in a way that the latter two do not.

Ayn Rand is emphatic: "This is the key, the entrance to the conceptual level of man's consciousness. *The ability to regard entities as units is man's distinctive method of cognition,* which other living species are unable to follow."[9]

Stanford: Suppose that A.R. is right in concluding that the ability to form units is distinctive to man and this is the key to the nature of rational thought: then it must follow that animals cannot reason because they cannot form mental units.

Doxa: That is correct. Leonard Peikoff adds that the higher animals have reached the first two stages of recognizing entities and identities, although "animals have no concepts, not even implicit ones. But the higher animals can perceive entities and can learn to recognize particular objects among them. It is this third stage that constitutes the great cognitive gap."[10]

Penelope: But does this three-fold system of classification rightly divide the difference between human reason and animal cognition? Many of the higher animals are in fact aware of kinds. They do note similarities and differences among the things with which they deal. They don't just smell some type of food once and then have to start the process of learning how to deal with that type all over again when they encounter it again. They don't just perceive a tree and then forget about it; the next time they find one they act on what they had learned about the first one. An animal fleeing from a predator has to know more than simply to identify entities, plus some similarities. It has to do more than merely identify rocks as a group; it has to connect them—if it runs into a bunch of them, it must be smart enough to go around. It has to understand that the rock it is hiding behind is opaque and the pursuer cannot see through it; that it must make no sound that its enemy might hear.

Doxa: Ayn Rand considers a study that was made to determine whether birds could understand numbers. When one man entered a clearing in the woods, the crows did not come out. When three men entered the clearing and only two came out, the birds were not fooled. But when five men came into the clearing and only four returned, the crows left their place of hiding. From this, she concluded that the crows were able to handle only three units; any more than that would confuse them. "Whether this particular experiment is accurate or not, the truth of the principle it illustrates can be ascertained *introspectively*: if we omit all conceptual knowledge, including the ability to count in terms of numbers, and attempt to see how many units (or existents of a given kind) we can discriminate, remember and deal with by purely perceptual means (e.g., visually or auditorially, but *without counting*) we will discover that the range of man's *perceptual* ability may be greater, but not much greater, than that of the crow: we may grasp and hold five or six units at most."[11]

Penelope: The fact that crows could discriminate as many as three units shows that they have some conceptual ability; and if the ability to consider existents as members of a group is man's distinctive ability, then crows should be classified as men with limited abilities.[12]

This is clearly the kind of problem that Objectivism gets into when it tries to account for the radical difference between man and animals in terms of units. Over the last thirty five or so years, since he first began studying Objectivism, Dr. Peikoff has, probably, heard this objection at least once. Yet, in his 1991 book, he says that in the absence of the implicit concept of 'unit', one would be unable to count or measure quantitative relationships: "Without the implicit concept of 'unit,' man could not....count, measure, identify quantitative relationships; he could not enter the field of mathematics."[13] But, as Rand herself conceded, some animals do have the ability to count, albeit in a limited manner. Also, Peikoff even admits that an animal perceives objects as a whole and can note some similarities and differences and may even be capable of a primitive focus on occasion.[14]

"But it cannot isolate or unite any group of concretes accordingly: it cannot *do* anything cognitively with the relationships it perceives. To its consciousness, the noting of similarities is a dead end. Man *can* do something: he makes such data the basis of a method of cognitive organization. The first step of the method is the mental isolation of similars."[15]

Peikoff is clearly wrong. It is true that the higher animals do not say words; but they do answer to them, sometimes. Furthermore, many of them seem to discern more than similarities. They do not, for instance, treat all humans alike; some, they are friendly with; some not. Furthermore, they know how to play with people. Most dog owners, for instance, have known their dog to allow them to put their hand in its mouth while the dog *pretended* to bite, but, of course, does not. This takes more than a perception of similarities.

Philosophus: Some further indication of Objectivism's inability to account for the higher animals may be found in Rand's criticism of the philosopher David Hume who had taught that he could discern sensations in the form of men and other moving beings, but that he could not perceive anything called *causality* in the midst of all this change; that there was no real connection between phenomena disclosed in consciousness, only patterns and customary associations—that the most permanent things in nature only seemed such because we have not to date perceived an exception. About Hume she wrote: "If it were possible for an animal to describe the content of his consciousness, the result would be a transcript of Hume's philosophy. Hume's conclusions would be the conclusions of a consciousness limited to the perceptual level of awareness, passively reacting to the experience of immediate concretes, with no capacity to form abstractions, to *integrate* perceptions into concepts, waiting in vain for the appearance of an object labeled 'causality' (except that

such a consciousness would not be able to draw conclusions)."[16] Actually, many animals have higher states of mind
than would a human being who had religiously tried to live
Hume's philosophy. Dogs and cats, for instance, are aware
of causality in practice, although they do not have any awareness of it as an abstract principle. The practical Humean,
however, would eventually stumble at tying his own shoes.
He might even choke to death on his own food; since breathing, he would have regarded as a mere habit.

Those who distrust the common sense of the work-a-day
world should consider the behavior of beavers, as reported
by scientists James L. Gould and Grant Gould in their book,
The Animal Mind. When these animals take upon themselves
to build a dam on a stream or lake, they usually look for a
log with which to begin their constructions; that, of course,
is consistent with the notion that they cannot really change
the nature of their surroundings. But observe! On page 129,
we can read that "in the absence of a starting log, beavers
take advantage of existing boulders or trees on the bank to
use as foundations. In these cases, however, they usually have
to cut long branches to act as downstream braces or the ver-
tical branches driven into the stream bottom. The scale on
which beavers can operate is remarkable: some logs are over
100 m long, and the record is 700 meters."[17]

Is this simply a matter of inborn instinct, responding to
signals? If that is the case, how then are they able to recognize that braces are needed, unless they are able to form the
idea of a substitute and then find one?

Animals seem to be able to reason without words. Something is amiss in the Objectivist position on this point. Peikoff
says this of a man who knew no words: "Every time the man
would want to use his concept, he would have to start afresh,
recalling or projecting relevant similars and performing over
again the process of abstraction."[18] Referring to the case of a
child too young to speak, Rand argues that his implicit concepts become solid when the child discovers that a *"perceptual* symbol"—words being audio or visual percepts—can

be made to represent a vast number of concretes which he is trying to comprehend.[19]

Stanford: A.R. seemed to be on surer ground when she expressed agreement with whomever had said that an animal may be able to perceive two potatoes or two oranges, but is incapable of comprehending the concept "two."[20]

Philosophus: It is true that animals cannot grasp hold of the abstract ideas themselves and work with them as human beings do, through words. Man's distinction from the brutes is not rooted in the nature of the Randian *unit*.

This back-and-forth recognizing and not recognizing of some abstracting powers by animals is indicative of a scratching in the dark, a scramble to hold on to a height.

Stanford: But we should not conclude from this that her theory of the centrality of the unit is false. It may be that all that is wrong is that Objectivism's account of the animal mind is in need of some revision.

Doxa: Good.

Philosophus: Men are born with the ability to form words, although it is not likely that they are given an innate language. Before a child will be able to speak, he must first be able to understand the need to use a sound-percept as a mark for a meaning. That is remarkable; yet, everyone in this restaurant appears to have done it. Rand herself goes so far as to admit that young infants are not at first able to learn words. "Before they begin to speak, you observe that they are trying to make sounds, inarticulate sounds, as if they were trying to communicate something."[21] Wouldn't this be an implanted ability? This does not have to be an innate idea, fully blown. It could simply be an inborn capacity which, given the right stimulus, will produce the desire to learn words. Clearly, the infant who cannot speak must be forming some abstractions; otherwise, he would lose this desire to communicate almost as soon as he was prompted by it and soon sputter to a stop. But if that were the case, how could he sustain his concentration long enough to go forward and form the Randian concept? There would have to be a time when he must be able to think without words.

(Some, like Sir William Hamilton, the great mathematician, would go farther, holding that the "idea of order, with its subordinate ideas of number and figure," are born within in us in a very rudimentary form, although not possessed by everyone to the same degree.[22] I *disagree* with him as far as the idea of number and figure is concerned. I think that such ideas are apprehended in experience).

Doxa: It may be that science has learned more about animals since her death. But they are different from humans, and whatever limited conceptual powers they may be shown to possess does not change what has already been learned about man's. Ayn Rand has much to say about this, as we shall see.

At this point, let us consider Ayn Rand's teaching that the mind begins *tabula rasa*. According to Objectivism, all knowledge comes from sensations of a world originating outside of consciousness. Whatever is learned through introspection consists only of observations from perception or from concepts formed out of percepts. The content of a concept of consciousness, in other words, of a concept pertaining to the faculty of awareness itself, she asserts, is either an aspect of the world external to the person, or is derived from it and can be measured only by the means appropriate to the external world.[23]

Philosophus: What about memory? This is not extrospection—it is not an immediate cognition of what is presently happening in the outer world. Rand puts it under "introspection," which she describes as "a process of cognition directed inward—a process of apprehending one's own psychological actions in regard to some existent(s) of the external world, such actions as thinking, feeling, reminiscing, etc."[24]

But placing it under a category does not make it solely dependent on sense perception simply because Objectivism defines it that way. What is disclosed as memory is an awareness of the past—yes—of a time which no longer exists. When a man remembers a former action, he is simultaneously aware of two facts: that those events did happen and that they are not happening while he is recollecting them. Even if it is something which he regards that is still happening, like the roll of the waves in the sea, he knows that it is not just exactly those same waves that are now coming together and dissolving. This is especially the case if he is standing on the shore and remembering a former scene. Sometimes, it is not the experience itself that we recall but the fact that we have had it. For instance, a student may not remember the proof of a proposition in geometry, but only recall that he had already proved it. This duality between our apprehension of a fact and the memory that the fact was apprehended is important. If the student only got a re-play of the proof which he had learned without the temporal significance implied by the "re" in re-play, then he would be simply be repeating his actions, like a wheel, without even a hint of *deja vu*.

In the absence of this power, we could not live as thinking beings at all. History would not even be thinkable; the student of mathematics would be unable to follow the second step in a demonstration, even if, *impossible*, he could grasp the first. One could not hear a melody, for to do so, it is necessary to hold certain notes in mind in order to understand the meaning of what follows.[25] One could not even have a normal dream.

Memory is an ultimate power of mind. It cannot be reduced to a set of internal perceptions; there are no tags attached to the data coming from the external world stipulating that it is something present which will soon be converted into a past event. The designation of an event as having taken place in the past is internal and is in no way borrowed from observation of the external world. Something was added to the stored experience, this being cognizance of the fact that it was stored—a recognition that cannot be further reduced to something more primitive without canceling the sense of it. John Stuart Mill was one of the relentlessly empirical philosophers of all time. He attempted to analyze every mental fact into simpler phenomena derived ultimately from sensation and the laws of association. But even he understood that this was impossible to do with respect to memory. He recognized that this ability to retain and recall ideas must be classified as an ultimate power, outside of which no other account can be given. Any contrivance for testing memory's veracity eventually presupposes the very thing to be explained. In other words, that remembrances of states of consciousness past, exist. He knew that the mind has to be more than a series of coexistent and successive sensations, as extreme empiricism would have it. It is aware of the fact that it is a series. Memory should always be distinguished from Imagination. My recollection of having read some lines from *Atlas Shrugged* yesterday is altogether different from the mental gymnastics performed when I put together the following complex ideas: myself—having read from that book—and the day-before today.[26]

This impression that the event was in the past is immediate and does not come from the external world; nowhere in that world has anyone found a percept called "pastness." It is conceptual in nature and is implanted within man. It may be that there must first be a sensory awareness of the external world in order to start its action, just as it may require the turning of the ignition key before a powerful automobile can start, but once the necessary amount of experience has been had, nothing contained in the objects being perceived brought about the idea of the past. Rand and the Objectivists have overlooked an important exception to their teaching.

Yet, it is not accurate to define it as introspection in the manner of Rand, in other words, as merely just another case of apprehending one's own mind in relation to the external world. The mind declares that the event is in the past. And that is not merely an apprehension of a subjective state, but also, by implication, a statement about the external world itself. *That is why it makes sense to inquire whether the memory was accurate or not.* The distinction between extrospection and introspection does not describe the phenomenon.

The fact of recollection immediately makes one conscious of TIME. The comparison of what is disclosed by memory and what one is immediately experiencing in the external world gives the notion of the *present*. With those two in hand, recognition that there is a *future* springs into awareness. This awareness is implicit in the disclosure of the past. Rand herself recognizes the legitimacy of implicit concepts which contain the possibility of conclusions which are yet to be inferred.[27]

The phenomenon of reminiscing is partly independent of sensation from the external world —a fact which Rand failed to appreciate. Her understanding of time was faulty. "'Time,' she said, "as the widest or parent abstraction of all subsequent and narrower measurements of time, is a change of relationship. You observe that certain relationships are changed, and you form the concept of 'time.'"[28] This is wrong. The fact of time is not first recognized by noting just any change in the external world; no comparison of any two states of some external phenomenon could have originated the idea of time without any recourse to the faculty of memory. Time is not a synonym for the relationship that exists when an object changes its position. It is true that time is used in the calculation of velocity; but so is displacement or distance. Then too, change of position is also used in the calculation of time, whether it be the movement of a shadow across a sun dial or the hands of a wrist watch. Her failure to understand the significance of memory is responsible for many of the errors of her system, as will be shown later (if your schedules allow).

Peikoff declared that "...there can be no reliance on *any* mental contents alleged to have a source or validity independent of sense perception. Every step and method of cognition must proceed in accordance with facts—and every fact must be established, directly or indirectly, by observation."[29] This declaration is in serious need of amendment. He fails to see here that observation can be of events which are originated by consciousness itself. In the words of John Stuart Mill: "The difference between Expectation and mere imagination, as well as between Memory and Imagination, consists in the presence or absence of Belief; and though this is no explanation of either phenomenon, it brings us back to one and the same real problem, ... the difference between knowing something as a Reality, and as a mere Thought...."[30]

Note that in addition to Memory, the great empiricist discovered that Imagination and Expectation were also ultimate and not further analyzable. These other two, we will not discuss in this place, although they do figure in the problems of induction and universals.

Cognition of time does not arise exclusively from our experience of the external world. Recognition that something had happened in the past is innate—it is an *innate idea*. But this does not mean that we need to accept the notion of Immanuel Kant that time is simply a subjective form in which the mind organizes its contents—that transcendental reality outside of that disclosed by the senses might, for all we know, be *timeless*. That would be a non-sequitur. The faculty of memory is a necessity for understanding existence. When we remember something—say attending a concert featuring Wagner's *Rienzi*—we *apprehend* the fact that it took place in the past. The concert is no more. We may not even be able to hum the famous opening melody. We know that we have heard it; and when we hear it again, it will seem familiar. The memory is an apprehension of the concert, although not of the same kind as the original experience; this requires an awareness of the past, the primordial apprehension of time. As John Cook Wilson put it: "Time is not seen, felt, heard, or experienced in general, in this sense of experience; it is apprehended along with the apprehension called experience, and as apprehended it is an apprehension of particular time."[31]

Rand disagreed with Kant that space is an innate and pre-given form in which experience is organized. On this point I concur with her, although she took the wrong direction from there. Later on, if there is sufficient interest, I will show that in a way different from Kant, she failed to understand that space is an objective fact, independent of human consciousness.

Yet, consider: Percepts disclose the existence of space. Two or more objects cannot exist at the same time; therefore the display of existence as manifested in the form of percepts does not show them all jumbled together in the same place, but as occupying distinct positions. Stereoscopic vision reveals 3-D directly; even if a man were born with only one eye, he would still perceive depth in space because whenever he moved his head he would experience parallax. A man born blind could discern distance through the differing sounds; for instance, in his infant state, what the increasing loudness of his mother's footsteps meant, as she approached him. Even a person deaf and blind at birth, like Helen Keller, would not be at a loss as far as the recognition of space is concerned. An infant's arms and legs move, and there is a consciousness of room; it will also show that the human body and the crib are more solid than the air, which may even seem to the infant as made up of absolutely nothing. The blind man who had reflected about the breeze could realize that air is not empty but only less solid than the ground, which in turn is less solid than the stone wall at the property's edge. It is from such experiences that one can derive the idea of density and empty space. These realizations come from perception of the outer world and do not require any explanation in terms of an innate and pre-given power of mind.

Space is simply a fact which the perceptual mechanism takes into account; this it does, whether one senses oneself stepping on a stone, feeling warmth while drinking a heated liquid, or looking down at some rolling hills from an airplane. It is a realization which comes in from the external world as experience and does not need to be brought into action by a preceding experience, as was the case with time.

Doxa: Ayn Rand may have been remiss in not taking into full consideration the innate nature of time, but I want to think that this is only a small error, a simple addition which cannot have much effect on the magnificent whole of her edifice of thought. Furthermore, her consideration of the metaphysics of space and time cannot be understood without reference to her thoughts on the subject of context.

Tomorrow, we will consider the role of context in cognition.

DAY IV

FORMS OF PERCEPTION vs. *PERCEPTION*

*T*he four are meeting together at the same res-
taurant. In front of each is a tablet of paper
with notes. Two have also brought books with them. Out-
side the restaurant, the pennants advertising the coming basketball game between the local team and its biggest rival have been
repaired. The rain is steady, but not threatening.

Doxa: Objectivism teaches that the senses are valid. Sensations come first and are then combined by the brain into
percepts. But it is through these percepts that the familiar
world of entities, attributes, and actions is experienced. To
question the senses is to question all conceptual knowledge,
since the latter is built upon them, even the words used by
the skeptic in the course of his questioning.[1]

"A sensation," Ayn Rand says, "does not tell man *what*
exists, but only *that* it exists."[2]

Philosophus: Rand's statement is a little careless. If the
percepts are to give us knowledge of the external world, then
the sensations supplying materials for the construction of
these percepts must also be knowledge giving. If they are
not, then the external world disclosed through perception is
a dream. And that, surely, Rand never wants to say! The statement is also a little curious, in that it brings to mind that the
Objectivists join together with the Hegelians in denouncing
Immanuel Kant for supposing that he could know that there

was a thing-in-itself beyond the phenomenal world while also supposing that it is unknowable. If it is unknowable, they ask, then how can one know that it exists? To know that something exists is to know at least one fact about it. A similar question could also be asked the Objectivists: if the sensations do not tell us what exists, how can they tell us that it exists, especially if, as Rand also says, man is probably not aware of an isolated sensation?

Doxa: All that the statement means is that it is through the integration of sensations that we are conscious of reality, not through them in isolation, and the reference to sensations telling us only *that* instead of *what* is there merely to point out their insignificance. A block found amongst the ruins of an ancient building would tell us very little about the former structure by itself; some companion pieces will be needed to make out of it, sense.

Penelope: To which the reply is that sensations are not all alike: some come from sight, some from hearing, some from taste, some from touch, some from smelling. They differ in more than hardness or softness, too. Therefore, since they are not interchangeable, they do tell us something specific.

Doxa: I think a writer of Ayn Rand's demonstrated ability should be allowed a few remarks which, while they may not stand up to the hardest analytical light, help make a valid and useful point. All she meant was that an isolated sensation is, ordinarily, too bare to give us knowledge of entities; that it is only when they are integrated by the brain are we presented with a multi-dimensional world filled with objects and actions. Even if there were a single sensation that we could recognize without needing to integrate it with anything else, such as, say—a pin prick, a tiny drop of acid on the face, a single ray of light in an otherwise total darkness— these would not invalidate Rand's statement, since it concerns the massive facts of perception, not a few minor experiences of little more than clinical interest.

Stanford: Yes, let us concentrate attention on the major points, lest we get lost in minutiae.

Philosophus: Very well. Just the major points, then.

Penelope: Yes.

Doxa: Objectivism opposes the arguments of those who question the validity of the senses. But it also denies that the senses produce knowledge of the thing-in-itself, pure and unalloyed. In the words of Leonard Peikoff: "Our sensations are caused in part by objects in reality. They are also—an equally important point—caused in part by our organs of perception, which are responsible for the fact that we perceive objects in the form of sensations of color, sound, smell, and so forth. A being with radically different senses would presumably perceive reality in correspondingly different forms."[3]

"Ayn Rand observes, however, that a difference in sensory form among perceivers is precisely that: it is a difference in the *form* of perceiving the same objects, the same one reality. Such a difference does not pertain to cognitive content and does not indicate any disagreement among the parties."[4] The senses of a color-blind man do not contradict those of a man with normal vision. Should the latter see an entity and remark, "It is red," his meaning would be: " This entity possesses a nature such that its action upon my senses causes me to perceive it in the form of the color of red." And that is exactly what it is. In the same way, should the color-blind man say, "It is gray," he would mean: "This entity is of such a nature that its action upon my senses causes me to perceive it in the form of the color of grey." What the color-bind man says is also true. Neither position contradicts the other. Each man perceives the same thing as the other, but in a different form.[5]

Philosophus: This example nicely illustrates Peikoff's point, but it does not prove that different forms of perception are equally valid. For one thing, both men have very similar light sensory mechanisms and the same kind of brain. In fact, color-blind sight is usually regarded as a deficient or degenerate case of normal human vision.

Doxa: I think it does. But to make my case clearer to you, let me consider another one of Dr. Peikoff's illustrations. What if—he asks—the scientists had finally found the ultimate nature of reality and it was discovered that the familiar world of three dimensional objects, of entities, of actions—full of people, trees, animals, and the like—were really but the product of "meta-energy energy puffs". Even so, he answers; this would not invalidate his hypothesis: "The process of sense perception, by this account, would involve a certain relationship among the puffs: it would consist of an interaction between those that comprise external entities and those that comprise the perceptual apparatus and brains of human beings. The result of this interaction would be the material world as we perceive it, with all of its objects and their qualities, from men to mosquitoes to stars to feathers."

"Even under the present hypothesis, such objects and qualities would not be products of consciousness. Their existence would be a *metaphysically given* fact; it would be consequence of certain puff-interactions that is outside of man's power to create or destroy. The things we perceive, in this theory, would not be primaries, but they would nevertheless be unimpeachably *real*."[6]

Philosophus: Peikoff uses the meta-energy puff fantasy as his final example because it is consistent with his case. It neither proves it nor makes it probable. It only makes the theory more vivid. What if instead of energy puffs, scientists in a later age found out that dualism was right and that matter and thought turned out to be radically different in their origins? That would indeed make a difference to Objectivism, both metaphysically and epistemologically.

And now we come to the real problem. The Objectivists want to avoid saying that a perception is just in the mind because to do so opens the road to skepticism. Neither do they want to say that it is a direct revelation of external reality. To say that introduces the problem of correspondence.

Penelope: What is the problem of correspondence?

Philosophus: The problem is this: If one were to assert that the content of a percept duplicates external reality, the skeptic would ask: how can you say that your percept corresponds to the original without being having both in front of you with which to make the comparison? Which is impossible, of course, because, if the mind could perceive the original directly it would never need the reproduction.

The Objectivists hope to bridge this gap by postulating an interactionism in which subject and object are united together in a special relationship. That way, they hope to deny that sensory qualities are either in the object or in the mind. In Peikoff's words: "A quality that derives from an interaction between external objects and man's perceptual apparatus belongs to neither category. Such a quality—e.g., color—is not a dream or an hallucination: it is not 'in the mind' apart from the object; it is man's *form* of grasping the object. Nor is the quality 'in the object' apart from man; it is *man's* form of grasping the object. By definition, a form of perception cannot be forced into either category. Since it is the product of an interaction (in Plato's terms, of a 'marriage') between two entities, object and apparatus, it cannot be identified exclusively with either. Such products introduce a third alternative: they are not object alone or perceiver alone, but object-as-perceived."[7]

And this brings up the question: Where is the product of the marriage, the object-as-perceived, located? Is it out in space somewhere between the mind of the subject and the object-as-unperceived? Or is space itself just a relationship among energy puffs?

Getting down to earth, how is the object-as-perceived different from the original object in its unperceived form? Suppose that I am sitting in an audience at a concert. I hear an instrumental solo, but I cannot see the performer and his or her instrument because the conductor's podium is in the way. Neither do I recognize the instrument that is being played. Obviously, the source of the sound would not in this case be the "object-as-perceived," since that is, by hypothesis, unperceived. What of the compression waves in the air that are striking my ear? Are they the object-as-perceived? And if they are, how do they differ after the encounter with my ears than they did before? Obviously, the physical result of the collision of the air with the ears will modify them to some degree. But very similar changes would result if they struck an anatomically exact doll or a totally deaf person who was seated in the audience for some strange reason. Rand and Peikoff and the rest of the Objectivists do not, of course, want to say that the air, being the marriage partner in this interaction, had picked up some elements of consciousness from humans.

But this is what their words suggest. They try to escape skepticism by, in effect, making the relationship between the object and the subject into what amounts to a third thing inserted between the two. Objectivists deny that the object can in and of itself be known independent of consciousness, because any form of consciousness has an identity; and that identity requires that we must perceive it in a specific form; and that, so they believe, requires an interaction. The object out of reference to consciousness is known as the "intrinsic." Now, the interesting thing is that the same thing can be said of the subject; it too is an "intrinsic." When studying one's personal psychological states, one must look upon oneself as an object; which means that here too there would have to be an interaction between what one is studying and oneself. This means that for the Objectivist, the real thing, the thing which can be grasped, is this third thing, the relationship between the two—the *marriage* and not the two partners, subject and object. Peikoff almost says as much: Consciousness, he avers, does not create either its content or the forms in which that content is perceived. The sensory forms are the joint product of the perceiver's sensory equipment and the external object(s) with which it is interacting. He concludes: "The source of sensory form is thus not consciousness, but existential fact independent of consciousness, i.e., the source is the metaphysical nature of reality itself. In this sense, *everything* we perceive, including those qualities that depend on man's physical organs, is 'out there.'"[8]

Penelope: What does "out there" mean?

Philosophus: It may mean that the sensory awareness exists independent of human wish. But to say that the sensory-perceptual mechanism operates without regard to human wish or tinkering—that the process is automatic—does not mean that it is valid. The mechanism could be wholly natural and still produce distortions. On the level of common sense, we see it every day. A brain becomes cancerous and the man goes insane; a dog gets rabies and snarls at its master. Within the "context" of an advanced alcoholic's delirium, shadows on a "ceiling" can appear as pink elephants. Obviously, Peikoff does not want to mean that.

Doxa: What he means by 'out there' is that there exists a relationship between the subject and that of which the subject is aware. The relationship is what it is and is no other and cannot be perceived from that standpoint in any different way. To take an example, the color one sees, one cannot help seeing, given the perspective, the ambient light, and the nature of one's sensory apparatus; this experience is as rigorously fixed as anything in the universe.

Penelope: Of course, the same thing can be said of the relationship between the consciousness of a diseased brain and external reality. The hallucination is the form in which the afflicted person perceives reality.

Doxa: Dr. Peikoff is, of course, referring to a physically normal brain. The sensory apparatus of the color blind person is normal, although it may lack certain powers of discrimination possessed by others, just as people cannot smell all that dogs can.

Philosophus: The root of the matter lies imbedded in the Objectivist notion of objectivity. By "objective," they do not mean what the object is without reference to human consciousness. That is the most common meaning, and it is the aim of the quest for truth. For Peikoff, to be objective is to willingly and intelligently stick to the facts.[9] Objectivity, then, for him is not the goal but the means. Consistent with this, he gently ridicules those who hold the other definition. Referring to the popular identification of the "objective" with that which exists "independent of consciousness," he remarks that it causes no harm, but is not technically correct: "Strictly speaking, existents are not objective; they simply are. It is minds, and specifically conceptual processes, that are objective—or nonobjective."[10]

This squeezes out the more common meaning of "subjective," namely, that which pertains to the contents of human consciousness, whether it concerns the reaching the sum, "2 + 2 = 4", the observation of a tree in a garden, the construction of a novel, or the ravings of a madman. "Subjective," in the common sense, refers to the private data of consciousness, regardless of whether that data is valid or not. To Peikoff, the "subjective" is the arbitrary, the hallucinatory, the irrational. According to Objectivism, while man can be objective or subjective, external nature is never either. It simply is!

Defining this way makes it easier for Objectivism to dispense with the old idea that a percept, to be objective, must correspond with the object-to-be perceived. Instead of being confronted with the problem of how the percept mirrors or otherwise represents external reality, a relationship is posited between the object and the subject. It is this third thing, this relationship that is perceived. Of what does this relationship consist? Those intrinsic characteristics of the object un-conditioned by the psycho-physical processes of the organism are not part of that relationship.[11] Objectivists denigrate the intrinsic. Peikoff ridicules the notion that a correct apprehension of reality would be one in which the object contributes all the information and the subject merely receives it without contributing anything of its own.[12] What matters to Objectivism is the relationship, not the two endpoints.

Stanford: Let us step back and ask, What is a relation? It is a fact about two or more other facts.

Philosophus: That is a philosophically accurate definition.

Stanford: Relations may be classified into two categories: dispensable and indispensable. An example of the former would be the relation of a rug to a floor, to be specific, its being on top. But the rug can be rolled up and removed from the vicinity of the floor and both would still exist. Another example is the relationship of distance between an automobile and its parking stall; the car can be removed without damaging either. An indispensable relationship is one in which no term to a relationship can be removed without the destruction of one or more of its terms. An example would be the relationship between a surface and a volume of a solid object. If the surface would vanish, so would the volume.

Is this relation between the intrinsic object and the intrinsic subject indispensable in the above sense? In most cases, obviously not. After the subject has smelled a flower, both man and plant can survive. A child encountering a hot stove for the first time may be discomforted for a while, but in most cases he will survive. The cognitive relation between subject and object is usually dispensable.

Doxa: I think I can accept that. But the relation in question is still *absolute* in the sense defined by Dr. Peikoff, namely that it cannot be other than what it is, given all the conditions which had brought it about.[13] The same can be said of the relationship of the rug to the floor on which it is lying. It is that and nothing else. If the relationship is not indispensable, then it is still absolute, since, given all the factors, it cannot be other than it is.

Philosophus: That is the Objectivist position. Peikoff defines percepts as "products of a relationship between existence and consciousness; they are a grasp of entities in a specific sensory form."[14] This is the key to the whole thing. To the Objectivist, the content of consciousness is not a presentation of the object as it actually is in external nature, but of what it is in a specific form. "Consider taste," asked Rand. "It relates to the way your particular nerve ends react to certain chemicals or certain components of the things which you eat. Tastes as such do not exist apart from your sensory apparatus. But that which arouses a certain sensation of taste in you, does it exist or not?"[15] Every quality we perceive, is like taste, she argued, even length.[16]

Doxa: According to Objectivism, we perceive reality in a specific form, a form which may differ from species to species, and even differ between men with slightly different neural systems, yet in every case be a valid reporting of reality—relative, of course, to the context being considered.

Philosophus: But exactly what does it mean to perceive something in a some specific form? Clearly this is not like the three forms in which a butterfly may appear in its brief life: first as a worm, then as a chrysalis, then as the beautiful delicate thing most of us admire. Each is real, but the same insect cannot be all three at once.

Neither is it like a piece of modeling clay which remains what it is, though it may be formed into the shape of a sphere one day and a cube the next; if the potter reshapes what was, yesterday, a clay sphere into a cube made of clay, we are indeed perceiving something in a new form, but the something we have been perceiving all along is *clay*. We would see the clay just as plainly if it were in the shape of a parallelopiped, or had no descriptive shape at all. The analogy is too weak to be of much help; the change of shape fails to yield any new information about the material out of which it is made.

Is this form of perception similar to a translation, as what we term "earth" is called "zemlya" in the form of Russian? But these two words bring up the same thoughts and images, regardless of which one uses. And the person who knows both has no trouble recognizing the underlying idea when one word is substituted for the other. The two synonyms are but audiovisual symbols, marks calling up to attention the same facts. In and of themselves they give no knowledge. Imagine that our civilization had collapsed—that even our language had disappeared from print. Were an explorer in a jungle to find two stones, on one of which was inscribed just the word "Earth" and on the other stone was found in Cyrillic script, its Russian equivalent, he would not have a clue that they meant the same thing. Nothing in the pattern of either word would show such a person its meaning. It is, therefore, impossible to compare the process of language-translation to deciphering what it is that is appearing in another form—assuming that we can even speak of a *what* or of an *is*. And if we cannot speak of these without adding a closet full of qualifiers, how in reason can we speak in a straight-forward manner of *form*? Rand's solution is quite mysterious!

Objectivism's solution amounts to what used to be called "objective relativism," a philosophical position which enjoyed a great vogue among Anglo-American intellectuals early in this Century who were anxious to catch the Einsteinian wave. This idea was thoroughly refuted by Professor Arthur O. Lovejoy in his magnificent work, *The Revolt Against Dualism*, which had its first edition published in 1930.

Lovejoy saw that such teachers would either have to come up with a criterion for distinguishing between what was contributed by the subject and what was contributed by the object, or they would become incoherent:

> "...in the doctrine of the universal perspectivity of data—if consistently carried out—any reality as it is apart from the special circumstances under which it is perceived or thought of becomes completely unknowable. The 'object of reference' becomes a mere x, like the Kantian *Ding-an-sich*, and is in the end likely to suffer the same fate. For if the nature of all the content (whatever it be) through which the subject of experience represents that object or locus is itself determined by his special standpoint, the latter swallows up even its own object of reference, and the knower is left confined within a 'point of view' from which nothing whatever outside that point can be viewed. And even if the relativist does not carry out his characteristic logic so thoroughly, he is still committed to the proposition that what appears from *any* standpoint is 'objective,' and that all such appearances are equally objective."[17]

Rand herself held consciousness or awareness to be one of her three cardinal axioms: that it is a fact so basic that any attempt to upset it would itself be uprooted by the axiom, since the skeptic would at some level be presupposing it. It is obvious that there must exist a fact of some sort which is passed through accurately to consciousness, a fact which is not intermixed with the effects of the sensory apparatus. Otherwise, the conclusions of men are permanently ensnared in context. What does "form" mean if shape has no necessary trans-contextual reality but is only the way we perceive a certain aspect of reality? Or to change the metaphor: If I place a drop of oil in a lake, at the moment that is resting atop the waters, it is in the place that it is and in no other. But as the waves and other foreign matter in the waters move about, the drop of oil may be joined to something else, split into smaller droplets, or at least change its shape. It may be that a person with a camera could follow it through its vicissitudes and proclaim that the drop was what it was and that the changes wrought were all in accord with its identity, that a clear line of causality led through each of the changes. But if man and camera were in a position analogous to that of the droplets, no such report could be made. To say, then, that within a given context of knowledge, the awareness is of what it is and can be no other is no answer. There has to be something more.

Penelope: Concern with *context* makes sense when one is referring to the use of mere words, since the same symbol is frequently employed to represent significantly different elements. But it cannot without confusion be applied to such elements themselves.

Stanford: It is one thing to show that A.R.'s theory comes short. It is quite another to show the right answer.

Philosophus: A just remark. But clearly, Rand's theory of the forms of perception is wrong. To determine why, let us inquire into the object which is disclosed in perception. That object may be a star which had passed out of existence before the rays of light we perceived reached us. What we would be experiencing in such an instance would be our apprehension of the light emitted by that star, its pattern, brightness, etc. This, of course, is a relationship, but it is subjective; it is entirely on the subject's side. It is the subject which has the apprehension; this, the subject does not in any way share with the object—not the star, not the ray. What became of the light which struck the eyes and triggered the movements within the eye and the brain does not matter for cognition.

Doxa: Objectivism has an answer. Once the light has reached the eyes and its presence has been taken notice of, a relationship exists between the two, regardless of the origin of that light. Objectivism does not sink into a boundless relativism. It has principles. It denies that the senses can err. As Dr. Peikoff puts it: "But percepts are automatic; ... they involve no deliberate method of cognition and cannot depart from reality. Normative terms, therefore, such as 'objective' and 'nonobjective',' are inapplicable to them."[18]

Penelope: This conclusion is contrary to common sense. Sometimes, our eyes have experiences which cannot properly be made into a consistent images. This is the case with certain moiré patterns, in which the image wavers, a false motion is perceived in a still picture. A few years ago, there was an artist who made a reputation by working with them. It was called, "op art."

Stanford: The automatic aspects of the brain can err. Even though memory is essential to life, many of us have come across situations in which we discover that some detail had not been remembered by someone correctly; this is a manifest failure.

Doxa: It is not the senses that have erred, but our interpretation of them. Even if a brain were diseased, it would still get some information from the external world; and that information, however slight, would be valid within its own context. A worm receives a little consciousness from its tiny nervous system; a rabid dog is still in contact with reality to some degree.

Philosophus: This, of course, is just an application of the familiar objective relativist argument that, given all the conditions, the effect is just that; a person with cataracts in both eyes receives some impressions; and given the full context, what they receive is just as valid in its own way as the person with more complete vision.

My answer: it is true that a person may not remember correctly because of lack of attention; but it can also happen that the failure is organic; in which case, it is reality that is misrepresented. It is true that one can understand the make up of moiré patterns. But it is still the case that the sense of sight in its normal perspective gives a false percept of motion which has not taken place in the object. Part of the sensory system has missed its take. The fact that it can be understood does not alter the conclusion.

The Objectivists try to get around these facts by excluding objectivity from percepts and confining it only to voluntarily created concepts. But the older definition of objectivity shows the inadequacy of the approach used by these thinkers. In the words of Alfred O. Lovejoy: "...a datum is, by definition, epistemologically objective only if it serves to give up information about a character that the object has within limits of time and place, or both, which do not include the percipient event, and independently of the occurrence of that event...."[19]

Penelope: Just because a person cannot help perceiving something wrongly does not make the percept right.

Philosophus: Most of us have been told by people who ought to know that the interior of the atom consists nearly entirely of empty space. Yet we see solid objects. Is this an illusion? Not at all. A wad of cotton is more solid than an equal volume of air and less solid than a cube of wrought iron of the same dimensions. What we perceive about this by means of our senses has never been refuted. In the end, the laboratory physicist depends upon his eyes to recognize the readings on his instruments. Nobody would attempt to build a forge for making steel out of *thin* air nor wipe the sweat off his face with wrought iron. The student of geometry sees the shape of the triangle he is constructing on a sheet of paper. That the ink which appears so continuous to him is actually mostly empty space does not figure here. It is the shape made out of ink that he sees. Should this student go to the science lab and look at a small section of that ink drawing through a microscope, he will begin to see that all the surface of the paper has not been covered; he will also notice irregularities in the paper. Because of the magnification, he will then apprehend light from objects which are smaller than what he would normally see. Yet, it is the same eyes that allows him to see both. It would be a mistake to conclude from this that *sight as such*, while valid in its own little context, is actually a contextually impoverished form of some mysterious somewhat.

Stanford: Couldn't it be argued that what we perceive as a triangle is what we perceive it from our context; and that it is valid within our context, with the implication that some other being in another context may use what we perceive as three connected straight lines as something different within its context, but just as validly, because, as A.R. had put it, "A is A"?

Philosophus: If extension is not what we take it to be, but only a representation, then what is the status of a proposition of geometrical proof? Suppose that following Euclid in Proposition 1 of Book I, we construct an equilateral triangle on a given finite straight line: If extension be only a representation of something that is not extension, then what are we really proving? Bishop Berkeley had the advantage over us, for he supposed that there are only sensations, with nothing behind them for them to "represent." If it be answered that the construction of the triangle is valid only within the specific context of extension, which is itself only a representative of an existent yet to be understood, then what does the triangle tell us about this ultimate reality? The construction tells us only about how to draw an equilateral triangle; it enables us to infer more properties about triangles in general and figures made out of them, such as squares and rectangles. There is not even a glimpse here of the supposed reality which the Objectivists think may lie beyond extension. If man did not know what he was really perceiving, then relation or no relation, he would be blind.

Length or extension is a primary quality and cannot be treated the way that Objectivists and other objective relativists do.

It was the 17th Century theorists, most prominently John Locke and René Descartes, who brought much clarity to the distinction between primary and secondary qualities. They concluded that we perceive certain primary qualities, such as form or shape, motion, and extension directly, but that the secondary qualities, such as color, sound, and heat are perceived indirectly through their effects on our sensorium. Heat is the effect of some motion of the molecular particles on our bodies; sound, from compression waves; color is the reaction of certain parts of our nervous system to certain vibrations of light.

Stanford: Let us pause here for a moment while I try to understand your point by elaborating on one of your examples! The shape of an object, its geometry (you state) is a primary characteristic. This, we receive directly through our eyes. Light, which travels in straight lines (except in the presence of a sufficiently strong gravitational field) brings us the shape of the object sending it. But there is another part of that same ray of light, acting at right angles to the direction in which light is propagated; this part, the transverse part, vibrates in certain frequencies. Unlike the other part, we do not perceive this transverse motion directly. All we see is their effect on our optical systems; and this effect is known as "color."

Philosophus: I accept your illustration of the distinction between primary and secondary qualities.

Doxa: Your position is old-fashioned. Ayn Rand puts both the primary and the secondary qualities on the same level.

The following is her argument: A primary quality like length is perceived by the same eyes that perceive so-called secondary characteristics like color. Like heat, another "secondary characteristic," length can be perceived by touch. Therefore, since we learn about both types through the senses, both are on the same level; neither is in a cognitively preferred position.[20] With length, no less than with taste, she thinks we ought to conclude that the form of perception is set by the context—both are the way that the underlying "X" is perceived. She writes: "The primary-secondary quality distinction is a long philosophical tradition which I deny totally. Because there isn't a single aspect, including length or spatial extension, which is perceived by us without means of perception. Everything we perceive is perceived by some means."[21]

Philosophus: Her argument is a non-sequitur. Just because length and color are both perceived by the senses does not make them alike with respect to the depth of reality apprehended. Reason is not simply concerned with similarities, but also with differences.

Doxa: Ayn Rand points out that "the primary-secondary distinction in fact starts from the idea that that which we perceive by some specific means is somehow not objective."[22]

Philosophus: No, it does not start from that idea. In fact, it was Rand who actually believed that if reality were perceived by some means, then the nature inherent in the means must enter into the final product produced, yielding up Objectivism's mysterious amalgam, the object-as perceived.

The primary-secondary distinction holds simply that some qualities are perceived directly and others are not. The distinction is emphatically dualistic and does not reduce them to the same level.

The distinction is not based on the idea that if the primary qualities are perceived directly, that portion of the apparatus of consciousness which receives them can have no identity, that it is simply a receptacle with no specific nature, a blank nothing.

Let us put aside for a moment the question of the secondary qualities and concentrate attention only upon the primary qualities. Consciousness there has a specific identity. But its *identity* consists in its *ability to apprehend* reality. This does not mean that neural processes do not exist. Quite the contrary! It is because of this apparatus that perceptual consciousness has the identity it has.

The two terms of the relationship are that which apprehends (the agent) and that which is apprehended (the patient). Unless the two are distinct from each other, the relationship could not exist. Take away what is apprehended from the act of apprehension and there is nothing left.

This is the real solution to the problem of correspondence, to the question of how one knows that his perception of reality is correct if one does not have the reality in front of one with which to make the comparison? The point is not that what is disclosed by consciousness is like that which it purports to disclose, although this is true. The point rather is this: between the act of apprehension and that which is apprehended, there is no room for any third action to be inserted which somehow combines them.

The relationship is simply that or it is nothing. Objectivism's third thing would itself have to be apprehended, which would make it like a set of facing mirrors.[23]

British empiricism failed to understand this. Locke, although a great man in many other respects, taught that the mind looks at the impressions which it receives from the external world rather than the real world itself. This is wrong. The mind does not perceive by perceiving its impressions. It is not its impressions which it perceives. Rather, to put it bluntly, its perceptions *are its impressions.* The error led to the clever but clearly wrong innovations of Bishop Berkeley and the disastrous emendations of David Hume. The attempt by Rand was also mistaken, for her's involved reifying the relationship between consciousness and existence, the illicit conversion of a relationship into a third thing.

With the primary qualities, the apprehension is direct. With the secondary qualities, what is apprehended is an effect. There is still no third thing between the act of apprehension and that which is apprehended; it is just that instead of being conscious of the external object which brought about the effect, what one is conscious of is the effect itself. That which produces the effect is necessary for it to be produced. Simultaneously, the perceptual mechanism is necessary for the production, since the latter is an experience.

Doxa: Could one not say that the secondary qualities, at least, reveal the external cause in another form?

Philosophus: That is misleading. The effect *is* one's perception. It is not the cause in another form, which would be absurd. First, one perceives the effect; second, through a complex process of reason, observation, and even experiment involving additional facts, one can learn about that which lies behind it. But this is abstract; let us consider some examples, beginning with color.

Doxa: Ayn Rand also says: "Color is a form of perception—something caused by one existing phenomenon, namely wavelength, acting on another phenomenon, namely, the retina of our eye. That does not make color a 'secondary quality,' as if one could say color isn't in the object but extension is."[24]

Philosophus: Note the manifest differences between what we call "color" and what scientists identify as wavelength, which is the other way of referring to its frequency. Try to imagine what we perceive of as *length* as the effect produced upon our sensory apparatus by a mysterious somewhat. That is the short answer.

Now for a longer answer. Color is perceived as existing over a specific area—as an extension; the area is not perceived over a specific color. As the great British logician, John Cook Wilson, put it, "the perception of colour is impossible without the perception of extension, not at all as an inference but as a necessary part or aspect of the same perception, and such extension again is absolutely unintelligible save as the extension of a *surface*—i.e. a real surface. If two colours are juxtaposed which do not shade off imperceptibly into one another, i.e. two colours homogeneous in themselves—as the colored blot on white paper, we necessarily perceive their common boundary as linear, that is really the common boundary of the surfaces to which we refer the colour."[25] Now, if extension is not final, but provisional, or as an Objectivist might put it, as an attribute which we perceive in a certain form in our context, then we cannot even speak of WHERE a certain patch of color is, let alone of its size. It can only be an indication of something we do not understand, to wit, of what we do not know. It appears that Rand's case ends up holding that in order to know anything, one must know everything. Otherwise, she cannot escape the position of Kant who held that we may never be able to know the thing-in-itself, only phenomena—that perception and every disclosure which it makes is solidly bound up in consciousness.

Putting the primary and secondary characteristics on the same level is worse than the error of Locke and other British empiricists who taught that one never perceives reality, only an image. It outdoes the Kantian *noumenon* as well, for now we have the attribute-in-itself.[26]

Rand holds that behind this reality which we perceive in the form of extension is a presentation of sense relative to our current context of knowledge, that extension is merely an integration between the intrinsic subject and the intrinsic object. Rand and Peikoff talk about entities. It will be recalled that she places them as the first stage in the development of her most crucial concept, "existence." Applying Rand's theory about the stolen concept: What could the term "entity" mean in the absence of such attributes as extension or solidity? It too would have only a relative contextual meaning. What then does it mean to say "X is the meaning of" in such a context, if *meaning* in Rand is supposed to be a reference to reality? All the Objectivist could say would be that what is perceived as "extension" in this context refers to an "X" known only in this way, and science may sometime reveal the final form as being something different. Which brings up the question touched upon earlier, what then would have been proved in geometry when one begins Proposition I of Book I of Euclid with a given finite line and upon it one constructs a triangle?

To put it simply: color is explained by physiologists as the way our body responds to vibrations of light. Now, frequencies, length, and the rest are, all of them, primary characteristics. Color is made intelligible in terms of the primary characteristics. Remove the primary ones from the realm of explanation; put them on the same philosophical level as such secondary characteristics as color, and the whole process of explanation becomes relative, rubbery, and eventually dark. It appears that far from basing her philosophy on the acceptance of perception as the given, she has dropped it in favor of a universal relativism.

Penelope: The whole notion of perceiving something through a different form is a vain search for natural hieroglyphics.

Doxa: There is a pathway, however difficult, leading from the form that we perceive as "extension" to its base which could be known only when the science of physics has reached a final state of knowledge on that question. Just as with whatever we perceive as red, there is behind it what we, operating in our context, call a light vibration of a certain frequency, so, behind extension, there is something that exists in reality. A connection between the two exists, for existence itself exists.

Philosophus: Very well, let us consider this idea, although you have presented no evidence in its favor. Let us begin by acknowledging that, in most cases, a one-to-one-relationship exists between light frequencies and the appearance that we call "color". In other words, a change in the vibration of light that is within the perceptual range of a human being will, for the most part, produce a difference in shade or color.

But this is easily explained as a secondary quality. A change in the underlying cause produces a different effect on the optical system. Yet, even here, the primary-secondary theory has the advantage over its Objectivist opponent. Colors are commonly perceived as something solid. Look around you and you will see what I mean. Yet, what is commonly solid is supposed to be something essentially vibratory in a different form. The theory does not add up. (In only a few cases, such as fire, is there even a hint of the undulatory character of that which underlies it; and there, it is not the undulations characteristic of the wavelengths of light that is perceived. Rather, it is rapid combustion which gives fire that indescribable evanescence.)

Nor is it even true that the eye's productions are always in lock step with the underlying wavelength. As dyers of rug weaving material and pointillist painters have noted, when two colors are placed next to each other, they may blend in the eye into a different color; sometimes, complementary colors—such as red and green— are placed close to one another by the painter so that they will cancel each other, producing a rich color called an "optical grey." The pigments retain their original colors despite their strikingly different appearance when viewed at a distance.

Doxa: Nonetheless, close inspection of the canvas or rug may show the facts anyway. All one has to do is walk up close to the painting and perceive. It is through the use of one's eyes that the illusion is detected.

Philosophus: Why is the view that is taken from up-close accepted as the true account rather than the sight from farther away? The answer is obvious: we accept the closer up view because it *is* closer up—and that has to do with extension—with space and time. We cannot accept the simultaneous existence of two colors in the same place without an alteration in shade, at least.

My next question: If all the Objectivists were offered were the optical grey, how would they be able to know that it was only the juxtaposition of red and green in a different form?

Doxa: I don't think I would have guessed it.

Philosophus: What does color show? It does not reveal light waves, not even their interaction with the body. It is not the interaction that is apprehended. That part of the so-called "interaction" which produces changes in the object is usually not relevant to the act of cognition; what happened to the photons after the encounter is immaterial. What is apprehended is the effect on the light sensitive parts of the body. The nerves carry the impulses from the eyes to parts of the brain reserved for their apprehension. The channeling is selective. And, as has been emphasized above, this impression is knowledge giving. It gives position, time, intensity, variety of types, etc.

The resulting perception of color stands in the same places as the wavelengths and at the same distance from them and at an intensity proportional to it by some scale. The effect apprehended varies across the visible spectrum from violet to red. The effect varies as the underlying frequency varies, although not point by point but interval by interval: in other words, greens are bounded on one side by bluish greens such as ultramarine and turquoise and on the other side by yellow greens, such as olive and apple. It is because of the timing and location of color, together with its intensity, the areas which it covers, its differing effects when run through solid glass, etc., that naturalists are able to get beneath surface appearance.

What is the same here is a primary quality—namely position. This is perceived directly. Calling it "relative position" does not change a thing. To suppose otherwise is to imagine that what we provincials call "position" is in reality some 'X' which we perceive in the form of position. But that would be arbitrary. In the end, there will be nothing except the very boundless skepticism which Rand had pledged to fight.

Stanford: Why is it that the light frequencies or light waves are not perceived directly? Here we have a secondary characteristic surrounded by various primary characteristics? Why are they not both primary?

Philosophus: This is the type of question that Objectivists are afraid to ask, because it is an inquiry into why non-manmade things are what they are and not something different. But a plausible answer can be given. The frequencies and their distinctions are too fast for us to perceive. We cannot perceive them. Our nervous system would be unable to distinguish directly between the various kinds of blurs produced by the different frequencies. So, instead of rummaging around in the blurs in order to pick up a discrimination or two, we have before us a beautiful world in which certain ranges are shown by a natural technicolor. We do directly perceive vibrations produced by those things which repeat themselves at a slower rate, such as a pendulum or a metronome. Musicians also perceive beat and rhythm. Larger periods such as the rotation of the earth on its axis we recognize by our clocks or by the changes of light and shade. But the transverse vibrations of light are too fast for our physiology. We do not perceive something in a different form, unless it really has two or more forms. A butterfly has its three forms. But a light frequency has only one. That, I offer as an explanation. It fits the facts.

Doxa: Light is a complicated topic. Let us look at heat. It tells us something about the world. The scientific explanation is molecular motion. It is not just an effect on the body. It tells us something about reality. It is the way that we perceive molecular motion.

Philosophus: But that is false. If it were really the way that molecular motion is perceived by us, then there would not have been that long debate as to whether heat is a substance, at one time called "caloric," or what scientists now tell us it is. The holders of the caloric theory would simply have been told to use their senses, to perceive what they are perceiving, and the debate would have been over then. Sir Francis Bacon's claim to have produced evidence for the idea that heat is motion through inductive processes would have seemed to his contemporaries an utter triviality, and no historian of science would have recounted Count Rumford's observations about cannon bores.

Heat and cold are effects which certain levels of this type of action produce on our consciousness. Ordinary language reveals this too: we say fire warms us and snow cools us. To suppose that these are Randian forms is to suppose that we perceive one of the causes as the effect, an inversion of the actual facts. Note also, that there is nothing like a one-to-one relationship between the heat and molecular motion. Suppose it is winter; we are out in the weather and are caught in a snow storm. While the wind howls about we note that it is getting colder and colder. Then, if we find an unheated, drafty building, we do our best to close all the openings to the weather and place a fire in the fireplace. Soon, we feel it getting warmer and warmer. A quarter of an hour before, we felt cold; now we feel warm. Yet, the underlying molecular motion has been fairly continuous. But because of our bodies, we feel two scales, one of coldness; the other of heat, with a neutral section in between.

Suppose such primary qualities as extension were standing on the same level with the physical feelings which they help generate? Were that the case, the conclusion that the experience known as heat is the result of changes in the mean velocities of the motion the body's molecules would be in-decisive. Being on the same level, we could just as well ex-plain the action of the molecules in terms of perceptions of heat as the reverse. If we took the account provided by rashes and chills to be the final one or, anyway, as good as the other one, then instead of measuring temperature by the differing expansions of metals, we could measure the expansions of metal by our feelings of cold or warmth.

Taste is not the form in which we perceive certain chemi-cals; it is the effect experienced on the tongue and mouth. As before, if we had no experience of the primary qualities, we would know nothing about the chemistry involved. A natu-ral scientist's explanations are in terms of the primary quali-ties.

Sound is even more obvious. When we hear music, we are not perceiving compression waves in another form. It is the same with non-musical sound. With a shattering noise, we experience the EFFECT of the waves upon us, resound-ingly.

Let us turn once more to memory: Think of a painting which you remember. Perhaps it is da Vinci's "Last Supper" or his "Mona Lisa"? Michelangelo's Sistine Chapel? Raphael's "School Of Athens"? Rossetti's "Monna Vanna? "Van Gogh's "Starry Night?" A work by Seurat, then? Whistler's portrait of his mother? Perhaps you recall neither the name of the artist nor its title, but only the picture. Does your memory store these memories in the form of light waves or just the effect which they made on you? If the latter, then a clear dif-ference in kind exists between the color and its origin. If that is the case—and I do not know for certain—then color does not always involve light vibrations, as the Randian must suppose. How different it would be with extension and shapes; there, what we remember is similar to our original impressions.

The same would be the case for music. If it is not the physical waves that are remembered, but the effects, then sound is not simply and in all cases even the effect of compression waves on us; in which case, the Randians would be even further removed from reality.

Stanford: Is there anything about the greater subjectivity of sound and color which makes them seem different to us in our ordinary lives than that which has to do with primary characteristics?

Philosophus: Before I answer your question, I should repeat my point in order to obviate misunderstanding: sound and color are subjective, but not in the Objectivist sense of being the hallucinatory or the arbitrary; rather, they are effects upon us of certain physical causes. To find out what caused them, scientists have had to trace them back to the underlying primary qualities.

Yet, this subjectivity has made it possible for much of our art. It provides for a certain... playfulness. Music stirs us in ways that the *perception* of compression waves would not have. The literature on the role of color in fine painting and the psychological effects of certain combinations is too vast even to summarize here. Color studies have made it plain that subtle perceptual differences can be brought out by changes of background. For instance, the same shade of grey will look different when surrounded by a blue-green than when surrounded by a red.

Doxa: But doesn't what you have just said about color backgrounds bring us back to context?

Philosophus: Context plays a role in the perception of color, but not in the way outlined by Objectivism. Colors are sometimes perceived differently against different backgrounds because of the physiology of the eye, of the ways that the receptors in the retina work, which change the effect that physical light has on our senses. They are not the forms in which we supposedly identify specific certain light waves, which would be a contradiction, anyway.

Doxa: Not all art is based on what you call and Locke called the "secondary qualities." Statues, for instance, are frequently uncolored. They rest on the discernment of shape, a primary quality.

Philosophus: Very true. But note that most statuary is not designed to produce playfulness. Much of it exemplifies ideal types, as was the case with the Greco-Roman statues of their gods and goddesses. In the 19th and early 20th century, statuary was used extensively to provide decorative allegorical representations, often with figures showing such themes as "Commerce and Industry" or "Justice and Peace"; this use was employed in earlier times too; witness the allegorical figures of "Dawn and Dusk" at Michelangelo's Medici tomb. Another use is that of larger-than-life representations of people in order that posterity remember them. This is the case with ancient Greek and Roman funerary sculpture.

Penelope: I am reminded of a poem by Shelley which I once memorized:

"I met a traveler from an antique land
Who said: 'Two vast and trunkless legs of stone
Stand in the desert... Near them on the sand,
Half sunk, a shattered visage lies, whose frown,
And wrinkled lip, and sneer of cold command
Tell that its sculptor well those passions read
Which yet survive, stamped on these lifeless things,
The hand that mocked them, and the heart that fed.
And on the pedestal these words appear:
'My name is Ozymandias, King of Kings:
Look on my works ye mighty and despair.'
Nothing beside remains. Round the decay
Of that colossal wreck, boundless and bare,
The lone and level sands stretch far away."

Philosophus: Sometimes, statues are meant to bring awe and terror. (I have not seen a monolith that was produced largely as a frivolous diversion, unless it was some of those crazy modernistic things which tax exempt foundations think are good for us.)

Doxa: What about architecture? Great buildings have been described as "frozen music."

Philosophus: Form lacks the changeability of sound and color. For that reason, colored marbles, painted walls, and materials which handle light in interesting ways are often incorporated into the design. The Greeks who built the Parthenon did not stop with its shape; the building was painted gorgeously, both inside and out.

Music and painting are also capable of summoning up feelings for the heroic, or inducing a sense of awe and respect, but they have certain other ineffable characteristics which the primary qualities cannot show as readily. On the other hand, it is easier to show the ideal through the primary qualities. The characteristic of Intellectuality is hard to exhibit with music, though many classical composers have succeeded at that. It is shown more often in fine painting where the light and shadow predominate over color, as is sometimes the case with Rembrandt. In Raphael's "School of Athens," the color is used more to delineate the figures than it is to induce feeling—although the yellow arches inside arches in the background suggest intellectual strength and beauty.

Doxa: Does anyone else have anything more to say?.... No. I see by the clock on the wall that it is getting late. Let me close this discussion for all of us by stating that next time we will discuss Ayn Rand's theory of concepts. This contains some revolutionary discoveries which civilization needs if it is to survive the stormy night of irrationality which has been descending upon us. No writer is perfect; but this one was one of the luminaries of the 20th century.

DAY V

THE CONCEPTUAL LEVEL
OF CONSCIOUSNESS

*T*he *four meet again at the same restaurant. Now they all have books as well as notepads and writing instruments in front of them. Outside, the storm has calmed. The other people in the restaurant are either discussing business, romance, or the coming game.*

Doxa: Ayn Rand's theory of the concept rests largely upon her use of the term "similarity." This concept is the linchpin of her whole system. Go back to your childhood when you were learning the basic things we all take for granted—to the time when you were first grasping the concept of a simple everyday object, such as a chair—before you had even learned the word for it: You observed these four entities resembled each other but were different from some other entities which you would later identify as tables. Your mind focused on a particular attribute of the entities which you would later call "chairs", this attribute being their characteristic shape. You isolated them in accordance with their differences and integrated them into distinct groups as units in accordance to their similarities. Although, you did not know what to call it at the time, what you were engaged in was the process of concept formation. In its essentials, this is the same process used by the most astute businessman, the most brilliant scientist, and the most creative artist. Differences of shape are mathematically reducible to differences in linear measurements. Cubes, spheres, cones, etc., are similar in that they can be measured linearly. Here again, note the unifying nature of the similarity. Ayn Rand defines *similarity* as: "the relationship between two or more existents which possess the same characteristic(s), but in different measure or degree."[1] (She adds that when people form concepts, they do not have to know that it is based upon mathematical differences.[2])

Similarity stands behind the concept of the "unit", which is all important to Objectivism. *"The ability to regard entities as units is man's distinctive method of cognition.... A unit is an existent regarded as a separate member of a group of two or more similar members."[3]*

Similarity is the answer to the chaos brought about by modern academic philosophy. Ayn Rand did not want to return to the old idea that universals in some sense exist apart from their particulars; that, for instance, the quality "redness" itself exists in some way apart from the material things that are red or that *colour* itself enjoys some lofty characteristic—a quiddity, perhaps—other than is found in the separate colored objects and colored lights to which it has reference. She has been praised for this even by writers on philosophy who dissent from certain features of her thought. In the words of Wallace Matson, Professor of Philosophy at Berkeley: "The notion of apprehending the particulars subsumed under a concept as its 'units,' which is 'man's distinctive method of cognition'..., and of measurement (in a very broad sense) as implicit in the unit, are of great interest and an improvement on other similarity theories, in as much as by this means, the temptation to explain similarity itself in terms of identity of parts can be successfully resisted."[4]

Ayn Rand stresses that in forming a concept, man needs to take two instances of a type of existent and differentiate them from all that they are not.

Philosophus: Is this necessary? Suppose that a small child is on a family car trip. And as they are traveling through a forest, suddenly the road opens and a steel girder bridge comes into focus.

Now the child has never seen a bridge before, not even in a picture book. As they go over it, he looks down at the chasm and sees far below him a river. He knows enough that to understand that it would be probably impossible for the car to travel down the sides of the steep canyon, ford the creek, and then climb up the other side. He recalls how, last winter, the car got stuck in the mud and Daddy got help from some men in a tow truck. He asks his father, who is at the wheel, "What is that?"

D. "It is a bridge, Johnny."

J. "Blig?"

D. "No, Johnny, brriddge."

J. "Brridge"

D. "Yes."

In this instance, Johnny did not need two instances to form the idea of a bridge. Looking down at the obstacles, he knew its primary use. The next time, they go over a different kind of a bridge—perhaps a flat concrete bridge or an ancient wooden covered bridge—his understanding of what is a bridge may grow richer or more abstract, but these would only add refinement to his apprehension of that same basic fact. This could also be the case the first time Johnny encounters a balloon. He would not need to see two balloons in order to get the idea.

Raising it to a more adult level, suppose it were early in the 20th century, just before WWI: standing on a hill, overlooking part of a non-mechanized backward agricultural area of the Austro-Hungarian Empire, is a twelve year old shepherd boy and his small flock. He looks up and sees for the first time a bright object in the air, moving toward him. At first, he wonders if it is one of the mythological birds which he has heard about. But he decides to look some more before he runs anyway. He notices that the wings are not flapping, just gently swaying; what's more, the two straight wings on each side are joined by ropes. The side nearest him of the strange object is flashing in the sunlight. Metal! He has never seen a locomotive or an automobile. But he knows that it must it is man-made. Then he notices an open window and the figure inside. He doesn't give it a name, but it is registered in his mind. If he were to spot two of them that hour, he might learn a little more, but one is enough to convince him of its identity. He waves at the pilot. The latter rocks his wings.

Raising it to a more abstract level: suppose for the first time, one encountered a solid pink. It would not be necessary to contrast a pinkish-white and a pinkish-red in order to form the concept. It would be enough to contrast it with a solid ruby or a deep orange. The next time one saw another instance of pink, one could remember that one had seen it before and if one had not gotten the name before, one could get it then.

At an even more abstract level: How much more would we learn about a circle if we saw more than one of them at the same time? The fundamental properties of each are the same. The only thing one could learn from seeing more than one is that they can come in different sizes, a property which one might have discerned from examining the first one. In order to form an idea of it, a close look at one should suffice.[5] Consider the triangle: if one saw only one, an equilateral triangle and no others, one might not have guessed that isosceles and scalene versions are possible, but the fundamental fact that it is an enclosed figure with three sides could have been apprehended. From that example, all the properties inherent in the figure could have been determined, including the fact (by construction) that triangles with different proportionate lengths can also exist.

Doxa: Your examples give the impression that a concept can be formed with only one instance. But I will show you that this only seems to be the case. In the example of Johnny and the bridge, for instance, he probably had already noticed that he could overstep objects that were in his way like a toy which he had earlier abandoned on the floor. In doing so, he may have already obtained an implicit concept of a bridge. I should be given time to develop my point.

The principle that there must be two or more instances of an attribute(s) is crucially involved in Ayn Rand's concept of the unit, where entities must be viewed as units, and a unit is that which is considered to be part of a group with two or more members. It will be recalled that she holds that the idea of a unit was something which the animals below man could not attain, that they were stuck with perception and the observation of a few similarities.

Philosophus: Of course, the sighting of one bridge cannot be a group, neither can a single sighting of a balloon, an airplane, the color pink, or the observation of a single circle—none of these events can qualify as one of Ayn Rand's units.

Penelope: Yes. How can a philosophy which has so much trouble accounting for memory keep track of the first instance? If the Objectivist child who was learning to conceptualize was in a poor household that had only one chair, she would stumble over that object in wonderment.

Stanford: Let us hear the rest of the Objectivist position on the formation of concepts. It may be that what is left to explain might either redeem what seems to be an insurmountable problem, or if not that, it might be true on its own account and could be incorporated into a true philosophy.

Doxa: The second part will make the point clear. Ayn Rand writes: "With the grasp of the (implicit) concept 'unit' man reaches the conceptual level of cognition, which consists of two interrelated fields: Conceptual and Mathematical."[6] In her theory, the formation of concepts is, to a great extent, mathematical.[7] Ayn Rand does not spend a lot of words on a discussion of the nature of mathematics; that, she leaves to the specialists in the field. But she does define it as "the science of *measurement*."[8]

The purpose of measurement, she announces, is to expand man's understanding; this is done by relating easily perceivable measurements to greater and greater magnitudes; for instance, from the inch, the average person can get the foot; from the foot, the mile; from the mile, the light year. Or using the metric system, the scientist can go from meter down to the micron, or below. Man cannot directly perceive light years; he cannot even travel anything close to the speed of light; neither can he perceive a molecule with his unaided eyes; but through measurement, he can put the immensity of the universe within his compass. To paraphrase Protagoras, man is the measure of all things, but in an epistemological sense, not a metaphysical one. Everything, if it is knowable, must be brought down to a humanly perceptible scale.[9]

This brings us to the important principle of "unit economy."[10] Consciousness is limited; there is only so much that it can deal with at any given time. Percepts condense the vast data provided by sensations into units men can deal with; similarly, concepts condense the multitudinous array of percepts into manageable units. This explains man's power.

Mathematics and concept formation come together through the notion of the *Unit*. " A 'number' is a mental symbol that integrates units into a single larger unit (or subdivides a unit into fractions) with reference to the basic number of 'one,' which is the basic symbol of 'unit.'"[11]

Ayn Rand brings measurement and units together with concepts. This can be seen in her definition of a concept: "*A concept is a mental integration of two or more units possessing the same distinguishing characteristic(s), with their particular measurements omitted.*"[12] The idea of measurement omission is that when one forms a concept, for instance, the color red, one takes two different instances of red—say an apple and a sunset—and forms the concept uniting both. The two shades are similar, but not identical. The specific measurements wherein they differ are omitted. "Bear firmly in mind that the term 'measurements omitted' does not mean, in this context, that measurements are regarded as non-existent; it means that *measurements exist, but are not specified.*"[13] Man does not even have to know how to measure them; it is enough to know that they exist.

In the formation of concepts, men have long noticed that the concretes being subsumed under a concept are different; contrast, for instance, an armchair with an old-fashioned rocking chair. Yet they are also significantly alike. As Dr. Peikoff phrases it: "The puzzle has been: what is the same? Ayn Rand's profound new answer is that the relationship among similars is mathematical."[14]

This is why, despite what was said earlier, two or more instances of a kind are necessary in order to form a concept. In order to make similarity crucial in the formation of every concept, two or more not quite identical instances are required; thus, when we formed the concept red for the first time, we needed two shades. The difference between the two shades is only a matter of measurement, of number. The two shades are blended together in the mind to form a single unit.

Stanford: This seems to be analogous to how the brain takes the two different perspectives afforded by the two eyes together and blends them into stereoscopic sight. Just as two flat images are turned into a 3-D, so the unit does the same; it combines the two existents mentally into a unit.

Doxa: Yes, but it should not be forgotten that this is only an analogy, because stereoscopic sight operates on the level of the perceptual, whereas the unit stands at the entrance of the conceptual, which is potentially unlimited in its range.

Philosophus: Yet, it has been shown that the requirement that there be at least two instances to establish what Rand called a concept is not necessary from the standpoint of epistemology. It remains to show that it is also *metaphysically* unnecessary. Rand's concepts are supposed to be mental integrations of percepts based upon the fundamental similarities between two or more of them. This is a carryover of the old idea that the universal is a unity among many. But she is wrong.

The characteristics of a circle do not result from the fact that there are more than one circle. If there were only one in existence, it would have all the basic characteristics necessary for it to be what it is. There is no need for a plurality. Were all the rest to disappear, this one circle would have every one of its characteristics intact. The same would be true for the triangle. What is common to all of them is that they each have three sides. But if all but one triangle were to be destroyed, the one remaining would still have three sides, even though it would then not have the defining characteristic *in common* with any other existent and could not be grasped on the basis of any similarity, whatsoever. Rand's confusion on this matter can be discerned in her attempt to regard triangles as units. She argues that triangles are distinguished from rectangles on the basis of their particular shape. She said: "If we observe various shapes and find a difference between triangles and squares, how do we separate the two categories? By regarding all triangles as units of one group and observing that they have a characteristic in common—a certain kind of shape—that distinguishes them from another group which are squares. In that sense we do regard triangles as units."[15] That is true, of course; triangles do have their characteristic shape. But, this is not how Euclid defined them. He defined triangles as rectilinear figures contained by three lines, rectangles are rectilinear figures contained by four lines.[16] The important point here is that triangles do not have a *similar number of sides*; they each have the *exact same number* of sides. Yes, they do have a similar shape, although of different sizes and proportions, but what sets them off is not a similarity (since this includes difference) but an identity, that is to say, that they each have the *same* number of sides. Any one triangle meets this criterion. No blending of one's percepts of various triangles is necessary in order to recognize them.

Rand's two-minimum requirement is just a modern attempt to solve the problem of universals. But, as I will show later, it is not necessary that an attribute be present in many particulars. One instance is all that is needed. Aristotle's wording, κατα πάντος , is misleading here.[17]

Similarity is not needed in order to blend two or more percepts into a unity. This is the same fallacy that we have found with regard to Rand's discussion of context. She supposes that there must be some third thing interposed between the apprehension of existence and existence itself. Her concepts deal with what it is supposed to be general between two or more existents. But the truth is that if necessity is not in the particulars themselves, then it cannot be in any comparison or contrast made between them. (The reason why it often takes more instances than one to discern facts not readily disclosed by perception is because most things are more much complicated than lines in two or three dimensions and their implications. The second instance is needed as a check against error, not as a partner in a blend.)

Penelope: If two or more instances were required, a person could never arrive at a concept in a Randian sense, *unless they were presented simultaneously*. If one first perceived a single case of a phenomena, a shade of red, for instance, one could receive it in memory with sure accuracy. But how could one know enough to pull the earlier impression out of memory, unless one had already recognized it? The second shade is not required to enable us to see red as *red*. It can give us knowledge only of purity, intensity, and the like.

Philosophus: Rand's unit cannot serve as a bridge between the epistemological and the metaphysical. According to Rand, "...units do not exist *qua* units, what exists are things, but *units are things viewed by a consciousness in certain existing relationships*."[18] In her philosophy, the units cannot exist in external reality; if they did, the concept would not require the blend at all. There would simply an identical part of every existent referred to by a concept and a non-identical part. Thus the concept blue would refer to that aspect in the conventional blue object or light which possessed this attribute in all its purity; the non-identical part would comprise that aspect of a particular shade of blue which lacked purity; pure blue would be inherent in all shades of that color. As was just pointed out, similarity in such a universe would just indicate the degree of purity; contrary to Rand's concept of it, it is not such a crucial step in understanding.

But when Rand says that the relationships exist but not units *per se*, she enters into even more difficulties. Units, she claims, are things viewed by a consciousness in certain relationships. But if they don't exist as such, then how can they be "viewed'"? It would appear that under her theory, conceptualization would involve presenting reality the way it is not.[19]

It will be recalled that she defines a unit as "...an existent regarded as a separate member of a group of two or more similar members."[20] She opens herself to the objections probably first brought out by John W. Robbins:

"If the relationships of similarity and dissimilarity exist in 'objective reality' then units *qua* units exist. Similarities (or dissimilarities) that are not there cannot be 'regarded.' And if the similarities and dissimilarities are 'there,' the 'groups' also are there. If the 'groups' are 'there' then units exist *qua* units, *i.e.*, as members of groups. If they did not, no process of concept formation could account for universals."[21]

Rand's idea of the unit is not coherent.

The difficulty is in supposing that percepts can be blended into units and that these blends are comprehensible even though they are not just perceived as amalgams, or as mere sums, but as integrations.

Yet, what is apprehended is reality. The unit must be in nature, not just in our mind. Otherwise, it is not an apprehension. Rand supposes that the mind constructs this third thing she calls a "unit" between the apprehension and that which is apprehended. This is unnecessary.

Doxa: The concept of the unit may not be the final answer, but Ayn Rand's linkage between the conceptual and the mathematical is still crucial to the understanding of the nature of the concept. Central to Objectivism's theory of concept-formation is that of commensurable characteristics. Measurements taken in the metric system can be converted directly to those in the English system. The two systems are commensurable, i.e., they can be reduced to common units. To take an example from Ayn Rand, tables are mentally separated from such kinds of furniture as chairs, beds, rugs, etc. by means of the shapes peculiar to them. A table, whether it be a cheap thing made out of aluminum and plastic or Italian marble, is, for all of their differences, a flat level surface with supports. These shapes are established as the characteristic distinguishing tables from all other objects, with the measurements of the shapes of individual tables omitted. A particular shape represents a certain range of geometrical measurements. Shape is certainly an attribute; and any differences in shapes ultimately reduce to differences in measurements, whether it be spheres, cubes, or whatever. And these measurements are expressed in numbers.[22]

Ayn Rand calls this commensurable characteristic, the Conceptual Common Denominator.' She defines it as "the characteristic(s) reducible to a unit of measurement, by means of which man differentiates two or more existents from other existents possessing it."[23] In the first case, tables are differentiated from the other kinds of furniture by the Conceptual Common Denominator of shape; then the table in turn becomes the Conceptual Common Denominator for the various subcategories of tables, such as end-tables, coffee tables, desks, etc. Similarly, color is the C. C. D. for the reds, blues, yellows, etc.

To make this clear, Objectivism teaches that concepts are formed by distinguishing two or more similar instances from their Conceptual Common Denominator, which consists of an attribute which the two or more similar existents also possess. Thus the concept of "red" is formed when two shades—say carmine and maroon—are separated on the basis of some other color. The greater the contrast with other colors, the more maroon and carmine will look like each other. Against a background of green, this similarity will be especially vivid. Color is the Conceptual Common Denominator. (Centuries had to pass, Ayn Rand suggests, but eventually men finally learned how to measure colors mathematically, that, of course, being in terms of the wavelengths of light.)[24]

Stanford: Enough has been said about A.R.'s requirement of there being at least two or more instances.... Let us now focus on the Conceptual Common Denominator.

Doxa: What, according to Rand, happens when someone attempts to differentiate two existents which are not commensurable, i.e, do not have a common unit of measurement? To see this, let us take her illustration: "No concept could be formed, for instance, by attempting to distinguish long objects from green objects. Incommensurable characteristic cannot be integrated into one unit."[25]

Penelope: Why couldn't there be a category called "long-green objects"? A golf fairway would seem like a long-green object when compared to a single blade of grass. It would not be very practical, but it is not a contradiction in terms like a square circle.

Doxa: What Ayn Rand means is that there is no Conceptual Common Denominator in terms of which the concept of a "long object" could be formed by distinguishing it from "green objects," or *visa versa*, in the same way that the color blue could be differentiated from other colors because they both possess the same Conceptual Common Denominator, color.

Stanford: A.R., however, made the matter too easy by taking a case of overlapping categories. Some green things are short.

It is conceivable, although unlikely, that a small child could be kept in special quarters so that all the tall things were green and all the short things were of some color other than green. There could be no windows. The nurses would come in wearing green costumes, including green stockings, green gloves, and green hoods. Then, when the child formed the concept, "long," he might note that all the green things possessed this attribute in contrast to the other things. He would have to be able to differentiate the attribute of length from the color green....

Philosophus: In a conversation which is reported to have taken place between Rand and a person identified only as "Prof. A" at an Objectivist workshop, the latter, somewhat apologetically stated that length and color do, after all, have a commensurable characteristic: both are attributes.

In her answer, Rand began by saying that, "it isn't that characteristics which appeared at the first level to be incommensurable suddenly become commensurable."[26]

The game was given away right there. If the fact that they are both attributes is not enough to provide the basis for reducing them to a unit (in terms of which the two are supposed to differ only in measurement), then the Objectivist account is wrong.

So Rand attempted to avoid the difficulty by arguing that one would not attempt to unite them by forming the concept, "attribute," right away: "In that process [concept formation], you cannot form a concept to unify concretes into one category except by means of a commensurable characteristic. And two characteristics that appear to you, on the perceptual level, as incommensurable (like length and green) will be incommensurable at any stage. But you will be able to establish certain relationships between them through many other intermediate concepts. But by themselves those two will remain incommensurable. If we take just the referents of the concepts 'length' and 'green,' there is nothing that you can establish as a commensurable characteristic between them."[27]

This is irrelevant. An attribute is an attribute. It would not matter how long it would take to reach the magical Conceptual Common Denominator; the two would remain what they are throughout. Rand may have thought that she could get away with it simply because it is probable that a child forms both the ideas of green and length before they discover the idea of an attribute itself.

Let us take a plainer example. Sound and shape can be distinguished from each other, although they have no immediate Conceptual Common Denominator. One is a secondary characteristic; the other, a primary one. A child could form the idea of sound by distinguishing it from shape even before he discovered that sounds were produced by material objects. If he could not distinguish the attribute of sound from that of shape, then how could he make discriminations among sounds? The same could be done with two secondary characteristics, like color and sound. All that is necessary is that enough difference be discerned in that upon which one is concentrating attention to apprehend it in contradistinction to the other quality.[28] One could, of course, use 'object of perception' or 'disclosed by experience' as a genus out of which one was differentiated in terms of the other, but if that were allowable, then so would be long from green.

And now for an example taken from Rand's own words: In answer to the objection that one can form the incommensurate concept "mental entity" from "physical entity," Rand answers: "But you don't form those concepts directly. You form the concept 'mental entity' only after you have formed the following concepts: the concept 'man,' the concept 'consciousness,' then you identify certain mental states or events in your mind, such as thoughts, let's say, which you call 'mental entities.'"[29]

Rand is wrong. In memory, we are immediately given the difference between what is here and what is not here now. There is also the faculty of imagination which yields an analogous result. It is directly in contrast to external reality that these two faculties give notice of themselves. Regardless of how faintly one discerns the disruption between the mental and the physical, sooner or later one is confronted with this duality. Rand's reference to "man" is a non-sequitur; and her citation of "consciousness" only adds irony to my truth.

In short, Rand's concept of "similarity" is a failure; it does not and cannot solve the problem of universals.

Stanford: I see that incommensurable ideas are no bar to the formation of concepts. But what of commensurability itself and its role, if any, in cognition?

Philosophus: In her discussion of the concept of length, Rand writes: "Let us now examine the process of forming the simplest concept, the concept of a single attribute (chronologically, this is not the first concept that a child would grasp; but it is the simplest one epistemologically)—for instance, the concept 'length.' If a child considers a match, a pencil and a stick, he observes that length is the attribute they have in common, but their specific lengths differ. The *difference* is *one of measurement*. In order to form the concept "length," the child's mind retains the attribute and omits its particular measurements. Or, more precisely, if the process were identified in words, it would consist of the following: 'Length must exist in *some* quantity, but may exist in *any* quantity. I shall identify as 'length' that attribute of any existent possessing it which can be quantitatively related to a unit of length, without specifying the quantity.'"[30]

There are two things to note about this definition. The first thing is that it is defined ostensively. This means that since it deals with a basic attribute which cannot be explained by any words more elementary than itself, the definition is made by in effect pointing at some thing which exhibits the attribute in question, namely length, and by saying in effect—"This is what I mean by 'length.'" Critics who do not appreciate this point sometimes say that it is circular, since it defines length as a unit of length, which is circular. These critics may not be satisfied with that kind of definition, but, none the less, I will leave it like this. That said, I will pass to a more important consideration.

The second thing is that it states that any given length can be related to a unit of length. This is to be done mathematically. Rand defines mathematics as the science of measurement and measurement as "the identification of a relationship—a quantitative relationship established by means of a standard that serves as a unit. Entities (and their actions) are measured by their attributes (length, weight, velocity, etc.) and the standard of measurement is a concretely specified unit representing the appropriate attribute."[31]

Doxa: That unit of length is the standard by which length is to be measured, whether it is to be in terms of the English system of feet and miles, the metric system, or a handmade system, such a certain stick of wood. Now, as we know, the units of the English system are fully convertible into that of the metric system. They are commensurate.

Stanford: There is no doubt about it; the concept of length is a crucial one for her theory. The traditional quasi-Aristotelian idea that the way to define something is merely to identify it by means of the characteristics common to its kind and separate from all that does not have these distinguishing marks, A.R. rejected as insufficiently mathematical, as vague, because not reducible to a unit.

She was committed to the notion that length can be reduced to a single unit and that any difference which may be found in the definition of these units, whether we use the metric, the English system, or whatever, are ultimately commensurable.

Philosophus: Rand's theory was exploded centuries before its formulation by some Pythagorean.

Consider the following drawing: What is the length of the third side?

By the Pythagorean formula, the square of the hypotenuse of a right triangle—that is the longer side—is equal to the sum of the squares of the two adjoining sides. Therefore, $1 + 1 = (1+1) = 2$. So the square of the third side is two. Its actual length, however, is the square root of two.

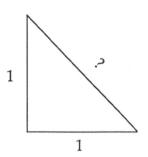

Now, the two adjoining sides of the triangle are each equal to one unit. This unit can be anything we like: feet, inches, meters, miles—whatever. What then is the length of the third side? We have found it to be equal to $\sqrt{2}$, but how long is that?

We know that its length exists. We can plainly see that it does. It touches each of the two adjoining equal sides. Place the length of one of these beside the third side! Note that the third side is a little longer. Exactly how much? Surely, there must be a way by which we can in theory, even if not perfectly in practice, determine how much longer the third side is in terms of feet, inches, meters, miles, etc.

Since $\sqrt{2} \times \sqrt{2} = 2$, we suppose that this square root of two must be a distinct magnitude, proportional to 1 as well. It does not matter if it is a long fraction. It is only that it must bear some fractional relationship to the unit one. Suppose we state it in terms of tenths. Then we can use decimals. Suppose we find it to be 1.4142 times as great. Then we have found that it is equal to one whole unit in the single digit place, to four tenths, to one-one hundredths, to four thousandths, to two ten thousandths.

But the truth of the matter is that $\sqrt{2}$ cannot be stated in terms of tenths at all. "1.4142" is the not the square root of two. It is only an approximation carried out to the ten-thousandth place. The truth is that no fraction of any kind, thirds, tenths, or whatever, can state the length of this third side of that triangle This number bears no fractional relationship to the unit length of the other two sides.

According to Rand: "A number is a mental symbol that integrates units into a single larger unit (or subdivides a unit into fractions) with reference to the basic number of 'one,' which is the basic mental symbol of 'unit.'"[32]

However, since the relationship between the third side of a right triangle to the other two sides is such that the former cannot be said to be a fractional part of the latter; there is no common unit.

The third side that did not fit brought about the discovery of irrational numbers. Rand's was a "rational" theory mainly in the sense that if reality were different and all quantities were rational, it might have been true.

How important are irrational numbers? Very. To give an illustration: The square is composed of two of these right isosceles triangles set along their diagonals or hypotenuses. Rand's theory of concepts is not for *squares*; it is for people who want to be hip. Incidentally, a similar argument could be made with respect to circles: the ratio of the perimeter of a circle to its diameter, namely, "Π", cannot be forced to fit into either the rational or the irrational numbers.

Length is not apprehended on the basis of a commensurable characteristic. Any characteristic used as a base would have to be consistent with the ratio between the length of the hypotenuse and that of the other two unit sides of the triangle. Length has to be defined ostensively, but not in relation to a unit of length. "Length" is a word which comprehends incommensurate systems of lengths; for this word, there can be no unit. It is not and cannot be a conceptual common denominator in Rand's sense.

One could take the idea of length and start by breaking it into two categories, "length 1" and "length 2". The first would refer to measurements taken in terms of rational numbers, the second, in terms of irrational numbers. Were this to be done, it is true that the infinity referred to in length 1 would all be commensurate, as would those in length 2. But if we tried to make a genus consisting of length 1 and length 2, there would be no commensurate characteristic. In addition to this, it would be impossible to build a measuring stick which would cover only those numbers commensurable with unity or one. If one takes a yard stick and runs one's hand over its length, starting from the "0" mark to the "36" " or "3' " mark, one will pass through the length of $\sqrt{2}$ feet, somewhere near 1.4142 inches; one will also pass through innumerable other incommensurable points along its length. A yard stick which did not include an incommensurable length would have to be invisibly cut in two at that point. This is called "the Dedekind cut," after the French mathematician who first conceived of it.

Doxa: Cannot one approximate? Even the most exact measurements can be made as exact as one likes.

Philosophus: Rand's concept requires that they not only be related to a unit as standard but that they be reducible to it. In no sense is the $\sqrt{2}$ a reducible to the unit of mathematics, which is 1.

Doxa: But if you made the differences ever so slight, you could potentially reach it through an infinite number of steps. Of course, there is no real infinity, but you can make the difference less than any number we can name.

Philosophus: Pragmatically, you can—but if you do, you are no longer employing exact mathematics. The unit in question will not allow it. The defeat of Rand's attempt is well described in this quotation from the 19th century British mathematician, Augustus De Morgan: "For, however, far you carry the subdivision, you do not, by means of the subdivision points, lessen the number of points which may be laid down. For each interval defined by the subdivisions contains an infinite number of points. Consequently, if you will suppose the infinite subdivision attained, you cannot do it without supposing an infinite number of points left in the intervals, or an infinite number of incommensurable quantities."[33]

I submit that if Rand's notion of the unit were really central to man's higher consciousness, we could not imagine such quantities. As we are now, we can understand that they exist, although we cannot calculate them. If we imagine a race of beings which could only think in Randian concepts, their minds would go blank while attempting to solve the problem. Their thoughts would turn into moiré patterns or something worse. Some people say that if everything were the color blue, we could not see any color, even that one. I do not believe this. If we can perceive blue, then we can perceive it, whether or not there are other colors available. But a race with in-born Randian conceptualizing equipment would be worse off. By contrast, should there drop into an-all blue world, a red object from outer space, the denizens, after a period of adjustment, would begin to see red too. Unfortunately, the born Randians would be incapable of recognizing that there were quantities which could not be stated in numbers, since they could only realize whole numbers and fractions. They would know that some quantities could not be stated as tenths of a unit and would have to be indicated some other way, but the idea of one of them being incommensurable to '1' would be unthinkable. Since, for them, the thought of magnitude would have been based upon the unit, they could never rationally realize that magnitude is not exhausted by number. They would be worse off than the village that voted the earth flat depicted in the Rudyard Kipling short story.

Let us take a mathematical concept where the two subcategories can easily be grasped together and where neither are commensurable: this is the concept of *figure*. Consider the two subcategories, rectilinear and curvilinear figures. There is no figure that is neither straight-lined nor curve-lined at the same place.[34] Even a mixed figure like a circle inscribed within a square is either one or the other at any one place. "Figure" is an attribute that is not reducible to one of Rand's units; it is not something mathematical which contains within it the base of what could be either straight or curved. Sometimes the straight and curved parts will meet at a point; in the square inscribed in a circle, for instance, there are four such points. But these points, either together or alone, cannot serve as a unit. Where are there two or more consecutive points belonging to both the curvilinear and the rectilinear? A real life tot could easily grasp the essentials of each and that both are alike in that they share something in common, but if he started looking for some underlying unit, his mother had better grab him quick.

Stanford: What is it that they share in common?

Philosophus: A line possesses two attributes: length and direction. A straight line maintains constant direction; a curve does not. Were they to cross at a point, the latter could not serve as a neutral point, as a unit, since a line must have some length. Neither is a bent line a curve. There is no quantitative unit to which constant and curved, crooked and irregular can be reduced. The point is an infinitesimal. What unites them is that they are lines.

Rand was wrong about numbers in general. This can be seen by examining the idea of the natural numbers: These are the whole numbers, 1, 2, 3, 4, etc. There, if any place, one would expect Rand's notion of the conceptual common denominator to hold up, because each number in the series can be reduced into so many multiples of one. Yet, even there, not all of the properties of even the first multiple can be comprehended in the One. But this mathematical reduction does not behave like a Randian similarity of being simply less of the same characteristic. The natural numbers are divided into the even and the odd.

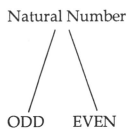

Natural Number

ODD   EVEN

The *One* does not include both the even and the odd; there is no way that a reduction can take place. Rand herself did not consider the 2 to be of importance: "The number 'two' is crucially important epistemologically, because to form concepts you need two or more existents between which you observe similarities. It's in that sense that the number two is very important, epistemologically. Metaphysically, it is all equal—there is no *metaphysical* hierarchy between one and a million."[35] But there is! It is the distinction between the odd and the even. Their properties are very different. Although 2 is but the double of 1, the properties of the number twice as great are not simply an amplification of the other. They are not like the varying shades of red. The difference between odd and even is of great practical and therefore metaphysical significance; one could not even tie one's shoes without this difference. Circuitry and labyrinth are also whetted on this difference. The implications of the odd and the even has been explored mathematically.[36] And finally, reflect upon this: two points can establish a *length*.

Doxa: Perhaps it is because of the way that you divided it. You made them both stem from a word.

Philosophus: Very well, then let us make them stem from a number. Obviously, we cannot use zero. So the only candidate left would be '1'. That would cancel the distinction between the odd and the even, since Rand's primal unit in mathematics is an odd number. Doing this would make it the Conceptual Common Denominator of all the natural numbers. But the C. C. D. is supposed to contain all the characteristics of all its referents, just as "furniture" includes all the characteristics of everything that is a table, a , a bed, a chest of drawers, etc. and "plant" subsumes all the characteristics of trees, shrubs, grass and the like. But this only brings back the same problem in a new guise: This *"one"* includes all the natural numbers mathematically, but does not encapsulate all of their characteristics.

The fact is that length, figure, and even natural numbers can only make sense if the Randian unit is dropped. This indicates that the base of mathematics is words rather than numbers. As a book which Rand did not like very much puts it, "In the beginning was the Word...." The fact that there are quantities which cannot be expressed by numbers is of great metaphysical importance. This, we can discuss later.

Stanford: A.R.'s theory fails in mathematics, but there still may be truth in her idea that the unit is somehow involved in both the conceptual and the mathematical fields?[37]

Philosophus: Only in an inexact manner of speaking. It is true that the number system is based upon the precise unit, "1". But it is also the case that whenever we use a word that is supposed to refer to reality in some way, it is implied that there exist at least one of that kind. If one speaks of a concrete object like an apple, it is presumed that there be at least one instance of it. The same is true for an attribute. One talks about a "red such and such." Even if one were reading about some presumably non-existent being like a hobgoblin in a book of fiction, one realizes that there is at least one reference to it in the story. But this situation is not unique to what she considers to be the conceptual level of consciousness. This is also the case on what she regards as the level of percepts. There is always at least one tree, one sight of the sky, one dog barking, etc. The same with sensations; here too, they must be specific in order to be registered upon consciousness.

Penelope: Rand defines mathematics as the science of measurement. "Measurement," she defines, as the identification of a quantitative relationship obtained through "a standard that serves as a unit."[38] But mathematics includes far more than quantities. For instance, there is the phenomenon of the *direction*, which cannot be reduced to that of so much or so many of this or so much or so many of that. Although

measurements can be made along a specific direction and
these specific directions can be numbered in terms of degrees,
direction itself is not a quantity. The reduction of geometric
figures to algebra in analytic geometry could not be accomplished without reference to the three axes covering the six
fundamental directions in space; vectors are based on that
fact. And yet, her notion that it is all a matter of differing
measurements seems to have been inspired by the success of
this kind of geometry.

Doxa: Ayn Rand's theory of the concept may be remiss
with respect to the more recondite subjects, but it handles
the nature of everyday attributes with great precision. This
can seen in her subdivision of the lowly concept of the table,
which is one of her main illustrations for her theory. The subdivisions she mentions are "the dining table," "the coffee
table," the "end table" and the "desk." She states that "in the
first three instances, the distinguishing characteristic of
'table,' its shape, is retained, and the differentiations are
purely a matter of measurement: the range of the shape's
measurements is reduced in accordance with the narrower
utilitarian function. (Coffee tables are lower and smaller than
dining tables; end tables are higher than coffee tables, but
lower than dining tables, etc.)"[39]

Philosophus: What is so different about "desk"?

Doxa: Ayn Rand writes: "In the case of 'desk', however,
the distinguishing characteristic of 'table' is retained, but
combined with a new element: a 'desk' is a table with drawers for storing stationery supplies. The first three instances
are not actually new concepts, but qualified instances of the
concept 'table.'"[40]

Philosophus: Why the special treatment for desk?

Doxa: "'Desk,' however," Ayn Rand explains, "involves a significant difference in its distinguishing characteristic; it involves an additional category of measurements, and is given a new linguistic symbol."[41]

Philosophus: What is the difference? The new characteristic is a statement of purpose. Yet, the coffee table has its peculiar height and shape because of the reason for its existence declared in its very name; the same for the dining table and the abruptness of the end table. In that respect they are no different from the desk.

Rand herself defines the genus table as "A man-made object consisting of a flat, level surface and support(s), intended to support other, smaller objects."[42] The reason for its existence is included in the very definition. It is one of the defining characteristics. Yet, on three of the species under this concept, she omits purpose.

Doxa: Earlier, she said that one can omit measurements because they are in her estimation all reducible to a unit.

Philosophus: And this very fact points to a fundamental problem with Rand's theory. She classifies purpose as a concept of consciousness. "A concept pertaining to consciousness is a mental integration or two or more instances of a psychological process possessing the same distinguishing characteristics, with the particular contents and the measurements of the actions's intensity omitted—on the principle that these omitted measurements must exist in *some* quantity, but may exist in *any* quantity (i.e., a given psychological process must possess *some* content and *some* degree of intensity, but may possess *any* content or degree of the appropriate category."[43]

Are the contents of a psychological process like purpose to be treated as omitted measurements? In general terms, can attributes be omitted like numbers? The whole point of her consideration of similarity was that because the differences reduced to only a matter of measurement, one could safely leave them out. But here we have the attribute itself left out.

Now, either the contents—in this case, the specific purpose behind a certain kind of table—are reducible to numbers or they are not. If they are not, then they cannot be dropped. There has to be a statement of purpose in the definition of each. In her definition of the genus, there is a reference to a purpose, but not in those.

Is this a minor inconsistency, or does it indicate something greater? Number and attribute are not real parallels. A number, as defined by Rand, is either a multiple or a fraction of a unit. The general category of purpose, however, is simply a fact about any specific purpose. A desk exists for some purpose; so does a coffee table and so does an end table. In no way are these collapsible into one of Rand's pseudo-mathematical units.

Yet, this is just what she allows the reader to wonder. In a discussion of categorizing tires by their physical dimensions, she said: "I think it is exactly the same process as I described in subdividing 'table' into 'dining table,' 'coffee table,' etc. Those are subcategories, with more restricted measurements, of the wider category, whose measurements are also limited within a certain range."[44]

Is this oversight due to inattention only or does it signify something deeper?

Doxa: In her definition of "concepts of method," she writes that they "are formed by retaining the distinguishing characteristics of the purposive course or action and of its goal, while omitting the particular measurements of both."[45] So the characteristics of a purpose *are* to be measured!

She does speak of evaluation as being carried out in ordinal rather than cardinal numbers, which means that evaluations are conducted in terms of what is 1st, 2nd, third,...nth, rather than in terms of mere statements of position, like 1, 2, 3, the end.

"Measurement is the identification of a relationship—a quantitative relationship established by means of a standard that serves as a unit. Teleological measurement deals, not with cardinal, but with *ordinal* numbers—and the standard serves to establish a graded relationship of means to end."[46]

Philosophus: But as to whether *the purpose which dictates the evaluations* is to be so reduced, she is silent.

If all can be reduced to mathematics, then purposes and, indeed all qualities are at bottom quantities of some fundamental stuff—the stuff of reality. (Peikoff illustrated this point with the hypothecation of energy puffs.) Just as water, which has the quality of being a liquid under standard conditions of pressure and temperature, can be changed to the quality of a gas if enough heat and/or pressure are applied, so it would be with everything.

Penelope: This would be the famous transformation of quantity into quality, one of the four fundamental premises of Marxism-Leninism. As Stalin put it: "Contrary to metaphysics, dialectics does not regard the process of development as a simple process of growth, where quantitative changes do not lead to qualitative changes, but as a development which passes from insignificant and imperceptible quantitative changes to open, fundamental changes, to qualitative changes; a development in which the qualitative changes occur not gradually, but rapidly and abruptly, taking the form of a leap from one state to another; they occur not accidently but as the natural result of an accumulation of imperceptible and gradual quantitative changes."[47]

(I thought that there was something like that in Rand's idea, and did not realize that this was the case until just a few minutes ago. But I came prepared.)

Philosophus: Rand most probably did not intend to go that far; but she made her theory consistent with such a state of affairs. It should not be forgotten that she was educated under the Soviets. Although she rejected much, she held on to some of it. Her theory sometimes points in that direction, although she herself did not care to investigate that avenue. She had too much respect for the independence of the human mind. Consciousness was to her a fundamental axiom which could not breached without contradiction. However, although she was not a declared materialist, she was uncomfortable with a dualism between Mind and Matter.

Rand's indecisiveness on this issue may not have hurt her fame. Many people, especially the college educated, came to the idea that the quantitative would soon dominate. Not willing to be held back with the reactionaries, they accepted this in some form, the more vulgar in that favored by the behaviorists, the more intelligent in the form brought forth by Rand; or they simply gravitated toward philosophical nihilism. So the word became secondary, even unscientific, something to be replaced, someday. Music could, of course, go on because it could generate emotions without words. But, with the reinstatement of the word, the way is open once more for real poetry. Sir William Hamilton, one of the most celebrated mathematicians of modern times, believed that poetry was as high an intellectual art as that of his own field. One does not have to accept all of his mathematical theories to understand the importance of this conclusion of his. Here are some lines from a longer work he penned:

"Spirit of Beauty! though my life be now Bound to thy
          sister Truth by solemn vow;
     Though I must seem to leave thy sacred hill,
     Yet be thine inward influence with me still:
     And with a constant hope inspire,
     And with a never-quenched desire,
     To see the glory of your joint abode,
     The home and birthplace, by the throne of God!"[48]

Stanford: Could you pull together what all this means as far as A.R.'s theory of concepts is concerned?

Philosophus: We have seen major parts of Rand's theory of concepts fall apart. This was because she did not hold the distinction between the physical and the mental to be absolute. Although she held "Consciousness" to be an axiom, she was open to the theory that all things can ultimately be reduced to one. The duality between apprehension and that which is apprehended in that act was too simple for her. There had to be some third. One instance of a kind was not enough. But, if this one instance was insufficient for conceptual knowledge to take place, why then were two enough?

In the formation of her "concepts", the percepts were to be combined into something which is supposed to be greater than a sum, an integration. The next question concerns the nature of the combination. They cannot be physically combined, because that would ruin the percepts used up in the process; the result would be a transmogrified superimposition of one percepts upon the other—an overlay which would make less sense than the modern abstract art which she deplored.

Apparently, information is to be abstracted from the percepts intellectually without destroying the underlying source. Similarity is to be the key. What the actual nature of the many-in-one that results is not really spelled out. It is to be a unit, but not like the definite mathematical units or units of physics. The percepts are to be "regarded" as members of a group, even though the group does not exist as such.

This vagueness is what can happen to a theory of knowledge when apprehension is regarded as an indirect process.

First, her percepts are sealed up inside themselves, as if she held that what we perceive is our percepts and not external reality. In Rand's theory, if a creature confined to the perceptual level of understanding had a "percept" of a tree, it could not go beyond the identification of this singular event and see it as a *tree*, even non-verbally. That is the task of what she regards as the first level of concepts. (These are concepts of entities like trees, rocks, grass, and the like.)[49] In her system, higher concepts are formed by abstraction from these;

thus, if man were an Objectivist, he might note that the colors of the foliage in the tree and the new grass in the field are both green and on the basis of that, in contrast with some other color, come up with the concept of "green."

But in the real world, the capacity to experience greater generality is not denied to the perceptual level. It is not locked away in a capsule. When we notice a certain particular, we cannot apprehend it merely as an isolated individual, but as having a certain quality(s). All that is required is that it stand out from the background with sufficient distinctness to be take notice of. Even if we have had but one experience of a thing or of an attribute or of the action of that thing, the fact that we are able to remember it when we later encounter another existent which we recognize to be like it or not like it in some respect, shows that the "percept" points beyond itself, that more is retained than stone-dead detail.[50]

What we have perceived about the particular contains within it all the necessity we later apprehend as a universal. There is no need to warp quantity or magnitude by trying to make it fit into Rand's unit. (If you approve, more can be said about this later.)

Doxa: In our next meeting, we will finish our discussion of Ayn Rand's theory of concepts and explore her studies of definition. These, I think you will find, contain more solid substance.

DAY VI

DEFINITIONS AND UNIVERSALS

*T*he scene is the same restaurant. In front of the four are books, notebooks, and writing instruments. About them are the other patrons, discussing the usual things.

Doxa: One of Ayn Rand's most famous statements is that essences are epistemological rather than metaphysical. By this she meant that the definition of a concept is not some principle inherent in the existent being defined which separates it from all that it is not or which makes it the kind of existent that it is. In her theory, essences are not metaphysical; they do not disclose a fundamental principle inherent in the existent which makes it what it is. Rather, the essence is simply the defining characteristic of the concept *within the present context of knowledge*; and that what is today taken as the defining characteristic(s) might be substituted by another formulation when a higher state of knowledge is reached.

The best way to explain this is with Rand's own famous illustration: At the earliest stage of learning what a man is, a child might define man as "a thing that moves and makes sounds." This is universally true of people; they do things which are audible and they do perform actions. Later on, after the child has learned more about things and has observed dogs and cats, he might define man as "a living thing that walks on two legs and has no fur." The child would still include in the list of man's characteristics, the fact that he moves and makes sounds, but these would no longer be defining characteristics, since they do not separate men from the household animals with which he might be familiar. Finally, when the child has reached his teens and has recognized some the things which men are able to do which other animals are incapable of performing, he may conclude that man is a "rational animal."[1] In each stage, the information contained in the earlier definition is retained and subsumed under the new definition which includes it together with whatever additional facts are learned, in a wider deeper, more comprehensive formulation. In short, definitions are contextual; later, more advanced definitions do not contradict earlier, more primitive ones.

Stanford: A.R. was not the first to come up with the idea that essences are epistemological rather than metaphysical, but she was the most emphatic and drew the most conclusions from it. There is even a debate as to whether Leibniz had preceded her on this point.[2]

Philosophus: John Cook Wilson, who was Professor of Logic at Oxford University early in this century and who died in 1916 had long anticipated Rand on this point. Here are some of his words on the condition of the empirical sciences: "We might possibly never have an absolute definition ...but we might have a relative one; we might, that is to say, unify the facts which we know about a given subject by dividing them into two groups, one of which conditions the other, and this assemblage of the complex of conditions we might term the essence. Growing knowledge of a thing might then sometimes widen and sometimes narrow this essence. New elements might be discovered which we could not derive from the old essence, or, again, some of the elements first included in that essence, might turn out to be derivable from others of the group. Thus the complex of the essence would be diminished. Definition then would be an ideal by aid of which we unify what we know, and this corresponds fairly to the present position of the empirical sciences."[3]

Penelope: Did Rand take this idea without attribution from Professor Wilson's writings?

Philosophus: I think not. She did read the work of another English logician, H. W. B. Joseph,[4] who had made several favorable allusions to the as yet unpublished work of Wilson. But Professor Wilson knew some things which she probably had never learned; had she read him, her philosophy might have been different.

Doxa: It seems to me that Ayn Rand's account that essence is a matter of epistemology rather than metaphysics was a more penetrating identification than Wilson's. His was in terms of the "relative" and the "absolute", which, it seems to me, is a little vague.

Penelope: If this is really such a great achievement, what degree of credit should Rand be given for it?

Philosophus: To answer this question, consider Albert Einstein's fame and the formula, $E = mc^2$: A German scientist, Friedrich Hasenöhrl, had discovered it earlier and reported it in a reputable journal of physics the year before Einstein published his famous paper of special relativity. Hasenöhrl did not publicly draw any conclusions from his formula than those germane to his experiment, namely, that it applied to radioactivity. Einstein universalized it, in other words, he held that it pertained to every form of energy, as Rand did with her idea about the essence. This is not to imply rivalry; this scientist who died in WWI is not reported to have said anything against Einstein. Since Hasenöhrl had drawn up what one physicist has called "a special case of Einstein's law,"[5] he must be considered an important precursor. Moreover, in addition to Hasenöhrl, the French mathematician, Henri Poincaré had ventured a cruder formulation of it in a paper published the year before Einstein's; furthermore, the physicist, Max Planck, was the first to correctly derive it.[6]

If Einstein could emerge as the only person to be remembered far above the others, then Rand's disciples would not be acting without precedent should they request that she alone be remembered for this insight of hers.

Stanford: Einstein might have universalized the formula, but I don't think that the doctrine that essences are epistemological is really capable of universalization, especially in the light of A.R.'s philosophy.

Like Einstein, she believed that the universe was finite, that the number of elements constituting it were not unlimited. That being the case, within a given science, complete knowledge would be possible. A full and final definition could be had. One might, for instance, start with the definition that ice is that which floats on water; but seeing wood do the same thing, one would quickly see that this characteristic does not sufficiently distinguish it from all that it is not. Moreover, it is not even an ice-characteristic which holds throughout all conditions; the scientists have found, for instance, under the extreme air pressures that can be created in the laboratory, that ice will not float but in fact sink.

Then when one discovered, finally, that ice is the solid form of water, it is, at least, arguable that one would be in possession of a final definition. If this is correct, and the definition of "ice" as "the solid state of water" proves indeed to be the final one after all the facts about it are known, then this definition would be absolute *per se*, and not simply within a context. This being premised, one could speak of a "metaphysical essence", even within A.R.'s understanding, for if definitions are contextual as she taught, then within a final context, that knowledge would indeed be final. Therefore, if A.R.'s denial of an actual infinity in nature were correct, then the statement that essences are not metaphysical would be relative to the epistemological context of our time.

Doxa: I don't know how Ayn Rand would answer that, but I find it convincing. The final definition of ice, once it was known to be such, would both identify it for what it is and set it in contradistinction to all that it is not. All of its properties would be tied to the facts stated in such a definition. The only exception which I can see would be if, in some particular science, there were two possible ways of organizing the facts and so two different essences. As an example: A triangle is defined as a closed plane figure consisting of three sides. It could also be defined as a closed plane figure with three internal angles.

Stanford: Yes, that could be done. And, as far as I see, either definition would allow one to discover all the remaining properties of a triangle. But even if this were so, the earlier definition is superior, metaphysically. An angle is determined first by the lines that form it. The notion of directions without lines is absurd. (A line cannot be without direction, but a direction requires two points; and that is all that it takes to establish a line; for, as Euclid defined it, a line is length without breadth.[7])

Doxa: That is correct. A direction cannot exist independently of a line; nor can length. But let us turn to another of Ayn Rand's important statements about definitions: *"The truth or falsehood of all of man's conclusions, inferences, thought and knowledge rests on the truth or falsehood of his definitions."*[8]

Penelope: One can agree with her that a bad definition can lead to mischief. This is especially the case with something that is not directly perceptible, like "government." In terms of Rand's "percepts," there are only buildings, men marching around with uniforms on, pieces of cloth flying in the breeze, documents, polling booths, etc. But nowhere do we see a thing called "government." Nobody, not even a child, is fooled into thinking that the cartoon of Uncle Sam depicts it. Government is a man-made institution, existing in various forms for thousands of years. Since Rand believed that the universe is finite, she should have been able to distinguish it from all other human institutions in a final and definitive way. Look at her definition of government: "A government is an institution that holds the exclusive power to *enforce* certain rules of social conduct in a given geographical area."[9] Note the phrase *exclusive power*! In the same essay, she states that the difference between governmental and private power, that is to say, the distinguishing characteristic, "lies in the fact that a government holds a monopoly on the legal use of physical force."[10]

Now, the original U.S. Constitution did not grant this monopoly to government: in the Second Amendment, it reserved the right of the people to have arms. The Declaration of Independence, the document upon which the Constitution stands, grants the people the right of revolution. In the Constitution itself, there is the second Amendment, which gives them the right to bear arms. According to Supreme Court Justice Joseph Story, who wrote his commentary in the 1820's and was only one generation away from the founders': "The importance of [the second Amendment] will scarcely be doubted by any persons who have duly reflected upon the subject. The militia is the natural defense of a free country against sudden foreign invasions, domestic insurrections, and domestic usurpations of power by rulers. It is against sound policy for a free people to keep up large establishments and standing armies in time of peace, both from the enormous expenses with which they are attended, and the facile means which they afford to ambitious and unprincipled rulers to subvert the government, or trample upon the rights of the people. The right of the citizens to keep and bear arms, has justly been considered as the palladium of the liberties of a republic; since it offers a strong moral check against the usurpation and arbitrary power of rulers; and will generally, even if these are successful in the first instance, enable the people to resist and triumph over them...."[11]

Under Rand's concept, the U.S., as originally founded, could not be listed as a species of government. If we retain the pre-Randian notion that the institution which George

Washington headed as its first President was a *government*, then one would have to conclude that monopoly of force is not a characteristic of government as such, but only of some or most governments. She could not even include it as one of the non-defining but universal characteristics of government.

(It is doubtful that a government with a monopoly of retaliatory force would long be a free society. Aristotle reported that there was a Greek intellectual named Hippodamus who had proposed dividing a city-state with a population of 10,000 into three parts—one of skilled workers, the other of agriculturists, the third of arms bearers for defense. Aristotle replied that trusting all the arms to this third class would put it into the position where it could seize power and rule.)[12]

Philosophus: Moreover, if, as Rand asserts, the truth and falsehood of an idea depend upon one's definitions, her argument on context is disturbed. Objectivity is more than a mere relationship of the perceiver with the object to-be-perceived. It is not enough to show that something is part of our experience. Those who err about the object also have a relationship to it. To take a mundane case, if one mistakes a girl for a boy because the former is wearing the clothes of the latter, there is still a relationship between this object and one's opinion, namely misapprehension. A false entry into the navigational data for the computer of a space ship might be fully contextual, might fit in so well with the other numbers that it is not noticed by the technicians, but the more frequently it is used, the more it jeopardizes the mission. A bad definition might continue to bear a relationship to the facts which they are misrepresenting, but the discrepancies would grow with repeated use.

Just because something is what it is from a given standpoint and cannot be perceived from that standpoint in any different way does not keep it from being subjective. When two colors are placed against each other, there is an area of darkness where they border each other; the more contrasting the colors, the more vivid this zone of darkness. Physiologists call it a "penumbra." The pointillist painters noticed this and duly placed it in their paintings; see, especially, the works of Seurat's disciple, Signat. One could say that it is a "contextual absolute," as do the Randians, in that the phenomenon is what it is and not something else, since A is A. But that would overlook the important fact that it is a built-in error in perception which does not correspond to the light coming from the world outside of us. It is a characteristic perceptual error resulting from the physiology of the retina; because of the inhibition of some receptors in the optical system, the information obtainable from that part of the object is lost.[13] To say that it is the way that we perceive those rays of light coming from the border would be a mistake; it would be closer to the truth to say that it is the way we do not perceive it.

It is true that contrast phenomena cannot be other than they are, given the nature of the human visual system, but they are still "subjective." They come from the side of the subject only; it is not the result of a metaphysical relationship. The fact that the phenomenon persists, even after the physiologist has made his report, does not make the phenomena objective from the standpoint of perception, *per se*. The objectivity lies only in the intellectual act of understanding, an accomplishment that does not result in one's perception of what is missing.

Most people still call two related phenomena,"sunrise" and "sunset", although nearly all believe the scientist's report; the Beatle's even made a song about it. Yet, the error is very contextual; in the work-a-day world, the thing that turns is usually perceived as much smaller than that in terms of which it turns; since the disk of the sun is a small part of the field of our perception in comparison with the vast expanse of the earth, the error is quite persistent, even though only a few, if any, doubt the scientists on that point.

Doxa: I think that there is one area of the Objectivist position on contextuality which is valid. Ayn Rand contends that if a man's grasp of reality is non-contradictory, then, even though his beginnings are modest, none of his concepts will contradict the content which those same concepts have in the minds of the most learned experts. A defining characteristic—for instance, *moving about and making sounds* in the case of a child attempting to define man—may later be replaced by a new and different defining characteristic—such as *a live thing without fur that walks with two legs*, which is also replaced in its turn when the child has acquired more knowledge, *a living being that can speak and can do what cannot be done by any other live thing*. Ayn Rand comments that the most recondite philosopher looking down at the child struggling to raise himself in knowledge will not find anything to subtract from that definition. Within the context of what that child knows, the knowledge is as secure as that of the philosopher. The toddler's definition of man is what Rand calls a *"contextual absolute."*[14] It is fully consistent with what its possessor knows about the thing being defined and is defined in terms of that which sets its apart from the rest of his knowledge.

Leonard Peikoff presents a graphic illustration of this contextual absolute. Many years ago, he reminds us, medical investigators had been able to identify four types of blood, which they labeled : "A," "B", "AB", and "O". All the individuals tested had one type or the another of blood. Each was incommensurate with the other. Should blood of an A-type be transfused into the veins of a B-type person, or vise versa, the result would be a bad reaction. The same with the other combinations. Sometime later, however, it was found that a bad reaction could take place even when A-type blood was introduced into the body of a Type-A person. From this, the RH factor was discovered, a factor which was present in the blood of some but not others. Only some A-bloods were compatible. "The principle here is evident," Dr. Peikoff points out: "since a later discovery rests hierarchically on earlier knowledge, it cannot contradict its own base. The qualified formulation in no way clashes with the initial proposition, viz.: 'Within the context of the circumstances so far known, A bloods are compatible.' This proposition represented real knowledge when it was first reached and it still does so; in fact, like all properly formulated truths, this truth is immutable. Within the context initially specified, A bloods *are* and always will be compatible."[15]

Philosophus: To understand why this is wrong, let us imagine ourselves back to the time when only the four basic types were known, when everyone was ignorant of that which would later be called the Rh factor: suppose that, in accordance with "latest discovery of medical science", the doctor gave an A-blood patient a transfusion of A-blood and the patient died; furthermore, that if the patient had refused the transfusion, he might have lived: What is the meaning of this?

Epistemologically the operation was a success, but metaphysically it was a failure. This, of course, is the human condition, which must be borne. Perhaps, if the doctor had not been so impressed with the "latest" and had spoken in a more tentative way, the patient might have refused the transformation and lived. (I once knew a man who, after having been badly injured in a traffic accident refused a transfusion because of fear of AID's contamination and survived it, although it took him many months to recover.)

Peikoff exalts: "If the researchers had decided to view their initial discovery as an *out-of-context* absolute; if they were to declare—in effect, as a matter of dogma: 'A bloods will always be compatible, regardless of altered circumstances'; then of course, the next factor discovered would plunge them into contradiction, and they would end up complaining that knowledge is impossible. But if a man reaches conclusions logically and grasps their contextual nature...."[16] The idea of the contextual absolute does not do much for the luckless doctor or his even unluckier patient.

Stanford: Could not the Doctor have said: "This procedure has been successful every time it has been tried in the past; and, although I have no specific evidence that it will fail this time, there is still the possibility that it will?"

Philosophus: Peikoff's definition of "possibility" rules this out: "A conclusion is 'possible' if there is some, but not much evidence in favor of it, and nothing known that contradicts it."[17] Were the doctor to say that since science has not exhausted the subject, something might be found which would make it hazardous to health to inject A type blood into an A type patient, the Objectivist would interdict that it is not enough that the proposed possibility be consistent with the known evidence; there must be positive evidence. Peikoff states that an idea which was merely consistent with all the known facts but not supported by any could not be labeled as "possible," only as "arbitrary."[18] An Objectivist cannot say "maybe," unless there is some specific evidence for it.[19]

Stanford: Trial and error cannot be written out of science by Peikoff's peculiar idea of possibility. If he wants to retain this meaning for "possibility," at least he should have a place for that which does not contradict known facts but has no positive evidence in its behalf. This could be called the "conceivable." The "arbitrary" could be left to refer to situations in which an assertion in made, regardless of what the facts are.

Penelope: Is there any truth to the Objectivist contention that it is possible for an intellectually inclined person to go through life without ever having seriously accepted an idea which was later shown to be false?

Philosophus: Consider the most famous scientific revolution of them all; that of Copernicus, in which the received theory that the sun traveled around the earth was reversed. The old theory was rendered consistent with troublesome data by supposing that the sun and the planets traveled around the earth in cycles within cycles, or epicycles. The theory of Copernicus was much simpler, although he was unable to prove his theory either. Then, while another scientist, Johannes Kepler, was studying the astronomical observations recorded and set down by his mentor, the renowned Tycho Brahe, he discovered that the ideas of Copernicus to be more consistent with the observed facts than those of the orthodoxy. Kepler had once believed in the old theory; but he was open-minded. So he was not an instance of the type of scientist that had never drawn a conclusion that was later contradicted by the facts. Copernicus was able to see that the same evidence used to support the theory that the sun travels around the earth would also support his simpler account. But I doubt that his biography would show that he never believed anything which Peikoff considers to be an error.

Penelope: What kind of person would fit Peikoff's ideal? Such a person would have to regard everything which had not been proven as neutral. Could this be a person of the type of a Kepler, a Galileo, or a Newton who would be willing to venture boldly into the darkness. More likely it would be the laboratory drudge who played it safe; who was willing only to test the ideas of other men, someone who was inclined to be neutral and tentative toward everything. Someone not like Rand.

But could such a person even be neutral? If the scientist believed that the currently winning theory was only considered to be provisional, he would run the risk of smashing into Peikoff's concept of possibility—he might end up doubting without reason. He might slip into the ways of a pragmatist (a philosophy which Objectivism abhors) and simply define truth as that which works. Such a scientist would be uneasy, to say the least.

Philosophus: But let us put these great questions of astronomy and cosmology aside and take the easier case of the apparent daily motion of the sun across the sky. In order for a child to make no mistakes, he would have to regard the apparent motion of the sun to be the equivalent of what grownups call an "hypothesis." Can this be?

A child who had not yet discovered relative motion might conclude that it was the sun which moved about the earth. To avoid having made this error, the child would have to have held every action he observed to be tentative. This is barely imaginable. And if he did, it would certainly effect the speed of his learning—his stride—if not its contents.

But, to continue. Such a child would not need to learn by trial and error. When he saw the sun appear to move across the sky, he would form no fixed opinion.

Penelope: How could he avoid becoming perpetually indecisive?

Philosophus: With regard to the sun, he might have noted the path of its light throughout the day. Then, one time, as he was sitting in a passenger car, looking out the window while his train was traveling through the countryside, suddenly, he passed a parallel train that was idling at the track. For a moment, he had the illusion that it was the other train that was moving and that his was stationary. Recalling the daily sun, he figured that either the sun or the earth was moving.

This is barely conceivable, and the Objectivist epistemology is no help here. Context or no context, the notion that the sun moves around the earth is always wrong.

And now, let us close our account of the contextual absolute. This conceptual contraption is supposed to be sound because a situation does not change any more than it does. If something is perceived a certain way, then it is perceived that way. A round penny will look elliptical from a certain standpoint; if it looked round instead, then the laws of perspective would have vanished, and so forth. The doctrine is at least as old as Hegel. It is a strange term, since it combines the absolute with the relative. John W. Robbins humorously suggested that it be called the "temporarily eternal" or the "momentarily everlasting."[20]

Humor aside, the contextual absolute is of no help to Rand. The words of Alfred O. Lovejoy are as true today as they were when they were written thirty five years before Rand published her theory: "To say, as the relativist appears to do, that all data are nothing but perspective aspects, that they are determined to be what they are by the special standpoint of the perceiver and the nature of the individual percipient event upon which they depend, seems equivalent to saying that no datum can ever inform us about the nature of anything not itself, *i.e.*, of anything not relative to and conditioned by the particular 'standpoint' from which it appears."[21]

Any attempt to make sense of the contextual absolute would imply that there be an abstract time beyond the flux of things which ties the varying contexts together. With the connection of *before* and *after*, which was the same for all participants in the scientific process, intellectual harmony would be conceivable. But Rand, as we shall see, rejects the notion of absolute time. Therefore, she must find another way out of the difficulty.

And, as has already been discussed, this is just what Rand's theory of the unit is supposed to give us. Two or more similar pieces of data are combined somehow in the mind to produce something that was not in either of them alone—a sterile amalgam is hypothesized, and a dead theory is hoisted to stand up in a semblance of organic integrity through an evocation of something resembling stereoscopic sight, but without its intelligibility.

The next problem is to determine whether concepts, such as Rand envisions, exist even when we excise from consideration her unit her Conceptual Common Denominator and her teachings on context.

Consider first, Rand's account of definitions: Assume that the defining characteristic of some Randian concept "X" needs to be changed because of increased knowledge: the question comes up, Does the concept necessarily remain the same? Rand admitted that in some cases, they do not persist through the changes, that there are reclassifications. She gave two examples: one was the Medieval theory of four humors which were supposed to classify men as personality types. Since modern psychology does not accept this theory, the whole system has been scrapped. The other was that the whale was originally classified as a fish, but was later re-classified as a mammal.[22]

Penelope: One wonders what the person who held all his knowledge perfectly in context was doing while the idea of man was being re-shuffled from the medieval to the modern?

Philosophus: Let us take Rand's idea of a rational child's first definition of man, *a being that moves about and makes sounds.* Suppose the little Objectivist sees a white bunny rabbit scurry across the grass. Recognizing the morphological difference between the bunny rabbit and the man, he knows, implicitly, that a substitution is needed. Suppose further that the family has no pets and he has not time to inquire as to whether or not the bunny rabbit can talk or make breakfast. Could the child not consider *moving about and making sounds* to be the genus—the central concept—of which, in some implicit sense the existent called "man" and the existent called "rabbit" would become species, in other words, sub-categories? Then, when the child discovers the electric train, which also moves and makes sounds, he will have one more instance of his "genus," his never changing underlying concept. Finally, having discovered the distinction between the animate and the inanimate, he can then divide his great genus into two subordinate branches, under one of which man could be placed as a sub-species. During this period, *man* would be identified by his basic shape pattern. Nor does this conflict with experience. Children frequently indicate people by stick figures.

Is it really the case that when we perceive a man of whatever description—male or female, young or old—this subject is classified under *rational animal* and then anything we notice about it is regarded as an instance of the species possessing this definition, that anything it does is placed under some sub-category of it? Is it not rather that the general physical shape or the sound of a human type voice enables us to recognize this as a man? And that we consider him as a rational animal only when we are cogitating about his mind, that the intellectual classification system stands besides the physical perception of the man rather than determining the whole presentation of the phenomena?

If the Objectivist child later finds that *moving about and making noises* is inadequate as a general category, this will only highlight what is being suggested, i.e., that concepts would be removed while the facts which they contain would be kept. During the time that the old concept was in place, "man" would be a sub-species of the genus, *beings that move and make sounds*. While the change in conceptualization was taking place, the child would still continue to recognize man by his morphology and other characteristics. When we see a creature approach us from a distance, whether it is clothed or unclothed, we decide that it is a man and not something else by its general shape; we do not wait until it utters rational sentences before we can identify it as a man. We assume all that on the basis of that generalized appearance. It is the same with the child reclassifying people.

Let us grant that man can be differentiated from animals by virtue of rationality. Now, suppose that a biologist identified man by some characteristic in his skeleton which differed from primates. How would he tell that the person who had defined man as a rational animal was talking about the same thing?

By the morphology.

Penelope: Naming man "the rational animal" distinguishes him intellectually from other animals. Why not then, if one is an atheist like Rand, define man as "the rational being"? This too would distinguish the concept "man" from all that exists in (what is for Rand) the present context of knowledge.

Doxa: Rationality might be enough to distinguish him from everything else that is known to science; however, characterizing him as an animal indicates more completely his place in the structure of life on earth.

Penelope: But that simply places it closer to the recognition of morphology.

Philosophus: Rand was once asked whether man should not be differentiated from other animals on the basis of the latter's type of consciousness being non-rational or perceptual. Her answer is very interesting: "Yes, but what would be the purpose of this? Here you have an evaluative consideration entering. Is the distinction by type of consciousness more important then [sic], let's say, the distinction between animal and bird, by feathers and ability to fly?".[23] Her unarticulated premise is the same as it is for most other people, i.e., that the role that morphology plays in the differentiation of men from other things is crucial.

Let us now briefly return to the C. C. D., an aspect of her theory of the concept which has already been refuted: The Conceptual Common Denominator for "rationality" would have to be "consciousness," which is one of Rand's axioms. The C. C. D. for "the ability to fly" would be "locomotion." There is no Randian Conceptual Common Denominator between that which distinguishes men from other animals and that which distinguishes birds and bats, etc. from the rest of them. In Rand's philosophy, these two being incommensurate, one could not be differentiated from the other.

Doxa: But one could make sense out of it simply by referring to "animality" itself, which Ayn Rand defines as: "A living entity possessing the faculties of consciousness and locomotion." [24]

Philosophus: Her concept of "animality" consists of two incommensurable C. C. D.'s, locomotion and consciousness. Where would there be the unit that would unite them? It wouldn't be a typical animal cell, since the later certainly does not possess consciousness. Once more, what really ties it together is the fact that we have perceived various beings which fit the definition. Most of them are identified by their morphological characteristics and their typical actions.

Doxa: This brings up a connected issue of fundamentality. Ayn Rand states that when there is more than one distinguishing characteristic, we should look for the one on which most of the greatest number of properties depend and use that one as the "*essential* distinguishing characteristic."[25] Both reason and bipedality—the ability to walk continuously on two legs—distinguish men from other animals. But reason is obviously the more comprehensive. It explains much better why men live in houses instead of caves, fly airplanes, study geometry, read books, etc. I know that you will answer that, on a day-to-day basis, it is by morphology, by shape, that men are distinguished from other things; that it is by the sight of such a being, not by hearing them utter intelligent words that those of us who are not blind recognize them first. I think we all want to hear you develop your main point, now.

Philosophus: I will now do so. Rand teaches that when a new defining characteristic is selected, the old one is still kept within the concept and not discarded. The question is this: under Rand's system, *with a new defining characteristic, is not a new concept made out of the old and the new information?* She taught that one can only differentiate in terms of a commensurate characteristic, reducible to a unit, that one cannot differentiate length from color, or *vice versa*. This being the case, one would suppose that when the new defining characteristic was selected (involving a unit around which the facts that previously belonged to the old concept would be rearranged), the old concept would disappear and a new and more comprehensive one would take its place. Remember, according to her, the very mental act which originally set up the concept of man in the first place was the isolation of two or more instances of some being *moving about and making sounds*. All that the concept refers to in reality is supposed to be mathematically explicable as units established with the two defining attributes. When the higher definition of *being able to do what no other thing which moved and made sounds could do* was realized, the concept was to be orientated around it as a principle.

But here, Rand was wrong. The requiring of new defining characteristics would not simply be an alteration from one axis to another, as when a gyroscope tumbles. It would be a different concept, since the referents now point to a different organizing principle. A concept is not like a sack, indifferent to the way that the percepts and sub-concepts within are organized. The new concept would not simply turn the old one to a new starting position; it would swallow the old.

The fact that we can recognize man through his bodily shape and can also discuss him in intellectual terms implies that there is something wrong with the whole notion of the concept as it is thought of, not only by Rand, but also by many other philosophers.

Penelope: Retaining the old concept while rearranging everything inside would be like the New Testament image of putting new wine in old bottles. In ancient times, fresh wine had been placed in bags made of animal skins, where it fermented. When that wine was gone and new wine was placed in it, some yeast from the old wine would be left inside. That additional fermenting power, plus the stiffness of the old sack would often cause it to burst.

Stanford: When the defining essence is changed, so must the concept. The reality which the concept is supposed to represent may remain the same; the facts referred to by the old concept will not be forgotten, but the concept itself has changed. The person who used to think of ice as that which floats on water has a new concept of ice when he discovers that there are other things like wood which also have this attribute. He comes to define it as the solid form of water.

Philosophus: The problem is greater than that. Much of the phenomena which Rand refers to as belonging to the conceptual level consciousness actually is not something which men deliberately put together after a survey of various particulars. Far from being a Randian construction which is supposed to result from a blending of concretes, they are facts actually experienced. Neither are they ghost-like things emanating from whatever is being perceived, as many Aristotelians suppose, or some sort of a general image as Nominalists would have it. *They are apprehensions of existence, usually of a type of necessity.* Later on, if you will, we will discuss the true nature of universals, but only after we have first considered Rand's position on axioms. But for now, a couple of examples should suffice: Consider force. Is this a concept which we deliberately put together by integrating particulars in the Randian fashion? We may define "force" as the tendency to change the state of a body's rest or motion; but this definition is only another way of stating *force*. If we only had this definition and no knowledge of what it was referring to except through the words used in it, we would not have a clue as to what it means. The answer to the question, "what is our conception of force?" is simply that it is FORCE.[26] There is no way we can get behind this truth and try to show what it is that makes it possible for a force to be potent. Anything which lay behind a force could only be a greater force. Force is not a conception put together out of number of observations. It is a fact that is noticed. It does not even require intellectual skill to discern. Many animals which

Objectivism supposes can barely discern similarities perceive it. Anyone who has ever had a dog or a cat for a pet realizes that they are quite conscious of force and react to it as such; they are not automatons responding to the push and pull of levers and switches. Nor are they passive, like plants. They experience it as part of their world.

Doxa: Don't physicists mean something different by it?

Philosophus: To contemplate force, however, does require a special act of attention, as distinct from merely recognizing it. Physicists have made discoveries concerning this basic fact and have distinguished it from momentum, then from work or energy, and eventually from power. But the fundamental experiences of exerting and resisting remain the same. And while the discoverers were making those distinctions, they were are aware of themselves doing it, and in the process making sure that they were apprehending real differences in nature and not just exercising their imaginations. (More will be said about this later.)

What is causality? It is simply the necessitation of action. Like "force," if we did not already know this, hearing the definition would mean nothing to us. Many animals, of course, are aware of this too. A smaller dog surrenders without a fight to the mercy of a larger one. It knows that flight would be futile and that resistance would fail. This animal is not able to reason about an action's necessity in general terms but it can discern this as a *fact*. It has been said that a dog will distinguish between a master accidently stepping on it and the intentional blows of discipline; which shows that it is not only immediately aware of cause and effect but even has what Rand would called "concepts of consciousness."

Causality would be a fact even if there were only one thing in existence. It is a universal only because it is a fact about everything which moves or undergoes some alteration in its characteristics. Whether there be one such thing or an infinite number does not alter this fact. In short, causality is experienced as a fact of existence along side such attributes as color, shape, and sound. No entrance to a Randian conceptual stage is required. We apprehend the necessity of simple actions almost as easily as the attribute of green color in fir trees.

(However, one should realize that it is metaphysically possible for a cause to *not* itself be an effect of other causes. But for this, we had best wait until we are ready to discuss free will).

Doxa: If causality is grasped so easily, if it can be "apprehended" directly, why is there so much difficulty in science with the term? Why is it as John Stuart Mill once remarked that in some cases a single instance will prove a point and in other cases, hundreds of observations are not enough?

Philosophus: What you are asking about is the famous problem of induction. The problem arises because a large number of instances cannot be equated with infinity. Simply because the occurrence of A has been followed by B every time we have found an A does not prove that it is the cause of B. Night follows day and yet one is not the cause of the other.

This problem was basically solved by John Cook Wilson. Whether others preceded him I do not know. His words on the subject are scattered throughout *Statement And Inference*. The following is my own adaptation of his idea:

With simple things like the lines and curves constructed in plane geometry and elementary arithmetic, algebra, and analytical geometry, the necessities are apprehended easily. In plane and solid geometry, for instance, the properties of points and lines are easily grasped. The attributes are so simple that quite complicated demonstrations involving them can be followed with ease. The truths are self-evident. In slightly more complicated areas like calculus, the answers obtained are obviously true, although there is some debate among mathematicians over the foundations; this last is due to the intellectual disorder in this century.

Much, much greater difficulties, of course, come in ordinary life. There, so many sides exist that many spend most of their time trying to account for it. This is one of the chief reasons for the seemingly endless number of stories about love between the two sexes, each author taking some tangent and exploring the consequences.

To a marked extent, this is also the case with the natural sciences (although they do not have free will to contend with). In plane geometry and solid geometry, a single demonstration is sufficient. Once we have proved the Pythagorean theorem, we need not do so again with a different triangle. It is not necessary to remember the proof; only that we have proved it once. But when one is studying the relationship between the green color of a plant and the role that light plays in vegetable life, many observations from many samples are necessary to convince oneself that it is not just an accidental association. Many more are required to find exactly what the connections are. When one is dealing with matters which are too small or too large to be seen with the naked eye or which cannot adequately be explored through touch, the possibilities of making a false observation are immense.

Then there is the problem of determining whether all the sides of the phenomena under consideration have been found. In some situations, there may never be a complete apprehension. If that be true, then, probability is all there can be in these cases.

This is why Peikoff's theory could not adequately account for the possibility that some unknown category of A-type blood might prove poisonous to A-type recipients even though the transfusion had always been successful in the past. Peikoff treats it as if the possibility were purely epistemological, i.e., that it were only a matter of whether or not there is positive evidence for a theory which contradicts no known fact. But the possibility here is metaphysical as well as epistemological. It is metaphysical because such situations can exist in an unfinished part of a science, and it is epistemological because we do not know in advance whether this is or is not the case. We do not know in advance how many sides or aspects to a problem there are. We may have found that A and B cause C with such A-types and B-types as A_1 and B_1 and also A_1 and B_2, ditto A_2 and B_2, the same for A_3 and B_1, etc. But whether all the types of A are basically the same and will result in the production of some type of C, we cannot know until we have gone through all the types. And this determination cannot be realized until and unless we have exhausted the phenomenon.

In a nutshell, this is the answer to the problem of induction.

It is not a question of the number of instances, *per se*. Were the individual instances all of the same quality, it would not matter whether one or a million repetitions of the same experiment were made.[27] If the experiment were reported correctly, any additional trials would only repeat the same results. The re-performed experiment would prove to the second scientist that the first one had done his job.

Third parties are given a little more assurance, since it then becomes less likely that the first scientist had reported something falsely.

There is a problem about memory, however. Sometimes, we only remember that we have proved something without recalling the actual steps which took us to that proof. The memory of having done something is not the same as the actual doing of it.[28] This poses problems when one is attempting to fully contemplate what one has been doing from start to finish. If one recalls that one has already proved a certain result but has forgotten how it is done, it is a rather easy thing to recover that forgotten proof in the case of plane or solid geometry. But when a number of researchers are working together and relying on each other's work, it is rather difficult for any of them to really say that they have checked out and verified their colleagues' conclusions to the fullest degree. At various points, they have to say, "according the so-and so, such and such is the case...." This adds to the previous problem in making scientific research work a matter of probability rather than certainty.

This is why research is more problematic than manufacturing or invention. If a group of men are building a machine, it is a relatively easy matter to determine whether everyone has been doing as advertised. If one or more of them has shirked his job, the mal-functioning part is likely to call attention to the fact that someone has been lying, and even which one he is. With an invention, a working model will show the thing as a whole, even if, for some reason, its creator was unable to contemplate the detailed workings of his invention in one continuous thought, tracing the operation of all its parts in their abundant intricacy. The problem is practical, not due to a freakish quirk in nature.

The universals which we have discussed are *apprehended necessities*. They apply wherever and whenever they apply. What Rand calls "concepts" are a hodge-podge of many things, not just apprehensions of necessity but also guesses especially theories which we think will correspond with truth when it is found. Unproven ideas lack some necessity; they are merely hypothetical. It is about these that we compare and contrast in the hope of reaching a correct conclusion. But for those apprehended as truths, one instance of a kind can be enough. There is no need to construct a theory as to whether memory and time exists. Consciousness of them is immediate. Causation and force are two more examples. Many of Rand's so-called "first order concepts" are like that, too. We do not, for instance, perceive a solitary tree and then another one and then through the Randian process, put them together. This is done automatically, because no complex particular is perceived just as a particular; when we perceive a particular tree, it is very much like perceiving a single triangle. Just as from that one triangle which we have constructed, we can discover remarkable properties, so with the particular tree, we can discern such properties as that its leaves have certain attributes of shape, color, and texture; its form, its hard and soft parts, and much more. Even a dog or a horse takes notice of some of the attributes of common things. These attributes express *universals*.

Stanford: With all due respect: Aren't you assuming that the experience of necessity in causality is real? I know that this must seem rather annoying to you, but Hume did point out the casual connection is not perceived by the senses like attributes of the objects of Rand's first order concepts.

Philosophus: With all due respect: It is true that causality is not perceived by men and horses through the senses like a sight or a sound, nor is it a construction out of them, as the Randians propose. But its factuality is apprehended, nonetheless. You suggest that this is an assumption. Well, what is that? To *assume* something is to perform a mental act of causality within one's own mind. It is to bring forth an idea which allows one to draw a conclusion one could not otherwise draw. This change in our subjective thinking is itself an instance of causality. Hume did not see this because he accepted Locke's notion that all we perceive is ideas. Because of this, he could only compare subjective this with subjective that. Rand probably did not either, because, for her, perception was an interaction in which the subjective was squeezed out and glued on to the arbitrary. But if we make a clear distinction between subjectivity and objectivity, and the former refers to mental events (rational or not), then the interposition of an idea produces a conclusion different than it would have been in its absence. How, then, were you able to raise the objection about what I have assumed or added?

Stanford: If you made an assumption of causality, so did I. How did I obtain it? I apprehended it. It would do my argument no good to talk about an "association of ideas" confusing the issue because "confusion" is both an effect of what brought it about and a cause where it is used within future speculation.

Philosophus: Exactly.

Penelope: I realize that this is not the proper time to go into the nature of universals. But could you point out what place, if any, concepts have in the scheme of things?

Philosophus: The trouble with the idea of the concept and, to a lesser extent, also with the idea of the percept in Rand's argument, is that they insert something between the act of apprehension and that which is apprehended, which brings about her enveloping context with all its attendant difficulties. Yet, there is a place in existence for concepts. The chief use is in certain matters where certainty does not exist, and the question cannot be resolved simply by repeating the observation(s) in order to rule out mistakes due to bias or inattention and the like.

Recall what was said about scientific research: Suppose that having found that A is B after testing several types of A, the scientist then suspects that all A is B. But he does not know this. It may be that there is a type of A which is not a B. He knows that he has not identified all the kinds of A that there are. But he has a belief that when he has explored all sides of A, he will apprehend the proposition, All A is B, to be true. Another name for this kind of belief is "hypothesis." And, if stated in an organized mode with all the supporting evidence, then it is a "theory." The belief stands apart from the evidence because that latter does not add up to a necessary conclusion. This is a "concept," in other words, it is something that has been constructed as a model in order to guide research and in some respects, anticipate it. Apprehensions, whether in regard to sensation or perception, or with regard to the necessities inherent in the data are not concepts in this sense. They are truths.

The situation with the work-a-day world is only less formal. People know what ice is by its appearance and its coldness; also by its melt-ability. They notice things about it. If they look it up in a dictionary, they may find it defined as the solid form of water. But it exhibits the same morphological characteristics that it always did. *That* is what the various definitions are referring to. A student may read about latent heat, freezing points, and standard conditions of temperature and pressure. Most likely, he will accept what the scientists say about it. This book learning will take the form of a conceptual construction. If he is careful, he will never confuse what he has apprehended with the plausible reports of other men, even experts.

The second case of concepts is with regard to works of the imagination to the extent that they do not depend upon apprehensions already realized. In other words, when Lewis Carroll has Alice conversing with a rabbit, certain characteristics peculiar to these animals are retained in our thoughts so that the story will be intelligible enough to follow. Belief (when it falls short of certainty) and imagination (where it is still intelligible) are the two kinds of concepts. Both are distinguished from apprehension. Remember that even in the case of the secondary characteristics, there is apprehension. (And, of course, there is apprehension while a concept is being formed and while its implications are being understood).

Stanford: Concepts, then, are somewhat hypothetical. They lack the element of necessity. Once something is really apprehended, then it has passed beyond the state of being a "concept." This implies that necessity is not everything, does it not?

Philosophus: Yes. But the apprehension of necessity is the one that is present most of the time. It is present in sensation and those aspects of Rand's treatment of the percept which do not make it into a capsule. One cannot be conscious of the presence of something in consciousness—even if it is only of a memory of a experience—without some degrees of awareness of some quality in it. When one is aware of the fact that this quality *belongs* to it, one has realized necessity in one of its lowest orders.

It should not be forgotten here that while the act of apprehension is "subjective", that which is apprehended is by definition, "objective." What is disclosed in perception is objective. So is necessity.

Apart from necessity, there is also the fact of possibility—more specifically, of metaphysical possibility. If necessity is that which cannot be other than what it is, possibility in this sense is that which can exist but may not. This type of capability is a fact, whether recognized or not. It is not a material fact, for it may never be realized, but it is real, nonetheless.

This truth is grasped best by the artist and the inventor. In both cases, what was not, was brought into existence, not by denying necessity but by taking advantage of it. This is what Michelangelo meant when he spoke of the carving out of the statue which implicitly existed in the stone; this statue being the highest and best possible use of the material, given its size, strength, color, veins.

Possibility in this sense is also different from epistemological possibility, which is concerned with evidence and its sufficiency of evidence, degree of probability, etc. Metaphysical possibility has to do with whether something is capable of existing, or not. It differs from imagination in that it is always in accord with necessity. Fictional characters can only be consistent with necessity in certain respects; they cannot as such exist; just to mention one reason, they have no real parents.

Objectivists themselves distinguish between the two possibilities, but their account is mired in the discussion of context, which is only partly objective. In the proper sense of the word, the objective is the reality apprehended in cognition. Rand and her school have reduced the objective to merely acting in compliance with rational method.

Universals, as we shall see in a few days, do not owe their existence to the human mind. Those which do not depend in any degree on human existence would exist even if there were no men.

Possibilities can exist without a mind being conscious of them. The dynamo was capable of existing even if Nicola

Tesla had never lived, and no one on Earth had taken his place. *But here is the paradox!* Were there no free will anywhere, there could be no possibilities of the metaphysical sort. If all that exists were strictly determined by its antecedents, there could be no alternatives whatsoever. A rock lying in the desert could not be a billionth of an inch away from its present position. It was necessary that it land there and in just that place and be of exactly that size and composition. At that moment, it would have been incapable of existing anywhere else.

Were there no mind anywhere, at any time, even if the blind forces of nature should come together and stupidly shape something like a dynamo, or a watch lying on a seashore, they would never have been possibilities, even moments before they started coming into being. They would have been necessary products of necessary forces at every moment. Even a billion years before they came together, they would not have been possible. They would have been necessary, as the result of inexorable forces, just like the spray of a waterfall lands where it must.

The Objectivists make a distinction between the metaphysical and the man-made, the first being that which cannot be changed, and the second being that which could have been different because it depends for its existence upon what is usually called "free will."[29] Here, I am farthest and closest to Objectivism. We pass by each other, but go off in straight lines, never again to meet—for directions do not double back on each other. The Objectivists have little to say about the metaphysical possibilities which are facts simply because beings with free will exist, regardless of whether these possibilities are ever realized, or even thought. But that will be postponed for a later discussion.

Doxa: Unless someone else has something to add or subtract—which I doubt— today's meeting is closed. Next time, we will discuss the axioms of Objectivism. I will make the strongest case that I can for them. It is here that Ayn Rand's claim to be a great philosopher of reason is strongest.

DAY VII

AXIOMS

*T**he four are sitting at the same table with books and papers and writing instruments in front of them. Most of the other patrons are wildly excited by the victory won by the city's basketball team.*

Doxa: Axiomatic concepts, Ayn Rand teaches, are at the basis of all objectivity. Without them, no real thought that connected with the external world would be possible.

The three basic axioms are existence, identity, and consciousness; all others are corollaries of these. When one says, "I am conscious," all three are implied, for by thinking it one affirms that someone is conscious (existence); that the one who possesses this capability is something specific, namely myself (identity); and that I am aware (consciousness).

One can find an axiomatic concept by asking oneself whether in the act of denying it, one does not presuppose it at some level. One cannot rationally ask "Does Existence exist?" for instance. The question answers itself; in order to ask it, someone must first exist.

Ayn Rand holds that whenever one engages in a complicated form of reasoning, recognition of axioms prevents the mind from wandering into unreality. Behind every school of mysticism, she teaches, one will find smuggled into their verbose declarations, mind-numbing denials of some fundamental axiom, usually identity. She states that this is particularly the case with Kant and Hegel.[1]

What is it about existence, identity, and consciousness that makes them axiomatic concepts? The answer is that each is an identification of a fundamental fact of reality which cannot be further analyzed, cannot be broken into facts still more basic.[2]

Ayn Rand is not the first philosopher to see the centrality of existence; others have noted that existence seems to be so full of mystery simply because it is everywhere present; that we extend the concept of existence to apply to realities which we have not experienced; and that when we so extend it, we mean more than that we have extended a word—but that the existents, known and unknown, are real.[3] She is, however, the first to assert it as the grand principle of what purports to be a thoroughly integrated rational system. It will be recalled that Ayn Rand would have called her philosophy, "existentialism," were it not first appropriated by another kind of philosophy.

Axiomatic concepts, Ayn Rand asserts, have no Conceptual Common Denominator; that is to say, they are not differentiated from anything else. This is because there is nothing from which the facts of existence could be differentiated in order to form the concept "existence." It is simply all the facts.[4]

This should be of interest to us. Although the Conceptual Common Denominator is fallacious, it may be that some truths can be found in this realm of her thought where there are no C. C. D.'s.

An axiom "is not the abstraction of an attribute from a group of existents, but of a basic fact from all facts."[5] One can say that an entity possesses a certain attribute; for instance, that an apple *has* a certain color, or a bird *has* wings, or a man *has* the faculty of reason. But it would not be rational to say that a vegetable, an animal, or a man possesses in addition to all their other attributes, that of existence. Existence is not an attribute because existence is implied by all the attributes themselves. It is a fundamental fact which runs through all that is.

Stanford: I can see how a man would still be a man if he lost his arm; how a rose would still be a rose even if its red color were chemically expunged and then it was dyed black. I can even see how a man would remain a man if he lost his capacity to reason; such men can be found in veteran's hospitals and old folks homes. But there are some attributes which cannot be taken away without changing the entity itself. For instance, the roundness of a sphere. Remove that attribute and what was once a sphere would be something else. The attribute of roundness permeates it just as much as the fact that it exists. When a block of ice melts, it is no longer ice.

Doxa: What is so crucial about these particular attributes is that their destruction simultaneously brings about the demise of the entity which possesses the attribute. The axiom, existence, is more fundamental. It is crucial not just to spheres and red colored objects, but to all that is.

How do we become aware of axioms? Ayn Rand is clear. "Their peculiarity lies in the fact that *they are perceived or experienced directly, but grasped conceptually.*"[6] For Ayn Rand, the fundamental building block of knowledge is the concept of the existent.

Penelope: At first glance, Rand's procedure seems to be perfectly reasonable. A person who doubts "existence" doubts everything, and by that doubt even doubts his own doubt, since that kind of uncertainty is part of everything. The absurdity of such a procedure is quite evident. But is this not also the case with many of those concepts which Rand does not regard as axiomatic? Suppose someone who is not blind or color-blind doubts "red." If the doubter seriously proposed to proceed along that line, she would destroy her consciousness of the continuity of the color spectrum. A blind spot in the mind would exist with respect to those hues which are normally called "red." One would also blank out orange, since the latter is a combination of red and yellow. One would also have to excise the purples and the violets. What would one see then? Not greys, because the supposition is that one is not color blind; what one would see would probably be a ghostlike appearance. What would such a one see if she caught a glimpse of Old Glory waving in the wind? A weak person might faint from the fact that she could not take it in. One could see the sun during the daytime, but it would be dangerous to drive at sundown, because it would then be invisible. Colors also effect emotions. Red is supposed to evoke strong feelings of desire. Doubting causes is a well-known way to induce mental disease.

Suppose one denied that the table was real. If someone actually doubted it in a systematic way, where would she eat? On the floor? But to do this, any idea of a raised surface would have to be suppressed. If this enterprising skeptic had a bed which was raised up off the floor, she would have to suppress or destroy the connections which would allow her to see the utility of placing objects on a raised surface. Her clothes would either have to be on hangers or lying on the floor. But since a slight connection exists between the pole running through the closet along which the hangers are strung and a table, this too would have to be stopped by some sort of mental block. If one methodically doubted the TV set and what it was about, at a certain point, one would simply lose the ability to understand electronics at a level much above that of the Edison light bulb. What of the person who doubted the existence of the Tiddley-Wink? Think of it! Such a person, if she were a conscientious skeptic, would have to block-off the ability to flip with her fingers a small plastic disk. This would eventually cause her to deny the physical laws covering the dynamics of rotating particles.

Doxa: Most of these things which you mentioned are percepts. And according to Objectivism, percepts are self-evident. Therefore, part of your illustrations do not make the point.

Penelope: The electronic workings of the TV set transcend the realm of percepts. But, let us not quibble. Let us instead take something that is neither a Randian axiom, nor knowingly perceived. Suppose we take a perfect circle, which we could never verify if it existed in nature. If one really doubted it, if one really thought it was an irrational idea—not just whether or not it existed in some Platonic realm of ideas, but whether it could even be realized in thought—I submit that one could not build so much as the wheel of an automobile without having extreme misgivings; one could not even drive a car without fearing that it would fail. One could not drive automatically; one would soon have to take to the back roads, because the slow lane on the freeways would be too much. Or if that is too concrete, doubt instead the quantity indicated by "Π". Much of exact geometry would be impossible. I do not need to repeat what was discussed at our fifth meeting.

The principle is the same when one doubts something without reason, whether it be a concept which covers all like existence, or less, much, much less, like the color red, or an object or only an abstraction. The more that is dependent on it, the more that is taken away when one systematically doubts it. What is true of a concept of the greatest generality like "existence" is also true of the humble tiddley-wink. A person like Hume may get by, saying memories are simply fainter than impressions and mean nothing else, but if he merely put what he remembered on the same level with what he was imagining, he could not even write his essays—soon, he would be burbling like a baby. The trick of such skeptics is to assume the attitude of defying reason without really being irrational, of talking about reducing will to mere sensations without really turning one's decisions into nothing more substantial than pin pricks on one's arm; of supposing that causality is nothing more than an invariable sequence without actually attempting to break tradition in a given case.

Doxa: But that is the whole point of axioms. They are present in not just a few facts, but the totality. When the mind is challenged as it is today by the irrational, there is a need to show that the intellectual grounds on which the skeptic is standing sinks because of his attack on reason. It may be enough in a few cases to stand one's ground by showing the absurdity of doubting something by pointing to what would disappear alongside of the level of awareness and knowledge which it requires, but if this is not enough, then we need to turn to the fundamental axioms.

Penelope: If someone insists on playing the skeptic, if they are not going to be stopped by my arguments, neither will they be stopped by your showing them their connection to the fact that existence exists or that they are contradicting themselves. Perhaps, the doubter is telling herself, "Eureka! At last I have found it—a contradiction that exists in reality. I will go down in history."

Doxa: Just because a man who persists at irrationality might succeed at destroying his mind does not mean that axioms of the greatest generality are useless. Even on the basis of your argument, it would follow that should the first line of defense give way, then one may have to go higher and higher levels of reality in order to remind oneself or one's opponent that they are questioning their own questioning.

Stanford: It is true that existence is a universal of greater generality than roundness, in other words, that it applies to more particulars. But it was by noticing the simple sphere and by attending to it that we were able to discern the universal, roundness, not by concentrating all of our attention upon the fact that existence exists. I still say that the universal roundness, limited in application as it may be, is just as crucial to a sphere as the latter's existence. Indispensable attributes are just as certain in their restricted range as are universals of greater generality.

Doxa: The degree of certainty about a specific attribute in a case like that may be the same as that afforded by the universal, existence, but they are not on the same level. Not only is *existence* of greater generality than these other attributes, but it is often implied by them. For instance, in the sentence, "that is round," it is implied by all three words, especially by the verb. The reference to the universal, roundness, has to be stated explicitly. That means that existence is more comprehensive.

Penelope: There are circumstances in which using axiomatic arguments creates more difficulties than it solves. Euclid himself stumbled into this error. This happened in the very first demonstration of the *Elements* (Book I.1). First, he proved that two sides of the triangle which he had constructed were each equal to a third side, that in triangle ACB, side AC and side BC have the same length as side AB. Strangely, however, he did not immediately conclude that they are, therefore, equal to each other. Instead of that, he drug in the axiom that two things that are equal to a third thing are equal to each other. Then came the majestic conclusion that the three sides are equal. But the introduction of this axiom was unnecessary. If we cannot apprehend the fact of their equality immediately, using the axiom would never make it intelligible to us.[7] The conclusion follows from the meaning of equality. If we were never able to draw the universal from the particulars, adding the universal in order to make the conclusion work would be an arbitrary act, almost as if we had tried to memorize the demonstration, instead of following it. It is from the particular that we derive the universal, not the other way around. The power in answering a skeptic by recourse to a universal as wide as existence is that it can be drawn from the very particular which they refer to in making their argument. In the present situation: it is not because of the axiom, existence, that we conclude that TV's and tiddley-winks exist—or that perfect circles can exist, or that there must be a quantity which we signify as "Π". Rather, it is by examining these that we can understand a universal like existence.

Doxa: In the case you mention, the axiom used by Euclid was a derivative. Once one has understood the meaning of "equality," one already knows that two things are equal to a third are equal to each other. In this case, the real axiom is just one word, not the complex proposition which depended upon it. Far from showing the superfluity of axioms, the example only underscores their significance.

Let us return to the examples of roundness and redness. Try to imagine a mind that is conscious of colors and also conscious of shapes, but is completely oblivious to the fact that they exist. Since metaphysical possibility means being capable of existing, such a mind could not even conceive of this idea. All that consciousness could have presented before it would be *happenings*. It could not even remember what had already transpired, for memory announces and gives notice that certain events had once existed.

Stanford: Yet, with all that, I still say that the degree of certainty is no greater than in the case of the axiom. If redness, for instance, were any less certain than existence, then the consciousness of the existence of that color in a given case would be contradicted, which would negate existence as well, for (according to the argument just presented) the two are inextricably bound together.

Philosophus: Rand made too much out of this very comprehensive fact. She spoke of axioms as "the *constants* of man's consciousness, the *cognitive integrators* that identify and thus protect its continuity."[8] She would have it that it is because round things and red things can be tied together through the fact that they exist that we can think of them together in a coherent way. To the contrary, it is because the human mind can apprehend all this that it is coherent. Axioms are not required.

Doxa: The challenge is accepted. Unless there is something which persists in the flow of thought with its ever changing content, the mind becomes chaotic. When one perceives a red entity, whether it be a beam of light or the surface of an object, what one is perceiving is that it exists. One does not perceive that it is red and also that it exists in the manner of a man noting first that the red object in question is an automobile and then that it is a Packard. What one perceives is the existence of the color; the two are inseparable, except through an independent act of thought. This is also the case when we cannot identify some important attributes of an object of perception. For instance, if something flashed before our eyes so fast that we could not recognize it, we could at least be certain that it existed, *whatever it was*. We cannot use our perceptive faculties without concluding that what they are disclosing exists. This is the case both when we identify certain specific attributes which it possesses and also when we are not able to do that.

According to Ayn Rand, the units of this axiom "are every entity, attribute, action, event or phenomenon (including consciousness) that exists, has ever existed or will ever exist."[9] (This is also the case with her axiom of identity, which we will come to later.)

Philosophus: From this, it might be argued that to be classified as an existent, the candidate must in some way affect the senses, even if only potentially. If it cannot even in principle agitate the retina or put pressure on the eardrum or touch the skin or affect the tongue, it cannot exist. This must be either through direct perception or indirectly through the medium of some instruments such as microscopes, cloud chambers, or telescopes. What this philosophy terms "conceptual knowledge" is ultimately derived from the external world.

Doxa: That is basically correct. Ayn Rand held that there was nothing that man could not know. If someone should argue in a theoretical fashion, however, that there might be something too large or too small for man to perceive with his instruments, I suppose that she would say that for the sake of the argument, that it too existed, although by hypothesis men could not be aware of it.

Philosophus: Rand would also have to assert that space and time have no independent existence, which indeed is just what she does. We have already seen the fallacies involved in her attempt to reduce time to a nest of relationships. Space also exists. It is a fundamental fact, independent both of matter and of mind. If there were nothing in the universe, there would still be that great emptiness. The Objectivists would emphatically reject the statement of James McCosh of the Reidian school of thought that "the intelligence does not create [time and space], and it discovers them as having an existence independent of the mind contemplating them, as having this existence whether the mind contemplates them or not, and an existence out of and beyond the mind as it thinks them."[10]

To Rand and her Objectivists, it is all matter of that mysterious "context" of theirs. But, let us go on and see what else her interpretation of the universal, existence, attempts to leave out. What of the negative? It does none of these things. Yet, it is indispensable in thought and discourse. Rand tells her readers to be on the lookout for those who commit the fallacy of reifying zero, of trying to treat nothing as a particular type of existent.[11]

Doxa: Ayn Rand answers that "nonexistence is not a fact, it is the *absence* of a fact, it is a derivative concept pertaining to a relationship, i.e., a concept which can be formed or grasped only in relation to some existent that has ceased to exist. (One can arrive at the concept 'absence' starting from the concept 'presence,' in regard to some particular existent(s); one cannot arrive at the concept 'presence' starting from the concept 'absence,' with the absence including everything.) Non-existence as such is a zero with no sequence of numbers to follow it, it is the nothing, the total blank."[12]

Philosophus: The quick answer is that the absence of a fact is also fact. A more developed answer follows:

Consider whether our idea of absence is formed fully from the notion of presence. If it is not, then it points to an axiom as well, and one that is not simply derivable from that of perceptible existence.

The act of forming a concept, according to Rand, involves differentiation; and differentiation is an act of negation. This being the case, the negative is as primordial for thought as Rand imagines the positive to be, although there may be no existents perceived by men that are negative. Differentiation cannot be reduced to a subspecies of its corresponding positive, integration, for the first involves something analogous to subtraction and the second, to addition. Is this not a negative fact?

Doxa: The Objectivist would probably answer that it is not. Subtraction is a positive fact, even though there is a taking away. In the ordinary work-a-day world, we see a man dig a hole and witness the withdrawal of earth by the spade and the placing it upon a pile. This, I submit, is a positive act. Throughout the whole operation, there are only concrete events taking place. It is only because the normal surface is so much larger that we think of it as a concavity. Valleys are not looked upon that way. But this cavity is as fully measurable as a hill, only it goes in the opposite direction, a scoop instead of a lump. Here is no real negation; this non-level is in actuality only a different sort of positive?

Philosophus: In the instance of the hole, negation may not be a necessary idea, but let us consider cases where it is. Rand considers the syllogism to be a hall mark of reason. Now, the premises of a syllogism consist of propositions. The affirmative proposition and the negative proposition are as different as they can be. While it is true that the negative cannot do what the affirmative can do, namely tell what existent A is and can do, there are things the affirmative cannot do which its contradiction can, i.e., it cannot tell what A is not and cannot do. If I know that A is B, I cannot know that it is not C, unless I have the requisite information supplied by the negative. The *reductio ad absurdum* argument in mathematics reduces the situation to two alternatives, one is disproved, leaving the other. The real world inventor, Thomas Alva Edison, thought that he was gaining in his knowledge of reality when he found that a filament of a certain material which he was testing for his laboratory would not work. Suppose that there were a number of things that were being tried in an experiment, and, after the whole list had been gone through, only one material was suitable; this would constitute positive knowledge that only *one* would work. If a substitute had been found, it could have been used in place of the other during a time when the latter was scarce. Now, Rand believed that the world was finite; which means that there are only so-many alternatives available, never an infinite number. Were she correct there, it would follow that if one were given a subject X with properties a and b, and one wanted to determine what other properties belonged to it, as we proceeded to test it for likely properties c, d, e, f, and so on, the ones that did not pan out would tell us something about the reality which we were seeking to uncover.

Doxa: What is it that you are trying to show?

Philosophus: That negation and absence are legitimate universals in their own right and not simply derivatives of the corresponding positives. These basic facts will become plainer from my next illustration. Rand and Peikoff both like to try to equate the negative with zero. Peikoff writes: "If gremlins, for instance, do not exist, then they are nothing and have no consequences. In such a case, to say: 'Prove that there are no gremlins,' is to say: 'point out the facts of reality that follow from the nonexistence of gremlins.' But there are no such facts. Nothing follows from nothing."[13] This argument goes too far; there are subtle errors involved in equating false or even impossible concepts all to zero. This stands out even in mathematics. Let us take the idea that sin x = a/ b where a/b is greater than unity. This is impossible, as every student of trigonometry has learned: sines go from 0 to +1 to -1 back to 0 in cycles; they cannot exceed one. Even so, to equate this and other fallacies to zero involves a double error: (1) In some problems, for instance +a + -a = 0, zero is absolutely the correct answer, as is sin 0° = 0; (2) To equate all these fallacies to zero would destroy all algebraic equations, as zero would take on all sorts of weird meanings.[14]

Consider once again the diagonal of the square, which is incommensurable to its sides. It is simply a negative fact that the quantitative relation between the two cannot be reduced to a common unit, yet there is a quantitative relation of a certain type. As Harold Joachim put it: "It is not a meaningless or an 'infinite' negation (like e.g. 'the diagonal is not hot'), because its negative form conceals a challenge to recognize this unfamiliar relation, and to attempt its determination by new methods."[15]

Doxa: What does this negative fact tell us about existence?

Philosophus: It tells us that quantity is not exhausted by number.

The negative simply cannot be reduced to non-existence in the sense meant by Rand and the Objectivists, *for they say that their axiom can have no contraries.* If the positive statement extends our knowledge of reality, so does the negative. If we consider the two forms of the positive propositions: namely, All A is B & some A is B and compare and contrast them with the two negative forms: No A is B & some A is not B, we find that both stand as species under the genus "proposition."[16] Both are equally real, although, in the final analysis recognition of the positive must come first in time. And, this is another case of a genus heading an incommensurate pair of species, affirmative propositions and negative propositions. This is something which Rand, like Hegel, seems to have been incapable of realizing. One cannot be reduced to the other.

Doxa: But if the only propositions we had were negative ones, we could never reach any conclusions.

Philosophus: That is true. But, at the same time, without the negative, the reality which we could appreciate would be poor indeed. To dismiss negative statements because they are not completely intelligible without reference to a corresponding positive is to confuse dependence-for-intelligibility with being nothing more than a consequence. But this, manifestly, is not the case.

Penelope: What is its origin?

Philosophus: Obviously, experience of the **not** began early. Two possibilities present themselves; the first is that it is inborn; the second is that it is not. As an example of the first, there is the fact that it is an indispensable part of the process of differentiation, which exists not only in Objectivist theory, but also in reality, (although two or more instances of the same quality are not required). On the other hand, if it were not innate and pre-given in experience, then it has its origin in memory, in the cognition of the difference between what *is* and what *was*. This could have come as early as the cry given by the new born after the physician's slap; it could even have come in the womb. Most likely, this memory was triggered by a pain, which is, in a different way, a negative experience and, of course, is also natural.

Doxa: But that pain would not be a metaphysical negative, the idea of a non-A.

Philosophus: True. To get the latter, requires comparison and contrast. And, that certainly involves memory. Pains unaccompanied by memory are ruled out. House flies seek to escape from the advancing swatter, having been warned by the rush of air; but this is probably merely an in-built mechanism, as Rand herself probably would have been glad to admit. The apprehension of negativity requires a comparison between the present state in which something is hurtful or a good is absent and the memory of the better time. In short, the idea of the negative arises either from a physical pain or the ruination of an expectation.

Penelope: The latter would not necessarily be the defeat of anticipated pleasure. Couldn't it be the non-occurrence of an expected pain?

Philosophus: Yes. But in either case, absence is drawn directly from memory, which is an ultimate power of mind. The negative is an implication of this, the result of the relationship between what is being remembered and what is immediately being perceived. And Rand does allow for this. Her concept of the "existent" is supposed to refer to entities, actions, attributes, and relationships.[17]

Negative terms can be shown to exist. It would follow then that in order to account for reality, the Randians would have to allow a place to both presence and absence as legitimate classifications of existence. Presence could not be derived from absence, nor absence from presence; recall that it took the use of memory, the recognition of what is absent, in order to bring into focus this fact. It would also follow that the same would be the case for the two principal categories of propositions, the affirmative and the negative. **A is not-non B** cannot be drawn directly from **A is B**, for there is always the **not** and the **non** to account for. Note that they stand as species under the genus, "proposition." Like straight and curvilinear lines, neither of these have a Conceptual Common Denominator. There is something in presence that is ineradicably removed from absence, and the same for the other. By Rand's own account, they would have to be at least co-ordinate.

This presents a new problem. If absence is a type of existence, it would seem that Rand would have to admit the independent existence of space. It is just a single step from the kind of an absence which exists because something has been removed to the kind of absence where there never was anything present in the first place. And with that, we have not only space, but empty space. But this, as we have seen, she cannot admit. She would not consider an absence abstracted from all entities and actions to be valid. To the Objectivist, the idea of absence is to be defined in a certain context; to take it out of that and declare that there could such an existent would be out-of-context.

One can intellectually abstract away all types of presence one by one. If one can do it with one particular entity in order to form an idea of its absence, one can do it with all. There is no reservation inherent in the structure of thought which would prevent this. After this abstraction, what remains is space (and time, which will be discussed later). The necessity of empty space is disclosed by perception, the very thing which Peikoff claims is the basis for accepting axioms themselves.[18] Empty space is posited every time we consider how much more dense a chunk of steel is than an equal volume of air. The image given through perception is of different parts, up and down, to the sides, and in-front-of and in-back-of. To deny this is to claim that the senses lie in a big way. What is this bundle of relations which we in our limited context are supposed to perceive as "space," but which creatures, presumably of a wider experience would perceive some other way? But we cannot do this, because the term "bundle," only to mention "wider," already presupposes the very fact the Randian is trying to analyze away. As was suggested before, geometrical demonstrations would have to be weird things: When we think we are proving that the interior angles of a triangle equals two right angles, we would not even know what we are proving. Instead, there would be a kind of parallelism words cannot express. If one attempted to explain syllogistic reasoning that way, reason would turn into a metaphor. What the two premises actually demonstrated when all facts are discovered might turn out to be something indistinguishable from what most people would think of as mysticism, the very thing Rand condemned the loudest! But the Randian answers, "Only within a context". To make sense, syllogistic reasoning has to be defined in trans-contextual terms.

Doxa: Wouldn't the *entity* help? Objectivism recognizes corollaries to axioms. These are axioms which are of less generality than the three main axioms. An example is that of *entity*. This, you will recall, was the first stage in the development of the concept *existent*, the second being *identity* and the third being *unit*. In this first stage, the child is supposed to become conscious of objects. The Objectivists regard the concept, "entity," to be an axiom corollary to "existence," which is logical, since it is held by them to be the first stage in the development of the axiom. It is an important corollary to Dr. Peikoff, because he asserts that entities make up the entirety of the world we perceive; we can observe nothing else, he says.[19] Couldn't this be a bridge across contexts?

Philosophus: Yet, Peikoff later through such cases as his "energy puffs" casts doubt on the finality of the entities disclosed through the senses as existing in space and time; if this were true, how can they be self-evident? Perhaps he is proposing to argue that it is through accepting the concept of the entity as self-evident, but provisional, that we are later able to use it as a launching pad to go deeper into the heart of reality. But if the first stage in the development of the concept of existence is eventually dispensable, what of *identity* and *unit*? Are they too only "contextual absolutes," later to be replaced? If there were no such thing as place and distance, then there would be no such thing as "no such thing" either. Later on, we will see what it is that the Objectivists plan to do away with and what they regard as final.

In short, Rand's version of the universal of existence is incomplete; her statement of it surreptitiously denies the independent existence of space and time, it also slights the metaphysical status of the negative. Furthermore, Peikoff has unintentionally compromised it.

Doxa: Let us turn to Ayn Rand's concept of the law of identity.

Ayn Rand teaches that identity and existence comprise everything; that they are just different ways of characterizing the same facts. Existence exists and every existent is identical with itself. For Ayn Rand, "A is A" is both a statement of a principle of logic and an ontological statement of existence.

Philosophus: Peikoff attempts to get as much as he can out of it. He even attempts to refute Christianity with it: "Can God perform miracles? A 'miracle' does not mean merely the unusual. If a woman gives birth to twins, that is unusual; if she were to give birth to elephants, that would be a miracle. A miracle is an action not possible to the entities involved by their nature; it would be a violation of identity."[20] This involves a fundamental misunderstanding of the argument from miracles. The argument is that since the result obviously was not from the perceptible entity involved, it must have come from some other source. This was the point of John Locke's famous essay on miracles. Miracles are not based on a denial of the law of causality; rather they are based on its affirmation. If a given result—say the sudden healing of a leper—cannot come from the words uttered by a mere man; yet, many are healed of various diseases that way, then there must be some power much greater involved. No sensible person would contend that a man was simply followed around by a number of coincidental events. If one believed that anything could happen from anything, then one could never be affected by any argument. Hume's answer to Locke amounted to the conjecture that maybe there was an unknown cause generated by some mundane laws of nature which had not yet been discovered. But Peikoff could not rightfully avail himself of this opportunity; his definition of possibility would forbid it.

Doxa: Couldn't an Objectivist argue that since conclusions based on a great number of observations, like, for instance, the supposed sight of the sun traveling around the earth—have been proved wrong, that this might happen in a situation like this too?

Philosophus: Consider, wisely: The Humean argument is based upon what Dr. Stanford has identified as a *conceivability*, which means that no evidence exists for it but it does not contradict the known. Drawing an analogy from other circumstances in which it has been found that what was widely believed because of what seemed like overwhelming evidence was later shown to have been overturned by subsequent knowledge, the Humean argument is that such might be the case with some apparent miracle. The prototype, of course, is the Copernican controversy. But again, if we have no evidence that this is the case with respect to a given miracle, that controversy cannot be enlisted as evidence. It is just conceivable. But even if we were waive this aside for the sake of the argument, it would still be the case that its sole support would be a rough analogy, with the overwhelming probability on the side of the miracle. Even if we granted it, this would be no help to Peikoff; he would have to abandon his argument over blood-types, and much else besides.

Penelope: Leonard Peikoff, shake hands with David Hume!

Doxa: Now, let us consider the law of contradiction, the negative form of the law of identity. Objectivism regards it to be merely a corollary of identity and therefore of little metaphysical significance beyond that.

Penelope: I beg to differ. I think that the law of contradiction has played a tremendous role in the development of Rand's thought. In her writing, I have found it in constant use. I do not say that this is wrong. I merely say that it is an important part of that philosophy. Many of Rand's ideas can be seen as having been formed in emphatic opposition to dialectical materialism which teaches that contradictions exist right in the heart of reality. She wanted to emphasize that they existed only in speech. In this respect, her position is like that of the German philosopher, Eugen Dühring, against whom Frederick Engels directed a long polemic, called *Anti-Dühring*. Dühring wrote: "The first and most important thesis concerning the fundamental logical properties of being, relates to the *exclusion of contradiction*. Contradiction is a category which can appertain only to a combination of ideas, but not to reality."[21] While under Soviet tutelage, the young Rand may have read these words in Engels' famous book and found some agreement with his antagonist. (Dühring also believed that the universe was finite).

Doxa: It does not follow that she had read him, either. It may be that this was only an earlier Marxist reply to a type of criticism which Ayn Rand was later to develop. However, to restate what I tried to say a short time ago, according to Objectivism, the principle of contradiction contains nothing that is not in the positive form of axiom of identity.

Philosophus: There is a question as to whether it can be stated without reference to time. Kant, of course, held that time might not apply to the real noumenal world that existed beyond that disclosed by the senses but that logic would nevertheless remain. Of that, we will not discuss any farther here.[22] Rand herself was in need of an analogous statement because her axiom of identity must hold regardless of context, but she thought that time is only a relationship; for her it could not exist except as a relationship among entities.

Her theory of time has already been refuted from the standpoint of memory, but it should be answered in a discussion of identity and contradiction as well. Many years ago, a writer named Martha Hurst found that there are two ways in which the law of contradiction is used. The first and less common use does indeed contain no necessary reference to time. This is the statement that A is not non-A.[23] Here, as long as A is understood to mean all that A is, known and unknown, it is correct. This can be done even if one is discussing a temporal matter. An example of this is the statement that a seventeen year old boy is not some other age. That is axiomatic. In this case, "A" stands for "a seventeen year old boy" and "non-A" means "some other age," i.e., "A is not non-A."

The second use that she found is that A cannot be non-A at the same time and in the same space. This use, I will argue, cannot be reduced to the first one. For instance, suppose "A" stands for the same youth. And that youth is now a certain number of years old, namely, 18 years old. Here, "A" is the same youth at each year of his life; he was not a non-A when he was 17 years old and will still be A, should he live to 90. Under the first timeless form, the 18 year old youth could not be the 17 year old youth (non-A). But, of course, we know that the same youth would have to have first reached his 17th birthday before he could turn 18. The second and more common form cannot be reduced to the first form. To attempt it, we would have to ignore the fact that it is the same person existing at different times. Another example: This stamp which you just saw me place on a letter which is intended for England cannot be here in the United States and over there at the same time, and so forth.

Let us ask: What does it mean to define time as merely a relationship between entities? When one says that the youth in question is 18 years of age, one could mean that since he was born, the earth traveled around the sun 18 times. But "since" is a temporal term. So is "was." How can this be stated strictly in terms of the relationship between entities without reference to past, present, or future as realities independent of these? I submit that this is impossible. The number of times that the sun traveled around the earth implies of necessity a relationship of temporal succession; also the youth is supposed to have existed simultaneously with each of these eighteen revolutions. No matter how one looks at it, temporality cannot be expunged. If the youth had died in the womb and never had been born, Rand would have had to agree that the earth would have made these revolutions about the sun, anyway. That being the case, the 18 revolutions of the earth was independent of that boy's existence at age 18. It would have happened even if all humanity had died, if all life had become extinct. It does not take any leap in logic to see that if there were no earth or sun, then during the time that it would have taken the earth to make its revolution around the sun, some motions would have taken place in the stars. Let us go one step farther. Suppose, *impossible,* there were no matter, no molecules of any kind, no atoms, no radiation, nothing. According to the physicists, one could make a reliable statement about this. The temperature would be at absolute zero. And it can be approached in a laboratory. So it is not nonsense to talk this way. Where would there be the contradiction in saying of such a situation, that throughout the endless eons of time, the temperature would be at zero? "Existence exists," you say? Very well. What about the temperature?

Doxa: The question of time and space should be brought up at our next meeting and discussed in more detail. There is one more consideration with respect to the Objectivist axiom of identity which should be attended to, however. Ayn Rand, following the early twentieth century British logician, H. W. B. Joseph, held that causality was the law of identity as applied to action.[24] Joseph's words were: "...it is no more than a corollary of the Law of Identity, that the same thing unaltered on different occasions, or two things of the same nature, should under the same conditions produce the same effect."[25] The idea is that A is what it is and because of what it is, it, in conjunction with B and C, which are also identities, is able to bring about effect X, which also has a specific identity with certain specific properties or powers. This is a shift from the normal formulation of cause as the necessitation of an event. Let us determine whether the Joseph-Rand substitution is an improvement over the old formulation.

Ayn Rand holds that "necessity" has a meaning similar to that of "identity," but that it refers to those things which are produced by the forces of nature in contrast to those which are man-made.[26]

Dr. Peikoff goes into more detail: "A fact is 'necessary' if its nonexistence would involve a contradiction. To put the point positively: a fact that obtains 'by necessity' is one that obtains 'by identity.' Given the nature of existence, this is the status of every (metaphysically given) fact. Nothing more is required to ground necessity."[27]

In its positive form, he seems to be equating necessity and identity. But this is not has actual intention, for he says a few sentences later that "the above formula does not apply to man-made facts; the antonym of 'necessary' is 'chosen,' chosen by man."[28]

Philosophus: At this point, I think Peikoff is in error. The antonym of the necessary should be the metaphysically possible. This last refers to what might exist but does not. To equate the realm of possibility with that which has been chosen by man would be a mistake. To give a couple of examples: an artist may die before he is able to realize his conception; a possible invention may be missed by everyone. This also has to do with bad as well as good. For instance, in 19th century France, there was this popular general whom the Paris mob had hoped would seize the government, but he turned his horse around at the last minute.

Stanford: Rand and Peikoff restrict the equation of the necessary and the identical to the non- man-made. The older idea had "cause" itself defined as "the necessitation of an action or event." The Objectivists use the term, "identity", as the second stage in the development of the concept, "existent," the crucial particular of their universal, "existence." This stage in the child's mental development, we are told, is characterized by an awareness of individual entities which he can identify and set out in distinction to other things in his field of perception.[29]

The child has not yet reached the third stage, that of the Randian unit, in which he can regard things as members of groups. Yet, Peikoff teaches that it is at this second stage that he implicitly recognizes causality.[30] And there is a certain plausibility in this. The child gives a gentle push to a ball and it easily rolls across the floor; he attempts this with a book and finds that it slides only with difficulty. Try as he will and he cannot make the book act as the ball. And now we come to the point: which idea of cause comes closer to the understanding of the child at this state, that of identity or necessity? To grasp it as a form of law of identity, the child will have to have reached Rand's third stage: he would have to see that the ball behaves as it does because of the *kind* of entity that it is; that the flat book cannot roll so easily because that in not in its nature. Under the idea of necessity, there does not need to be any such reference to generality; this particular object which he will learn to call a "ball" rolls easily, but cannot be forced open by his little hands like that other object, the one later to be known as a "book." The book will not roll; it will glide with some difficulty. No matter how hard the child tries to make it roll, it will not do so. This, I submit, is an implicit recognition of *necessity*. The connection with identity is a sophisticated notion predicated upon the notion that it is in entities that all properties may be found. To think that it would be a contradiction for an entity to act other than it is involves a fairly advanced knowledge. What the ball will or will not do comes first; then comes the realization that this is because of what it is. Necessity, then, is the earlier discovery.

Doxa: I disagree. Before the child could make the determination that it was impossible for the book to roll or for the ball to be opened in his little hand, he would first have to *identify* the entities in question as well as certain key attributes. Having made those determinations, any subsequent conclusions he might draw up concerning what they can or cannot do would be inextricably bound up with what he had identified, earlier. He would not have to conclude that it was because of the *generic* class to which the two items belonged that he was able to get the ball to roll but not the book. It would be enough if he could see that this was the case with these particular objects.

Philosophus: Try to imagine it: without an awareness of identity, you would have an idea of rolling without any connection to the object that was doing the rolling; you would perceive an inside being opened without a reference to a book. What that would suggest would not be necessity but *utter randomness.*

Penelope: From such an encounter, a child might form a notion of necessity. But at the same time, he would also note that he can choose while those two dumb things, the book and the ball, just respond. One could not form the idea of that which cannot be other than it is or act other than it does without simultaneously supposing that is opposite is at least thinkable. And with that realization, the child would come to understand that he (identity) was different from the book (identity) and the ball (identity).

Stanford: I see the point. But there are certain clarifications which need to be made before I can more fully grasp your argument. The man-made wooden children's ball has certain characteristics, regardless of its origin. These characteristics would be the same whether the tree was cut down or was blown over by a windstorm. There are also certain necessities involved in its continued existence. Some of these do depend on the kind of thing it is; but to ascribe the action of a thing to its What—to its essence, whether merely epistemological or ultimate, is also to argue from necessity. It is to argue that *because* it is such and such, then it must do this and that, etc. Reference to necessity is more immediate than identity.

Put differently: Those who accept Rand's metaphysics may continue to think in her terms, but they do not go deep enough. We say that "A and B are the causes of X *because*...." The Randians may add, "because of what they are, acting in accordance with their separate identities in a specific context." But the *because* is the more fundamental. We do not say "because of because"; we say "because of A", or "A and B", etc., that such and such happens. We also say "because" when we are not referring to actions, but to non-moving entities: for instance, that the sum of the interior angles of a triangle is equal to right angles because.... We could say, "because of its identity", but that would not give us the information.

Philosophus: The interior angles of a triangle are an identity. It is because of what they are that they are equal to 180°. Necessity apart from that which is necessary is unintelligible. When we say that A causes B *because*, this last word does not refer to a mysterious third which is inserted between A and B. The situation is simply this: Conditions A bring about conditioned B. The latter comes into being as a consequence of what the former is.

Stanford: I know that you are right, but let me continue. The law of identity is axiomatic because it cannot be breached without in some sense presupposing it. But is it really as fundamental as necessity? In a syllogism, two terms are necessarily united in a proposition by means of a third. The connection is experienced immediately. The identity of the terms is less important; one can use empty categories like "A," "B," and "C" to represent the three terms.

Philosophus: The syllogism has a certain nature. It is composed of two interlocking premises which produce a conclusion by necessity, as you say. To refer to the most common form: All A is B/ All C is A/ Therefore, All C is B. It is the identity of the structure, regardless of what A, B, and C are that produces the conclusion. If the two premises were: *Some* A is B & All C is A, the conclusion, All C is B, would lack necessity, since it is possible that some or even all C is outside of B. *Whether the conclusion is necessary or not depends upon the structure of the argument, its form, its identity—not the other way around.*

Stanford: One last point of clarification: Joseph and Rand take the familiar law of identity, which pertains to the use of language and apply it to ontology. In itself, this is quite legitimate. Language must refer to reality. And once this is done, contradiction comes to stand for an action which cannot happen—either that, or a reference to combination of elements which cannot be. No one to my knowledge has said this any better than Ayn Rand. But a simple concept which is incapable of being broken down into smaller elements, it manifestly is *not*. And that is Rand's own requirement for an axiom. Three elements can be discerned in it: (1) a reference to a particular; (2) a reference to the type under which the particular may be classified, (3) necessity, which is why the priority of the last can be shown with a flourish. The law of identity, both in its verbal and its ontological form depend on necessity. The two are inseparable, but they are not the same.

Philosophus: Note that the first two references you give, the particular and the type to which particulars belong, are both identities. They are what they are and not something else. The third element, necessity, is not as crucial as you suppose. Peikoff pointed out that the alternative is the man-made. It does not have to exist. There is no contradiction in the statement that the man-made need never have existed, the reason being that it results from human choice, which is free, not determined. To be sure, certain parts of an existent might be necessary. The material parts of a child's doll, for instance, would have to be consistent with the nature of that out of which they are made—which implies once more, the identities of the components. More to the point, whether or not the doll itself was brought into existence or not being depended on the choice of man; it was optional—it could have been otherwise. The decision to make that choice was not necessary; but once made, what resulted from it was fully determined. *Yet, both the necessary and the possible are identities*. Both are what they are and not something else. That is what provides the association required for rational thought.

Doxa: How early in life do you think that the idea of necessity arose?

Philosophus: In the crib or even earlier. It could have come in near the time that memory began, connected in some way with the experience of the *not*. An infant lying in a crib might have two toys, a rattle and a doll. The baby might find out that the doll cannot roll like the rattle. Furthermore, one day the adult might have put the rattle in a crib carelessly so that it was stuck in the ribs of the cage, and the baby was too weak to pull it free. Such experiences could give a very rudimentary notion of necessity. It must be remembered, however, that in this case, as in the others already discussed, the supposed experience presupposes that the infant has already discerned the identities of the rattle and the crib and also that the rattle can be freed through force—which means that a rudimentary notion of cause had already been obtained.

Stanford: I see that the basic Objectivist position on the axiomatic character of the law of identity and that causality is this law as applied to action is correct. I thought that Peikoff had equated necessity with identity and then had contradicted himself by offering free will as an exception. I did not see that he meant to include both necessity and free will under identity.

Philosophus: You were right in thinking that the Objectivist position is fuzzy, but it is not where you thought it was. It is her concept of entities is that is unclear. Immediately after stating the relationship between causality and the law of identity, Rand writes: "All actions are caused by entities. The nature of an action is caused and determined by the nature of the entities that act; a thing cannot act in contradiction to its nature."[31] But, as we have seen, she denies that space and time exist in themselves, but only as relationships among entities. What is left of an entity after it is no longer viewed as acting *in* space? How can the *before* and the *after* and the *at the same time* of causality be understood after they have been reduced to a part of a network of relationships? Peikoff, as was said earlier, made it more tenuous by agreeing that entities might not be the final truth. Then, to bolster up a compromised position, he resorts to the polemics of dogmatism. Witness this in his answer to the question, "Is God the designer of the universe? Not if A is A. The alternative to 'design' is not 'chance.' It is causality."[32] The answer to this question cannot be legislated in the manner he tries. It is a matter of the facts. We have already shown that number systems are not all commensurate. This could mean that the universe is made up of discordant elements. Were this the case, the original form might indeed have been chaos.

But there are complexities owing to the existence of free will, which I suggest we defer until this the proper time to discuss this issue comes up. Kant listed it among the three great transcendental questions.

Doxa: Ayn Rand thought that Immanuel Kant was the worst of the major philosophers. Is there anything you care to say on his behalf?

Philosophus: Kant has been rightly criticized by Rand for his denial that we experience ultimate reality. But he does have a point worth considering. This is that whereas traditional epistemology had focused on the idea that the mind should obey the object, he thought that attention should instead be focused on the extent to which the object "obeys" our mental faculties. This point can be accepted without drawing skeptical conclusions. If an object, such as, for instance, an atom or a molecule, is too small to be perceived directly by the eyes, then we see the surface according to its relative hardness; we see the shimmering metal, seemingly reflecting back light at every point; we compare that with the firm, but less hard plaster which we can scratch off with our fingertips, and that with the wood, through which we can perceive the grain; from that we look at wool which we can see deeply into and can easily take apart manually. Then there are things like op art, parts of which we cannot quite perceive. Other things, like pressure waves upon the ear, and heat, we perceive indirectly through their effect upon us. But as John Cook Wilson has pointed out: "Kant's standpoint is what follows if we start from the subjective side of knowledge only. Even starting thus, we cannot represent reality as other than what 'agrees' with the necessity of thinking and knowing, but the standpoint is indirect and incomplete. The true account of the necessity of thought explains why there must be the 'agreement,' and this shortly is that the necessity of thinking is the necessity of apprehension. Necessity of apprehension, then turns out to be unintelligible save as apprehension of a necessity, that is, apprehension of objective necessity or apprehension of what reality must be."[33]

Doxa: Ayn Rand's third axiom is "consciousness." Like her other axiomatic concepts, it is supposed to be formed not by differentiating one kind of existents from others, but by integrating all existents. For this axiomatic concept, as for the other two, there is supposed to be no Conceptual Common Denominator. This seems strange, however, because while she can argue with some initial plausibility that her "existence" and her "identity" stand for all the existents, this cannot be done with "consciousness," which pertains to a part of reality only. That consciousness can easily be differentiated from the non-consciousness, we observe in in-animate things and, apparently, in plants as well. Her axioms are not supposed to have contraries; but this one does.[34] Its rightful claim to the status of an axiom is that one cannot avoid implying it when engaged in stating the axioms of existence and identity. Then too, the person who attempts to deny that there is such a fact as a state of awareness defeats himself in the usual way.

Other problems arise. Although, at the beginning, consciousness is presented as a direct awareness of reality, this supposed "awareness" soon becomes encased in the mummy wrappings of context. We have noticed several difficulties with the Objectivist idea. If truth lies in the totality of context, then it will be modified by future experience. It may be answered that within a given context of knowledge it is what is and cannot be any different. That may be. But to refer to an earlier illustration of Mr. Philosophus': If I place a drop of oil in a lake, at the moment that it is resting atop the surface, it is in the place that it is and in no other. But as the waves and other foreign matter in the waters move about, the drop of oil may be joined to something else, split into smaller droplets, part of which enter the atmosphere as spray to be carried off by winds which also objectively exist—or at least alter its shape. At no point in this process is the law of identity or that of causality breached. It may be that a balloonist with a camera could follow it through its vicissitudes and proclaim that the drop was what it was and the changes wrought in it were all in accord with the identity, that a clear line of causality led through each of its changes. But, the scientist, being caught within the warp and woof of the context, unlike the cameraman, does not stand above the rolling context.

This statement of Ayn Rand's has always puzzled me: "A consciousness conscious of nothing but itself is a contradiction in terms: before it could identify itself as consciousness, it had to be conscious of something. If that which you claim to perceive does not exist, what you possess is not consciousness."[35] What she seems to be saying is that an awareness that one is aware and nothing more is impossible. I don't understand how that remark can be made an absolute. It may be that a human being needs to be conscious first of something different from herself or himself in order for consciousness to start itself the first time at birth (or, as, I believe, in the womb). But to deny that one can have fleeting moments of pure self-consciousness, that I do not believe.

Philosophus: Rand was referring to the first time. Any subsequent moment of pure self consciousness that we might have would be tinged by memory in case of human beings.

I agree with Rand. Consider what has already been ascertained: The act of apprehension is different from that which is apprehended. Now suppose that what is apprehended is the act of apprehension itself. This being apprehended, then substituting this for the place provided by "that which is apprehended," we would have: *the act of apprehension is different from the act of apprehension*—which would be a contradiction in terms. Even a mirror requires something besides itself.

Penelope: Under a system of objective relativism, however, in which consciousness is a relation between subject and object, this relation could be equality, i.e., subject and object could be the same. To rule this out, the Objectivists would have to be able to show that this relation could not take place under their system. But that is their problem.

Stanford: The relation would not only have to be an equality. Two apples and two oranges are equal in quantity but differ in other characteristics. It would have to be an *identity*. The Objectivists teach that what we are conscious of is a joint product of the form of consciousness supplied by us and the object of consciousness. If, as in the hypothesis given above, the two are identical, how would we be able to separate form-as-subject and form-as-object enough to be able to be conscious of consciousness itself? All there would be is the form of consciousness standing by itself. There is no way you could get something between the form and itself.

Philosophus: That is true. Here is why the apprehension-terminology is better. There is not in that any element of double-thinking about context. This last, Peikoff defines elsewhere, as "'the sum of cognitive elements conditioning an item of knowledge.'"[36] This theoretical idea allows Peikoff to question whether consciousness is ultimate while affirming its axiomatic character: "Even if, someday, consciousness were to be explained scientifically as a product of physical conditions, this would not alter any observed fact. It would not alter the fact that, given those conditions, the attributes and functions of consciousness are what they are."[37] It would be in the position of the drop of oil on the ocean being observed by the balloonist. But what about its stature as an axiom? Would it not alter that? Would it not change it into something that could be defined in terms more basic? "Nor would it alter the fact that in many respects these attributes and functions are unique; they are different from anything observed in unconscious entities."[38] How does Peikoff know this? If consciousness were discovered to be something radically different than that which it presents itself to us in life, if it were ultimately reducible to a physical explanation, how can one determine in advance what such a science would say about other beings? He is saying that his axiom of consciousness, although not reducible in terms of the words used by our scientists and philosophers today, might be made obsolete by some unknown future knowledge. Having said that, he cannot prescribe the course of the rest of that unknown knowledge. "Nor would it alter the fact that one can discover the conditions of consciousness, as of anything else one seeks to know, only through the exercise of consciousness."[39] Once more, if the difference between consciousness and the material objects of which it is conscious are shown at bottom to be both physical, how does one know that there is not another way besides that of using one's mind of finding this, since discovery is, by this hypothesis, ultimately derivable to a physical process?

The reason why doing the opposite is absurd is because, deep down we know that it could not be. But, if *ex hypothesi*, such a thing were possible—a complete redintegration of mind and body, one could get to presently intellectual truths through physical actions not involving the work of consciousness.

Peikoff cannot have it both ways; what allows him to imagine that he can is the doctrine of context. If consciousness were to explained in terms of non-consciousness, it would lose its position as an axiom. It would not be a truth that is self-evident, nor a corollary of the same. It would be a conditional theorem. The reason is that if it were really different from physical process, then a certain kind of dualism is affirmed.

To the Objectivist, Kant is supposed to have argued that since consciousness has an identity, it interposes its nature between the object and the mind. Rand says that "the entire apparatus of Kant's system, like a hippopotamus engaged in belly-dancing, goes through its gyrations" while resting on that single contention.[40]

I answer that this identity of consciousness the Objectivists fuss about is just the apprehension of reality. The primary qualities are perceived directly; the secondary, through their effect on us. Where the sensory system is sensitive, it is capable of picking up the knowledge giving data (sensation) and conducting it to certain areas of the brain in which the process of establishing awareness is completed (perception). Where the sensory system is insensitive, no awareness will exist; for instance, scientists tell us that there are certain sounds and light frequencies which men cannot perceive.

This does not mean that the mind in its operations is infallible. Memory certainly deserves to be classified as a subspecies of consciousness. Yet, no one would suppose that everyone's memory is perfect. In some cases, there may be an impairment due to physical dis-function; in other cases, the person was dishonest and started to enter into his mind false data. Love and anger have been known to do this. The same with modern pop-psychology with its penchant for visualization. But nobody would suppose from this that memory as such is simply a prejudice; in the very act of trying to explain his doubt, the skeptic would be using his memory. His interlocutor need only reply: "If I recollect correctly, you think memory in general is valid," a type of reply which the Objectivists also know.

Penelope: There are other situations besides those resulting from physical disablement or dishonesty or high passion. One rainy night I was quietly driving home along a dark stretch of road which I had traveled many times. Suddenly, I thought I saw ahead of me the largest load I had ever seen on a highway; I imagined that it must be part of one of those huge cranes that are used to lift bridges. A few seconds later, I saw that it was just part of an overhead bridge that slanted across the highway, a sight I had seen many times. I do not know how that happened. I had received certain impressions through my eyes. Obviously, the patterns they exhibited for those moments were similar to those of some presented by some sort of a truck. These parts of the brain sensitive to that sort of a shape were activated and a resultant construction of the monstrous thing in the roadway came about. I must say, however, that there was something eerie about it; I slowed down. This was an *error of perception*. The Objectivist might say that given the total context: the nature and contents of my brain, the condition of astigmatism from which I suffer, the light from the sky intermixed with the reflections from the pools of water on the road, etc., that what I called an "illusion" was exactly what it had to be within that total context.... But that would be fallacious. It was a miss-take, pure and simple. The information supplied by the light landed on the wrong place in the brain, probably due to a similarity of shape. The eerie feeling accompanying it was an attempt of my mental faculties to show it as an object. Yet, it was unable to do so, adequately. What was shown was a kind of a ghostlike image. It was a misapprehension.

Philosophus: You were not physically disabled, although astigmatism might have been a contributory fact—which only adds emphasis to your main point, that errors of perception exist. But in a larger sense, it should not be forgotten that illusion is counted upon by visual artists of the realistic school. If one stands in the focal point for the full perspective to come out, one can be fooled momentarily. Motion pictures depend on something similar; they want their audience to be so engrossed in the story that they tend to forget the failure of perspective, the lack of parallax, etc. Technology pitch-men now talk about "virtual reality."

Aside from those connected with art and entertainment, there are certain involuntary optical illusions. These can be divided into three classes: The first—and least common—is that of ambiguity. For the most part, these situations are specially contrived. An example is the line drawing which may be seen either as a beautiful young lady with a feather hat or an old crone. Usually, after seeing one of them, the viewer soon thereafter sees the other and discovers the trick. The second class is when the information points to something similar to what it actually is but different enough to make it a misapprehension. Frequently, the resultant misapprehension is usually unstable, thereby providing a clue that something is wrong. There are various causes for this class; most commonly, but not always, the viewer has not yet had enough experience to be able to discover the difference. Sometimes, it is triggered by a physiological defect. The third class is where the false perception persists even though the party knows what it is. (One can go on and distinguish these from mirror images or mirages in which we see the thing where it is not, but that would take us too far afield).

The important thing is that the existence of aberrant perceptions should not distract us from understanding that apprehension has no mediation. The message from the outer world may need to be analyzed and channeled. Mistakes may be made. But we cannot come to the idea of misapprehension without first apprehending something; a *mis*apprehension is not simply a non- apprehension. In this sense, the TV set on-the-blink doesn't misapprehend the signal; it simply does not receive it clearly, or at all. A misapprehension is not simply a failure of mechanism; it is a failure of consciousness.

Many more words could be said on this subject, should be said in order to make it plain to some people. Let us, however, meditate on these words of Alfred O. Lovejoy's: "There is nothing more paradoxical in the conception of a knowledge of physical objects by means of sensa not identical with those objects than there is in the conception of a knowledge of past events by means of memory-images not identical with those events."[41]

Rand claimed that a common element is abstracted from a group of similar percepts and then united on the basis of a mathematical similarity. But, before one can discern a similarity, mathematical or otherwise, one must first be able to identify the element, individually, which will later be held up for comparison. Recognizing that two existents have the same feature is just one more identification, not necessarily any more complex than the first realization. A definition will cover anything that has the features stipulated by it, whether there be only one or a million existents fitting it. Let us take once more, the example of ice. The defining characteristic is that it is the solid form of water; all instances of ice must have that attribute. But the ability to increase in volume is not universal; it fits the common form of ice, but not some of the more exotic forms of frozen water established under much higher pressures in the laboratory. One cannot deduce this fact from our knowledge of the identity of ice. One must first observe the relevant situation. Sometimes, only one

observation is necessary. In short, ONE NEEDS TO APPRE-
HEND IT. The processing of our mental faculties will either
succeed in preserving the apprehension or, as sometimes
happens, botch the job.

Penelope: Earlier, I offered some criticism of one of
Euclid's uses of an axiom. But this much can be said in behalf of his procedure. Euclid's axioms served only to limit
the extent of geometry, not separate it from that which is
nonexistent or irrational in thought. His axioms are "givens,"
not cognitive regulators. They do not attempt to define reason or what is rational. They only confine its application.
Rand tried to use her axioms to legitimate the whole process
of reasoning. She thought that by choosing axioms of the
greatest universality, she could provide certainty for the less
comprehensive concepts. But if the concept for physical objects and the psychological states of men did not already
possess this characteristic, how could they obtain it by being
connected to her axioms?

Philosophus: Rand's axioms are not only unnecessary,
but they limit what one can know. If Kant had wanted to
make philosophy safe for faith by shutting off knowledge of
ultimate reality and confining our experience of the world
to mere phenomena, while the greater questions were left in
the irretrievable darkness, Rand wanted to obviate faith by
limiting what the world could contain. Even "existence," her
highest and most comprehensive axiom, was so constructed
as to judge any contrary thought as out of bounds in advance of consideration.

Rand said that knowledge must be processed. This is true,
but if the necessity was not already in the sensation, all the
processing in the world would be not put a consciousness of
reality into it. Were that the case, then Kant would be right.
The world of phenomena we experience would be a joint
product of the object which is essentially unknown to us and
our internal cognitive machinery, which, being in its own

sphere a thing-in-itself, would also be an unknown. The known would be a zone of light, immersed in a total darkness. Obviously; necessity has to be on the side of the subject also. The sensory system has to be made to receive. Anything less plunges the mind into confusion.

Penelope: What is the difference between Rand and Kant?

Philosophus: The difference between the two, as one of her academic admirers pointed out, is that whereas Kant held that science could never get beyond phenomenal appearance because the mind is bound by its form of intuition, Rand held that he can, through the appropriate use of her axioms and the scientific method.[42] To this, I add that she believed that the universe is basically finite and therefore that science can, in principle, be finished.

But the truth is that the axioms are unnecessary. The *identity* of man's consciousness consists in the degree and extent to which it can apprehend reality. It is endowed with this capacity, just as the lodestone has the ability to attract iron.

This points to another difficulty with Objectivism. Rand and Peikoff hold that sense perception is the basic truth to which all the truths of the intellect must be traced; moreover, that it is the standard of proof itself.[43] But, as we have seen, this cannot be. There are errors in perception. Moreover, since the knowledge of the external world gained through the secondary characteristics is indirect, and is learned by discovering the appropriate primary characteristics behind them, sense perception in its fullness cannot be the standard of truth. Part of what they disclose are effects, and even this fact is not immediately obvious; it takes some observation and reflection to come to this realization. It would be closer to say that it is only the primary characteristics that can be regarded as final. There is nothing further to get behind. Those who want to get deeper can only take apart and analyze the physiological systems which make perception possible; no verbal discussion of concepts in general will be able to do it; and this knowledge of physiology would involve primary qualities. But even this would be an exaggeration. Perception of primary characteristics at its best is only one form of apprehension. The standard is apprehension itself; the scientific method is only a means of obtaining this, where possible, with difficult phenomena. Apprehensions through intellectual study can be just as certain as the perception of the primary qualities themselves. The standard is the duality of the act of apprehension and that which is apprehended, wherever and whenever it may be found. Even the secondary characteristics are real in that they are effects of certain aspects of reality upon our perceptual systems; in such cases, we do not directly apprehend the primary qualities behind them, except for those involving tempo, area covered, intensity, etc. In short, the secondary characteristics can tell us when, where, sometimes how many and how much, but not what.

The doctrine of context, which was supposed to supply the material which the axioms were to stitch together, turned out to act like a magician's scarf, veiling the real procedures which were occurring underneath. The introduction of context into a realistic theory of knowledge was unnecessary and therefore self-defeating. It made the deductive process cumbersome, to say the least, and transformed the ignorance and guesswork of the complicated inductive sciences into chaos disguised as degrees or stages in the advancement of knowledge. It fused two things which must always be separated if a rational account of learning is to be made: the distinction between apprehension and that which is apprehended.

The axioms were introduced in order to bring order to the relativity. If perceptions of color, sound, feeling and the like are all united through the perception that they exist, then chaos can be prevented. But this very experience—the knowledge that they exist—is not the product of an intellectual abstraction being applied to some data. Quite to the contrary:

it is part of the apprehension. One can raise it to the level of a high comprehensive universal, as did Rand; but this abstraction, once obtained, does not from that point forward direct the process of cognition. That process goes on anyway.

Although some of the things which Objectivism teaches about the law of identity and its parallel in causality are correct, it is not a Randian axiom. Neither does the intellect impose forms upon the raw data of sensation, like some sort of a spectral cookie-cutter. The action of the intellect, whether in the act of contemplation or in the act of creation where the implications of some possibility are being drawn out is as much an apprehension as is the perception of the external world.

Rand says that once the axiomatic concepts have been identified, then in all future processes of cognition, the axiomatic concepts direct it.[44] This brings us to Rand's third primary axiom, "consciousness." But here again, that axiom cannot be a director. Her "consciousness" is largely defined as a state of awareness. This is fundamentally passive. By definition, that which supplies the direction would have to be a *will*. (But further discussion of this point will have to await the consideration of free will.)

Stanford: To say that such thoughts direct the process goes past the facts. Don't her axioms also require the lesser concepts in order to make them intelligible? The axiom, existence, for instance, on Rand's own showing, is nothing apart from that which exists.

My conjecture is that rescuing her philosophy from the ravages of relativism was not A. R.'s only motive for coming up with her axioms. She was also trying to avoid any return to the old Aristotelian idea that when one perceives something, one perceives not only the particular, but through the particular, the universal; that is to say, that when I perceive something as red, I also become aware at some level of the universal, redness. One can grant that in doing so, one is simultaneously aware of the fact that this red thing existed, but this second universal would only be more comprehensive than the other. We are simultaneously aware of both the attributes and their existence because it is our nature to be able to apprehend such facts. The inborn capacity which enables one to draw the universals from the particulars preceded the identification of the widest and most comprehensive universals.

Penelope: The only way out for Rand would be to proclaim that the axiomatic concepts are innate and are gradually activated as more and more conceptual activity goes on until they finally become explicit. But that would contradict her prohibition of innate ideas and also render much of the rest of her epistemological paraphernalia useless.

Doxa: I think that Ayn Rand herself would have to agree, ultimately, it is the man himself—his will—that directs the process. To suppose that it is certain concepts that are doing it would turn man into a mere knowledge machine.

In our next meeting, we shall discuss time and space.

DAY VIII

TIME AND SPACE

*T*his time, the meeting is in the living room of Penelope's *spacious condominium overlooking the city. Outside the huge windows may be seen points of light in the darkness, suggesting the shape of some of the city's buildings. The eyes of the four are directed to the table in front of them, stacked with books and other paraphernalia.*

Doxa: Time and space have proved to be insuperable obstacles to Ayn Rand's philosophy. Yet there is a place in it where she pays scrupulous respect to time. There, she writes: "The measurements omitted from axiomatic concepts are all the measurements of all the existents they subsume; what is retained, metaphysically, is only a fundamental fact; what is retained, epistemologically, is only one category of measurement, omitting its particulars: *Time*—i.e.,the fundamental fact is retained independent of any particular moment of awareness."[1] By metaphysically, Ayn Rand means the reality of all that is referred to by the axiomatic concept. By epistemologically, she means the psychological. The axiomatic concepts "identify explicitly the omission of psychological time measurements, which is implicit in all other concepts."[2] By this, she means that when you form a concept, it is as such not dependent on the moment that you became aware of it. Thus, when you form the concept "chair", it is independent not only of the perceived instances from which the concept was drawn, but independent of all chairs which you may perceive at other times. But non-axiomatic concepts like "chair" are needed only when they are used. If the concept of a chair, for instance, is not required to identify an unfamiliar object or to direct one's attention to refer to some specific piece of furniture, etc., you do not have it in conscious awareness. It is there only as something that can be brought forth out of storage when needed.

But with the axiomatic concepts, this implicit omission of time measurements becomes explicit. "Time is involved in them epistemologically or psychologically in a more important manner: they have to be held in your consciousness at all times. It isn't only that what you call existence today you will also call existence tomorrow, but also that in all future processes of cognition the axiomatic concepts are directing that process. You cannot form another concept or utter a proposition without regard for your axiomatic concepts, once they have been consciously identified."[3]

Since her position on axioms as directors of cognition has already been examined, we are now ready to discuss her remarks on time.

Philosophus: Rand states that in an axiomatic concept, all categories are omitted, except time, sans measurements. Time is not just another word for existence in Rand, since it is supposed to be present in all the axiomatic concepts. Nobody would say that "time" means the same thing as "A is A." Consciousness is also one of her axioms; surely, that cannot be identified in all respects with time. One is entitled to wonder why Rand does not make time an axiom in its own right: if an axiom in Objectivism is supposed to be a fact which is abstracted from all other facts, then one might think that since, by Rand's account, it is present in existence, identity, and consciousness—all three—that time would the ultimate axiom.

Penelope: Was it because she recalled that time is usually thought to have a triune structure— past, present, and future—and if she had made it an axiom, she would have had a hard time explaining why the past does not exist, inasmuch as she thought that such a concept can only pertain to what is?

Philosophus: Possibly. But there is a problem for Objectivism that is more immediate than that. Time cannot even be a non-axiomatic concept for Rand. The reason is that a finite unit cannot stand for the present. If she used the "second" as her unit, part of the period comprised in it would have already gone. What we call "now" is mostly in the recent past. We do not remember events which took place a nano-second before, because our faculties were not constructed to be conscious of it. The metaphysical past intrudes upon the psychological present, since part of the latter is based upon memory. Any unit of present time we might choose can be divided infinitely. The real *now* is an infinitesimal.

Stanford: One is beginning to see why time could not have been included among the axioms of Objectivism, even though it cannot be denied membership without contradiction.

Philosophus: Let us turn to Rand's explicit characterization of it. "'Time,' as the widest or parent abstraction of all subsequent and narrower measurements of time, is a change of relationship. You observe that certain relationships are changed, and you form the concept 'time.'"[4]

Let us stop right there: (1) We have already seen that consciousness of time flows necessarily from memory, which is an original disclosure of consciousness; we become aware that what we are perceiving internally occurred in the past. It is not formed out of change as such. If there be any doubt that this is what Rand means, she makes it explicit on her preceding page: "If you see some stationary objects and one object that is moving, you grasp the fact that it is moving by seeing the changed relationship between it and the other objects, and that gives you the concept of 'time.'"[5] That is false. From your senses, you would be receiving impressions of motion, or at most the difference between motion and rest. There is no percept of time in that scene. The first "concepts" you would form, to use Rand's term, from the scene would be motion and rest. The origin of the consciousness of time is elsewhere. (2) All instances of change are not temporal. When we look at the corner of a house and notice a change of direction, we are not observing a temporal process; in any rectilinear figure there is a change of direction whenever one segment of the figure is not parallel to another. In a circle, there is a change of direction at every point. These are *spatial* changes. (3) Time does not always involve change of things. Part of the definition of the law of contradiction in its common form is that two or more existents cannot exist at the same time and in the same space. Here, the absence of temporal change is emphasized. Immanuel Kant, Rand's *bete noire*, knew that: "Time," he wrote, "has one dimension only; different times are not simultaneous, but successive..."[6] (4) Rand's notion of time is less sophisticated than Kant's, but his is not definitive. Temporal events are not the only phenomena which exhibit successions of states. In a line segment, there is succession. Yet, herein is not an idea of time, only of space. A vector is determined by the difference between two points measured in a certain direction. It is a succession without the idea of time. A succession of numbers—1, 2, 3, 4, etc.—is just that, a succession of numbers, but it is not a temporal one. We can say that the number "3" comes before "4", but there we mean that "4" is "1" greater than "3" or we simply indicate that "3" is to the left of "4"— not that the number three is *earlier* than the number four. We read them from left to right, The act of reading is a temporal process, but the principle by which the numbers are brought forth need not contain a reference to time. (5) Time cannot be understood in non-temporal terms. We sometimes speak of a "before" and "after" in space, but this is more accurately described as "in-front-of" and "in-back-of." Coexistence in space would describe a condition of simultaneity, but they are obviously not identical.

After relegating time to a mere change of relationship, she finds it impossible to give it any existence apart from motion. "Then you can subdivide it into speed or duration or any other measurements. Speed and duration are really two aspects of the same type of measurement. Continue with the example of an object moving past some stationary objects. To measure the duration, you would have to define the beginning and the end of this process—how long will it take this object to pass three stationary points. And you measure the total of the process. To measure its speed, you have to already have established a unit of time-measurement."[7]

Rand is right at one point: motion is a change of relationship; but it is not a unit of time, nor time a unit of motion. Motion is a change of position; time does not change in space. Motion can be in any direction, forward and back, from side to side, and up and down; time can only move in one direction, and that is just a figure of speech, for time is not a "direction" in space. In both motion and time, there is a change. But that does not make them the same kind of change. Motion and time are both incommensurable. Neither are they alone: space admits change in direction, for instance.

Rand accepts the idea that time is the measure of motion.[8] Let us examine it: Consider the standard formula, $d/t = s$ or distance divided by time equals speed. If it be thought that time is just a measure by which we calculate speed, one could as easily write, $t=d/s$, in which case, speed becomes a measure of time. One could also argue that time is just a relationship by which we measure speed, which was Rand's argument. It is true that time is measured by motion and motion by time; clocks have moving parts, and motion is measured by distance and time. But I don't think that Rand would have wanted to reduce distance to a measurement of motion, although it certainly is one of the two parts of the ratio by which speed, velocity, and acceleration is measured.

Suppose that time were an attribute of motion. Then, under this hypothesis, speed, which is an attribute of motion, would be the distance divided by another attribute of motion. It would follow that distance would equal one attribute of motion multiplied by another. If this is rational, then distance must be part of motion also. And if it is, then there is no motion—no motion because, by hypothesis, distance is part of the same. But that would be absurd. The car, as it moved, would carry its distance with it—a mind cracker of an idea if there ever was one.

Distance and time and speed are different existents. A body going at a certain speed will traverse a certain distance at a certain time. Velocity is simply speed in a certain direction. Time is not part of velocity; nor velocity, part of time. If they were the same, the whole process would be a vicious cycle.

Aristotle, whom Rand admired above all other philosophers, did not identify time with motion, but thought them to be inseparable.[9] Since the world we know is full of change, the question as to whether time and motion can be separated must be carried out in thought. In our most recent discussion, it was hypothesized that everything was at absolute zero—no macroscopic motion whatsoever—no change in the relationship of either with respect to each other or even with respect to space. Yet, time would still be a fact. One could say that there would never be any more macroscopic motion. "Never" is a term laden with temporality. Suppose there were no motion in the interior of the atom. This would be the situation: no motion, no change forever. (Indeed, if the universe is expanding, as some scientists believe, then that might well be the terminal point, as predicted by entropy). Suppose finally that there were no matter, no energy, no thing occupying any points in space, a blank nothing. What would be the situation? The Objectivist would quickly answer that existence must always exist and there would therefore be no such situation. But, in the phrase, "there would be," exists a reference to time. Time would still be a fact. It would be the existence that exists. And that would not be a negative fact, but a positive affirmative one. Time would not be canceled by a void, not even if the void were all that there was.

The intention is not to argue that time is more permanent or more fundamental than matter or energy; only that it is a fact in its own right, not any more derivable from them than they are from it.

Let us change the example. Suppose that there were an ultimate form of matter. Let it be Peikoff's energy puffs. In order to agree with Aristotle that time was inseparable from motion, one would have to argue that time concerned only the movement of the puffs, especially when they entered into new combinations, ultimately through complication upon complication producing the perceptible world. But of the puffs themselves, one could not speak of them being in time, since they did not change but remained indestructible. But to confine time only to the actions and interactions of the puffs would be an abuse of language, for indestructibility is a kind of eternity, and eternity is endless duration. The puffs, we could say, would always be.

And now, let us return from matter to mind. The syllogism, which Rand herself considers to be the paradigm of deductive reasoning, requires that time be independent of human psychological processes. Were this not so, it would involve a *petitio principii:* The syllogism would assume the very thing which is to be proved. This charge can be seen in the ancient syllogism: "All men are mortal; Socrates is a man; therefore, Socrates is mortal." The charge is that no inference has taken place, since if I know that every man will die, then the case of Socrates has already been considered. The answer is that I may know the minor premise about the manhood of Socrates before I know the major. But once I have discovered the fact about the mortality of men, then I conclude that Socrates too—being a man—will pass away. If time were not independent of everything else, the syllogism would not be a valid argument.[10] (And it is the form of reasoning which they claim to cherish above all others).

A definition may be contextual in the sense that it is limited by the amount of knowledge available at a given time; as was discussed earlier, so much might have been learned that the old definition would no longer be able to contain the facts and a new one would need to be originated. Time, however, cannot itself be contextual in that sense. Were that the case, all would be lost. One could never recover an earlier idea that was right in its own way, but not in the new way.

The entities which Rand celebrates either had a beginning in time or they did not. If no beginning in time, then the chain of cause and effect is eternal and infinity exists. If finite, it had a beginning.

Doxa: The Objectivists try to escape from this by once more pulling context down over everybody's eyes and saying that one cannot reason from the situations which we know in which every "before" is followed by an "after" and conclude, as you just did, either an *absolute beginning or infinite time*. Before and after, they say, are relative matters: but since the universe is everything, we cannot speak of it in such terms because we have nothing to compare it with.

Why not? If we cannot reason in such a way backwards in time, then how can we extend our reasoning to the future, which is also something we cannot experience directly? Once we have reached the moment which used to be the future, it is something different— the present; then, quicker than a flash, it is gone. The fact is that I can abstract away from the context in which I find myself to an absolute future, even though I cannot ever be in the future. Yet, I have performed the abstraction. Just as Peikoff said that the only proof of perception is that one can perceive it, so the only proof that I can abstract away like that is the fact that I just did it.

I can mentally project the future infinitely, even after my lifetime is over; the same, therefore, with the past. I don't have to talk about the whole universe—just about what succeeds me and my mortal remains—or what has preceded me.

If the latter were an endless chain of cause and effect, then since part of the physical universe would in that case be infinite and the whole includes the part, then in that case, the universe would have no beginning in time. If, on the other hand, the chain had an absolute beginning, then the opposite would be the case. "Context" is not going to keep me from being able to understand that any longer.

Stanford: As far as we know, elementary particles like photons vibrate. Peikoff does not know anything different. Since by his hypothesis, these rates of vibration would have to be finite, if a particle had vibrated an infinite number of times, the physical universe would extend back to infinity. If not, then the universe might have had an absolute beginning in time. All things considered, Peikoff's universe would have to be one in which there is no motion, only the webbing of coordinates.

Philosophus: A philosophy which grants the reality of time independent of human cognition could avoid these contradictions. Such a philosophy need not hold that the past exists in some ghost-like setting. It would be a fact which was, which had once existed, whether anybody remembers it or not. An ancient stone tablet which crumbled into dust when the discoverers opened the vault still had a message written on it once, even if there is no way it can be retrieved. Should the Declaration of Independence be forgotten, what it was and who wrote it and who signed it would still be a fact that it once was. The obvious truth is no puzzle to the ordinary American, but to some intellectuals, it is, indeed, a great puzzle.

Penelope: Strangely enough, Rand had more respect for time than space. She identified it as happening every time, (which, of course, cannot be really said by an Objectivist adept) a relationship was changed. We have seen that when she defined time as a change of relationships, she was oblivious to the changes found in static geometrical objects. This is not the category of measurements omitted to which her axioms were reduced. She did not say that the axioms were formed independently of the place where they were conceptualized—that they were valid everywhere. The reason is simple: for her, space is replaced by context. Space for Rand is only relative place, and that is for her the nexus of a relationship. This is an interesting consequence. Despite Objectivism's penchant for materialism, it has no place for body except as being considered part of a relationship.

Philosophus: Space also deserves axiom status, if anything does. It cannot be reduced to anything else that is not space. It is there even when matter is absent.

Space and time are similar in that both would exist even if matter and energy did not. The remainder of the sentence quoted from Kant was that "different spaces are never successive, but simultaneous."[11] This, as we have seen, is not right. There is such a thing as succession in space, but it is not temporal. The co-existent in space and the simultaneous in time can in a way of speaking be said to "meet," but they are not the same fact. Some people are confused because we sometimes use words and phrases drawn from one to describe the other; thus we speak of a "space of time." But music and art sometimes use terms referring to each other—"the texture of sound", "the tone of a painting," etc. And nobody supposes that they are the same. It is simply that one is used to point out a feature of the other.

If perception is the building block, as the Objectivists teach, then space has to be accepted as absolute too, since it is by means of them that experience is ordered. Otherwise, we are back to Kant, whose subjectivity Rand despised above that of any other. It has already been shown that time is inherent in memory and the entities disclosed by perception are arranged in terms of space.

Space cannot be at base a matter of relations. Were it so, objectivity would be destroyed. Without a space which lay beyond the interstices of the net of relations, every observation would be made from a point of view that was so completely unique that there would be no way that one of these could be objectively mapped out in relation to any other. Nobody could say, in the final analysis, that what I call "L 1" you call "L 5," etc. This is because the origin of the one could never be precisely determined by the other. It could not even be approximated. As Alfred O. Lovejoy put it: "If 'space' signifies only a mode of relatedness between particular entities, the 'all-embracing relations required by the advocates of the philosophy of the unity of nature' disappear; there is no longer any reason to suppose that, because the objects in my visual field are spatially related *inter se*, they are also related in the same way in the same space-system to the objects in my neighbor's visual field, or to the constituents of the world of physical theory. That all these fall into a single-interconnected spatial pattern, or 'mesh' of relations, becomes, upon the rational theory, a thing to be proved...."[12]

Space, like time, has an independent existence. A penny lying on the ground when viewed from a certain perspective looks elliptical. But real understanding consists in looking at an object from several perspectives so as to discover the true facts of the matter. Just because something is what it is from a given standpoint and cannot be perceived from that standpoint in a different way does not keep that viewpoint from being subjective. The formula in the die out of which the penny is cut or molded is that of a circle, not an ellipse. The shape of the penny must be single. True objectivity consists in seeing it *out-of-perspective*.[13]

Rand's strategy becomes apparent from the following statement: "Actually, do you know what we can ascribe to the universe as such, apart from scientific discovery? Only those fundamentals that we can grasp about existence. Not in the sense of switching contexts and ascribing particular characteristics to the universe, but we can say: since everything possesses identity, the universe possesses identity. Since everything is finite, the universe is finite. But we can't ascribe space or time or a lot of other things to the universe as a whole."[14]

Why it is so important to Rand that the universe be finite will be disclosed shortly. But first, the meaning of saying that it is finite must be brought out. The following is the essence of the case for the finite universe: take all the entities in the universe; all their attributes, all their actions, all the permutations and combinations of every aspect separately and all together in every way; more precisely, take all the electrons, neutrons, protons, all the units we have not discovered, all their possible interactions, conjunctions, separations, integrations and divisions: this magnitude, stupendous as it must be, is still something specific. And being specific, it is finite.

And now, let us return to Rand's grand strategy: If the universe is finite, it is in principle knowable to man. This does not mean that there cannot be magnitudes too great for man to comprehend directly. To the best of our knowledge, the greatest velocity is that of light and the nearest stars after the sun are several light years away. But given enough time, or in her way of thinking, the entering into enough relations, all these—especially the problems of man living on earth—could all be solved.

Rand characterizes the metaphysical idea of infinity, i.e., that it actually exists, as "another invalid concept."[15]

Rand recognizes infinity only as a potential: "An arithmetical sequence extends into infinity, without implying that infinity actually exists...."[16] But if it extends there, how can we say that it is not reached? In the case of numbers, the Objectivists might argue that since nobody on earth lasts that long, the process of counting numbers could not go on forever. But to use the term "forever" and understand what it means is to implicitly recognize the actuality of the infinity of time.

Penelope: Rand's talk of the infinite as a mere potential seems to mean little more than an interplay of images, held together by association.

Philosophus: Rand's idea of the finitude of the universe is destroyed by the idea of the endlessness of time and space.

Past and the future go on without end in both directions. There is no end to space. To count them as part of existence is to rupture her philosophy. But we have shown that they are!

You can even perceive an object which contains an infinity of measurements. Consider the right isosceles triangle discussed on our fifth day. Using some unit as a standard, we can make the two sides with a right angle equal to one unit each; but the third side cannot be stated in terms of that unit. I can look at a skyscraper and know that it must have a certain height, even though I do not know what it is. The same with the triangle. Indeed, it is possible that the actual elevation of that building is not exactly what it was supposed to be in the drawing, but that the distance when measured from the sidewalk is an irrational number of the units used by the contractor. And finally, as was pointed out earlier, a yardstick must pass the incommensurable quantity equal to the hypotenuse of that triangle whose two equal sides are one foot each in length. It would pass thorough innumerable others as well.

A distance or displacement, like the rest of space, can be divided into an infinite number of parts. So can a line segment. If one takes a line just a hundred yards long and divides it in half, one would have fifty yards; dividing it by a half again, produces twenty-five yards, and so on, *ad infinitum*. Now, suppose that a body is moving across this distance. The body passes every point of that distance at a certain time. Time, like distance, is infinitely divisible. There is a point-by- point correspondence between time and distance. There is no contradiction in a finite whole being divided into an infinite number of parts. (On this basis, the paradoxes of Zeno about space and time can be answered, but that is another question.)

Now, consider a point on a bird flying across this distance. The field across which the bird is moving may be made of a finite number of atoms or whatever; the air through which it is traversing may consist of a specific number of particles, but the distance is infinitely divisible, nevertheless. It is not the time that is moving; it is the bird. Time does not alter its position in space; it changes just as fast at the point at which the bird was a minute ago. The distance is not moving along with the bird; to use the argot of 20th century intellectuals, "it is stationary with respect to the object moving over it."

Motion is not reducible to space and time. It is change in position; it cannot be analyzed into something which is not moving. And, it has an infinite number of parts. So space, time, and motion are alike infinite, but still different. *Time is never reversible; motion sometimes is; directions in space are always reversible.*

Rand thought that there was no absolute space; yet; she supposed that everything that exists must be something specific. This could mean that ultimate reality was corpuscular in nature. But her idea that there be no empty space necessitates pure continuity, for in order that there be no empty space, matter must be continuous—not just continuous, but it would need to be packed in rectangular blocks. For, a system of spherical objects, even when closely packed, must leave empty places between them. Space has no breaks in its flow; the subdivision is infinite; the same with time. But, of course, if the Objectivists were to believe that matter was continuous, they would only enter contradiction at another point, since continuity requires space, also. (Neither could they suggest that it is neither. Since they have no evidence for this third, its hypothecation would contradict their concept of possibility; moreover, it would not even be conceivable, since it would be supposed that there exists something that neither stops nor goes on).

The infinities of space and time are not mere potentialities, because a potentiality for man implies that it can be realized. Potential energy can be turned into kinetic energy, energy in motion. If it could not, it would have no potential. That is the plain meaning of language. "Potentiality" is a time laden term; to exhaust it of this reference is to deprive it of all meaning.

The present is an infinitesimal. Absence in terms of time is greater than presence. Only space with its coexistence gives us a notion of an eternal present. Simultaneity is where space and time meet. Motion is not a fusion of the other two; it is something different.

We cannot experience motion apart from reference to space and time. The visual system does not register a pure continuity. When we watch the flight of a bird, our retinas do not mark each and every point of its flight path. Neurons are fired at specific points along the trajectory. If our visual perception were broken into its smallest parts, the trace of the bird's motion would be like a strip of film with its many tiny stills. Why do we experience the motion? Because the bird is at various places at different times. We do not reason that motion must have taken place because of the law of contradiction. Rather, we draw up this law from the particulars of our experience of motion. We are able to formulate that two or more events cannot occur at the same place and at the same time because we know that space, time, and motion are not the same, but different. To seriously do otherwise is like trying to remember things wrongly. It might crack our capacity to apprehend.

Stanford: Infinity is like necessity. It is there. We know it is there. We cannot analyze it completely. Yet, we know it exists. It is also like free will, which will be discussed later. It exists. You can experience it—even analyze it to some extent—but I doubt that you are able to fully comprehend it.

Yet A. R. says of this, "The concept 'infinity,' in that [metaphysical] sense, means something without identity, something not limited by anything, not definable. Therefore, the measurements omitted here are all measurements and all reality."[17]

A. R.'s grand strategy ran into the reality of the infinities of time, space, and motion. Having recognized this, she sought to reduce the first two to a matrix of relationships and tie the second to the finite behavior of a denumerable entity, when like the bird, the mind wants to soar.

Penelope: Rand's predilection for finitude may lay behind the static electricity motor invented by John Galt, the fictional hero of *Atlas Shrugged*.[18] This motor was supposed to draw static electricity from the atmosphere and convert it into current electricity, thereby providing unlimited power for mankind. But how could this conversion be done without an enormous expenditure of energy, which is the requirement of the first law of thermodynamics? The answer is in her metaphysics: If the universe is really finite and space is only a bundle of relations, then the removal of atmospheric static electricity would bring about a redistribution of forces, since on Rand's account, there can be no real vacuum. John Galt's problem then would have been to see that the type of redistribution of forces would lead to the replacement of the old with new static electricity. All that would be required, then, would be an initial push and a motor of some special configuration, and a tiny bit of energy to run the converter. In a universe with infinite space in which there are real vacuums, the motor might destroy enough clouds to produce drought in some places.

Stanford: Thus far, the infinity of time, space, and, in one respect, motion have been discussed. So far, we have reached agreement with the Stoics, who taught that the world + the void = infinity. It remains to discuss the question of the infinity of matter. Even if the total quantity of the stuff of the universe, whether matter, matter-energy, or what not, were finite, enough has been said to have refuted Rand's position, or anyone else, such as Hegel, who holds out for the finitude of the universe.

I do not know whether the quantity of this substance or substances which has yet to be understood by man, is finite or is infinite. It should be said that if the average density of space were only some definite amount per cubic light year, however tiny, the total quantity would have to be infinite. Moreover, if there were no ultimate "uncutable"—the original criterion for the atom—then matter would be infinitely divisible. Furthermore, if Rand were correct in thinking that the universe, including matter, has always existed, why then would matter only be concentrated in one part?

Penelope: The question of the infinity of matter can be approached indirectly. Let us look at the realm of the conceivable, in other words, an hypothesis which is without evidence but does not conflict with any known fact. We have already learned that there are quantities for which a corresponding number does not exist. We have seen that space and time are infinite. Quantities have been found for which there is no number. Infinity is a quantity for which there is no number. The infinity of matter is, therefore, conceivable.

The next question: Is it possible? Astronomers have never found an end. Every time they build more powerful telescopes, they take in more information. The infinity of matter is therefore possible by Peikoff's own accounting, since it is neither contradictory in itself, nor does it contradict any known evidence, and some evidence exists in support of it.

Philosophus: The evidence in favor of the infinity of matter is also consistent with the opposite thesis. It could also be the case that the amount of matter in the universe, while vast, has not all been observed. At most, your hypothesis is little more than a conceivability—a weak possibility.

Penelope: If that is the case, then the thesis that the quality of matter is finite is also a weak possibility.

Philosophus: Consider again. The argument that infinity is a quantity inexpressible in numbers was derived from certain facts about space and time—from such spatial considerations as that not all lengths are commensurate with unity, that a line may be divided into an infinite number of segments,—or from the realization that present time is like a point, an immediacy, not an interval. All these facts show that with respect to space and also with respect to time, there is no fundamental unit to which everything else is either an amplification or an aliquot part.

But what of matter? There, such notions as the finite and the denumerable fit. Matter appears to be discrete; this being premised, the idea of the unit (though not Rand's) is appropriate to it. If one were attempting to enumerate all matter—all forms of energy—not only the types but also the individuals belonging to each type, it would make no difference whether a particular elementary particle had a diameter of unit 1 and another had a diameter of $\sqrt{2}$ units; each would be denominated alike in the count.

Since the realm of the material is so different from that of space and time, the argument that the total supply of matter-energy is finite is the more probable hypothesis. Although the infinitude of matter is epistemologically possible, the majority of the evidence is on the side of the opposing idea.

Doxa: Let us look at one more subject, today. Like Ayn Rand, Albert Einstein taught the relational theory of space and time; and like her, he also held the universe to be finite.

Philosophus: In recent years—and, indeed, throughout the years, there has been much controversy over the correctness of Einstein's theories. There are other theories which do not disturb our understanding of time and space. The supposed confirmations are not as clear as is widely supposed. But let us not attempt to pass on the merits of Einstein's physics here. That would require a separate discussion. (Furthermore, the professional physicists would not like it, as they would regard it as an invasion of their "turf").

Doxa: Let us confine ourselves to the question, Is Objectivism really consistent with Einstein's theories of relativity? This will keep exposition down to a minimum.

Before we begin, there is a certain matter which must be discussed. It is often believed that Albert Einstein's theories are purely mathematical and cannot be discussed in words.

This is not true; it is a physical theory, as he himself had emphasized.[19]

His critique of time came principally in the form of an attack on simultaneity. "The concept [simultaneous] does not exist for the physicist until he has the possibility of discovering whether or not it is fulfilled in an actual case. We thus require a definition of simultaneity such that this definition supplies us with the method by means of which, in the present case, we can decide by experiment whether or not both the lightning strikes occurred simultaneously. As long as this requirement is not satisfied, I allow myself to be deceived as a physicist, when I imagine that I am able to attach a meaning to the statement of simultaneity."[20]

Note that Albert Einstein had asked that the definition itself provide a test by which the condition could be discovered in a specific case. Without this test, one could not say whether or not two lightning flashes could be classified as simultaneous.

Stanford: This is the same as the old positivist theory that the meaning of a statement lies in its verification. As such, it is inconsistent with Ayn Rand's theory of definition.

Doxa: But, let us not stop there. While the Objectivists do not agree with Einstein's definition, they nonetheless agree with his conclusion that no absolute meaning can be given to the concept of simultaneity, that, in his words, "Every reference-body (co-ordinate system) has its own particular time; unless we are told the reference-body to which the statement of time refers, there is no meaning in a statement of the time of an event."[21]

This implies that two events which appear simultaneous in one system of reference may not appear so from the standpoint of a system moving in relation to the first one. Those events which are taking place within the vicinity of a single observer may be regarded as locally simultaneous. If, while visiting a library, I see two bookshelves standing next to each other, that can only mean that they are standing there at the same time. I go outside and walk to a park; there, I see two children on a teeter totter. While one child is going up, the other is going down while the bar that holds both remains straight, all this in accordance with the law of the lever. I walk from there into a building fronting the park which harbors a chemistry laboratory. There, I see a scientist weighing something with a pair of scales.

But for an observer at a considerable distance and moving in a different reference system, the theory holds that there will be a discrepancy; events which I suppose happening at the same time may not be viewed as simultaneous from that standpoint. Whether the two bookshelves would not be standing together or the bar on the teeter totter might not appear to be moving in line with the children or something bizarre may be going on with the chemist's scales, is difficult to say.

It is not simply that events taking place across a great distance are difficult to measure with certainty—that an exact determination of when two or more light signals are taking place at the same time across stellar distances could not be had; that the best would be an approximation. The Einsteinian position is rather that each system of reference has its own time that is peculiar to it. In the words of one relativity physicist, we "'must not talk about the age of a beam of light, although the concept of age is one of the simplest derivatives of the concept of local time. Neither must we allow ourselves to think of events taking place in Arcturus *now* with all the connotation attached to events taking place *here* now."[22]

To the Einsteinian, there can be no universal time. We cannot even speak of the two reference systems moving with respect to each other, for that would imply that they possess a common duration. You cannot say that *while* certain events are taking place on system K, certain other events are happening on system K'.[23] Indeed, strictly speaking, there can be no local time either; even that supposition is based in the end on the classical notion of absolute time.[24] Two clocks set next to each other will never be completely synchronized. In the final analysis, the two books standing are not really co-existing.

Returning to large scale reference systems, each such system must have its own "while." One cannot say that one reference system is moving to the left of another, or even is moving toward it, for that implies a common form of time, which is contrary to hypothesis. There can be no one-to-one correspondence between certain events in K and some others in K'.[25]

If time is completely relativized, so is space. Einstein said: "On the basis of the general theory of relativity, on the other hand, space as opposed to 'what fills space', which is dependent on the co-ordinates, has no separate existence."[26] Earlier, it was logically argued that a certain region of space might be empty; that, in such a circumstance, there would be nothing in it, even a gravitational field. And if something moves into it, then it would be no longer empty. But with relativity, one could not say that. As Einstein wrote: "There is no such thing as an empty space, *i.e.* a space without a field."[27]

Philosophus: May I see Einstein's book for a moment? .... Thank you. .... At the bottom of the same page, Einstein wrote: "If we consider that which fills space (i.e. the field) to be removed, there still remains the metric space."[28]

Doxa: Einstein may have contradicted himself here, but I think the words which I had quoted were the ones which he had really meant. (It is permissible to point out conflicting data on the same page as what I am using for my exposition, as you did, but it should not be forgotten that this is not a discussion of the truth or falsehood of relativity but only whether Ayn Rand's Objectivism is the correct application of it.)

Now, let us see whether or not Ayn Rand's Objectivism is the correct application of modern relativity theory to the world disclosed by the senses.

Existence: Ayn Rand teaches that the world we perceive is one of entities and their actions. Einstein teaches that what exists is space-time coordinates. There is no entity that moves in space and time. They cannot move in space because there is no space through which it can move. It does not move in some universal time because it has its own time. In reality, there is no motion, just a maze of spacial-temporal coordinates. Each 'position' has its own 'time' that belongs to it alone and none other, and there is nothing moving between any pair of coordinates. We have seen that Objectivism's "intellectual heir" has been willing to consider that entities are not final. We have also seen that their doctrine on time is reduced to an attribute of motion and that motion itself becomes problematic, all of which is consistent with Einstein's theory.

Identity The form of the law of contradiction which held that two things cannot exist at the same time and in the same space is abridged. Only the weaker, attribute form remains as it was, i.e.., A is simply non-A. It would remain simply because it is defined without reference to space and time. "A" could be defined differently in different frame of reference. So *A is A* in the fullest sense of being A would pertain only to one specific system of reference. But within this reference-system, there would be no change of attributes—A would remain A.

Turner and Hazelett leave us with this thought: "If we were to follow Einstein consistently, we would have to conclude that there is no truth in any physical location *now* that is also true in other places, for the simple reason that there is no nowness common to all systems in which a common truth can inhere. If there is no common nowness, then plainly there can be no truth that is common in all places now."[29] We have seen that although Objectivists do not wish to hold this notion, in the end they do.

Consciousness Suppose for the sake of the argument that Einstein was correct and that Objectivism is the theory's correlate in the world of perceived entities. Were that the case, consciousness could not move without crossing a great chasm from the region of high level thought characterized by relativity theory to the ordinary world depicted by Ayn Rand. This would present a paradox: The more realistic person who "acted" on the assumption that there were no action and no entities acting would probably be destroyed in a traffic jam. This would justify the most resolute pragmatism. The bridge across the two would be supplied by that mysterious whatever called "context": one would have to take concrete determinations from the Einsteinian reality in order to function in the mundane world. To get back to the Einsteinian reality, one would have to add determinations.

This *move*, if we could talk about such things, would be the opposite of that under Hegel. With the latter, the process of thought began with indeterminate being which was so empty of its determinations that it was the same as nothing, and ended through a series of loops at the highest level of determination, the Absolute. With Ayn Rand, on the other hand, when you remove the greater determinations of context surrounding the "real' Einsteinian world of no motion, and move into the world of fewer determinations of context, you get a world of things in motion.

But this means that Ayn Rand could not be the philosopher for Einstein. She believed that the rational person preserved context at all times, with consciousness of the fuller context being better than of the lesser. The person who was fully conscious would not operate in the world of the lesser context of knowledge unless he, in effect *dumbed* himself down in order to operate in that world. But with this, the naive realist and the much despised pragmatist would have it all over the Randian philosopher who was trying to act in fullest context. Leonard Peikoff blasted the distinction between theory and practice, saying that it involves a breach between percepts and concepts. "Given such a breach, thought comes to be viewed as pertaining to one world (the world of Platonic Forms, or of Kantian 'phenomena,' or of linguistic constructs), while action is viewed as pertaining to an opposite world (the world of concretes, or of things-in-themselves, or of empirical data). In this set-up, one expects an idea to be schizophrenic. One expects it to be good in one world, but not in the other, good in theory, but not in practice."[30]

It would seem from this that Ayn Rand's Objectivism could not be the correlate of Einstein.

Stanford: Yet, there is a dreamy similarity between Einstein's static conception of the world and Rand's, connected to their common denial of the reality of space and time. A novel does not move; the characters in it do not act. It is your mind that supplies the action as it moves from page to page.

Philosophus: There is more than a dreamy similarity. Rand's epistemology is generally consistent with Einstein's results, although they differ somewhat in their approach. It is true that there is this split between the mundane world of entities and actions in which the Objectivists operate and the world of the space-time hypothesis. But we have seen that this also comes out of the Objectivist epistemology. Obviously, that split does not bother the Objectivists very much. Rand's theories, despite their polemical embellishments, make a pretty good fit with Einstein's. The Objectivists would not be far amiss if they said that their's was the correlate of his theories in the fields of metaphysics and epistemology.

Stanford: Consider what memory would have to mean in A.R.'s metaphysics. It could not be a supplier of information about what once was. It could only be a kind of "contextualizer—a supplier of relations. As a contextualizer, it would provide relations which reason must then spin into something consistent with the rest of the mental data which it has before it—if a phrase like "before it" still has any sense left to it. Try to imagine it! To do so is impossible. It would be a kind of a machine which would supply certain biases to experience with which reason must then work. To use one of her favorite concepts, she and Einstein are "similar."

Penelope: Rand's epistemology is certainly a lot closer to what the Einsteinian would require than is Dialectical Materialism. Yet, fifty years ago, a scientific writer, in a semi-technical exposition of the mathematical theory of relativity (including tensor calculus), wrote that "the Einstein Theory shows also that practical measurement alone is also not sufficient for exploring the universe. In short, a judicious combination Of THEORY and PRACTICE, EACH GUIDING the other—a 'dialectical materialism'— is our most effective weapon."[31] At our next meeting, if you all agree, I would like to present what I have learned about Objectivism and Dialectical Materialism.

All: Yes!

DAY IX

AYN RAND AND V. I. LENIN

*A*gain, *the meeting is at Penelope's condominium, high above most of the downtown area. In front of her is a pile of books, some notes, and a fountain pen. Before Mr. Philosophus is a similar assortment. The other two have before them only some notes and writing instruments.*

Penelope: Notice has already been made of some similarities and differences between Objectivism and Dialectical Materialism. Both of them hold that the world of nature exists outside of and independent of human nature; that consciousness is but the awareness of that reality. In Lenin's words: "To be a materialist is to acknowledge objective truth, which is revealed to us by our sense organs. To acknowledge objective truth, i.e., truth not dependent upon man and mankind, is, in one way or another, to recognize absolute truth."[1] If this were the only important point of contact, it would be of little significance; there are many realistic philosophies. But, as was shown earlier, certain implications of her theory of concepts point in the direction to the Marxist-Leninist doctrine of the transformation of quantity into quality.

The question should be raised as to whether significant portions of her philosophy, especially in the subjects of metaphysics and epistemology, have been drawn from Dialectical Materialism. I am not the first to suggest this. In his 1974 book, *Answer To Ayn Rand*, John W. Robbins raised this very point.[2] Chris Matthew Sciabarra, in his 1995 pro-Objectivist book, *Ayn Rand: The Russian Radical*, praises Robbins for his "ability to see some of the parallels between Rand and the dialectical tradition."[3]

There is no doubt that Ayn Rand was exposed to the teaching of the Bolsheviks at an early age. Born Alice Rosenbaum in St. Petersburg Russia in 1905,[4] she received her higher education under the Soviets. She entered Petrograd University in 1921 and left the U.S.S.R. in 1926 for America[5] at a time when few were able to depart legally. Indeed, the heroine of her first published novel was killed by a soldier while attempting escape.

Little is known about what happened while she was under Soviet domination. Barbara Brandon, her biographer, cites this story which Rand had told of her university days there, when she supposedly studied under Professor N. O. Losky, characterized therein as "a distinguished international authority on Plato".[6]

> "Professor Losky was a stern, exacting man, contemptuous of all students, particularly of women. It was said that he failed most students the first time they took his examination, and that he was especially hard of women. In the spring, his students went to his home for their oral examination.... Alice hoped that she would be questioned on Aristotle. But when she entered his study, he questioned her only about Plato.... After a while, although she had not stated any estimate, Professor Losky said sardonically: 'You don't agree with Plato, do you?' 'No, I don't,' she answered. 'Tell me why,' he demanded. She replied, 'My philosophical views are not part of the history of philosophy yet. But they will be.' 'Give me your examination book,' he ordered. He wrote in the book and handed it back to her. 'Next student,' he said. He had written: 'Perfect.'"[7]

There are several difficulties with this claim. According to Sciabarra's research, Losky, because of difficulties with the Soviet authorities, had not taught at the University in 1921; neither did he teach in 1922; nor thereafter, for in November of that year, he was forced to leave the country.[8] Furthermore, members of his family and even a distinguished American professor who knew him then dispute that he disliked female students.[9] Sciabarra offers the hypothesis that Losky might have taught that year, unofficially, but there is no evidence of the same. In fact the evidence so far counters that idea: Pitirim Sorokin, who had been present in Petrograd during those times, and who subsequently rose high in the ranks of American academia, denied that those professors who were ousted from their posts were allowed to teach anything else under university auspices.[10] The matter is cloaked in mystery.

Before we draw any solid conclusions, however, let us ascertain the areas where Ayn Rand's philosophy intersects in a significant way with that of Dialectical Materialism.

(1) Lenin's concept of "matter" and Rand's of "existence" are similar in certain fundamental respects. Rand taught that the existence of entities are given in perception, that perception is the basis of all knowledge, and that motion exists as a consequence of the specific nature of a given entity; that it is not something accidentally tacked on to it, something which could as easily be other than it is; the motion appropriate to a crochet ball is determined by the kind of thing it is, as is the quite different motion of a child's wooden block. Lenin's words are also very clear: "The concept matter expresses nothing more than the objective reality which is given us in sensation. Therefore, to divorce motion from matter is equivalent to divorcing thought from the objective reality, or to divorcing my sensations from the external world.—in a word, it is to go over to idealism."[11]

(Of course, Rand holds that reality is not contradictory and that there is no actual infinite. On these important points, the two are in conflict).

(2) As we have discussed, Rand's distinction between primacy of consciousness and primacy of existence philosophies probably came from Dialectical Materialism's distinction between the Primacy of Nature and the Primacy of Spirit.[12]

(3) The two hold strikingly similar positions on the interconnection of the phenomena of the world and also of knowledge:

According to Stalin, "...dialectics does not regard Nature as an accidental agglomeration of things, of phenomena, unconnected with, isolated from, and independent of, each other, but as a connected and integral whole, in which things, phenomena are organically connected with, dependent on, and determined by each other."[13]

According to Peikoff, "Metaphysically, there is only one universe. This means that everything in reality is interconnected. Every entity is related in some way to the others; each somehow affects and is affected by the others. Nothing is a completely isolated fact, without causes or effects; no aspect of the total can exist ultimately apart from the total."[14]

In the words immediately following those of his quoted above, Stalin adds: "The dialectical method therefore holds that no phenomena in Nature can be understood if taken by itself, isolated from surrounding phenomena, in as much as any phenomena in any realm of Nature may become meaningless to us if it is not considered in connection with the surrounding conditions, but divorced from them; and that, *vice versa*, any phenomena can be understood and explained if considered in its inseparable connection with surrounding phenomena, as one conditioned by surrounding phenomena."[15]

In the words immediately following those of his quoted above, Peikoff adds: "Knowledge, therefore, which seeks to grasp reality, must also be a total; its elements must be interconnected to form a unified whole reflecting the whole which is the universe."[16]

The two are similar enough to be restatements of each

other. (At this time, if you please, I would like to depart from my procedure to make a point. How did Stalin know that everything is interconnected? Did Lenin whisper it in his ear? How does Peikoff know this? We have been in contact with much, but no one can say with certainty we are in contact with everything. If action at a distance is true, then it may indeed be the case that all is connected. If it is not, then there may exist some matter which is completely independent of the rest of existence.)

And now to resume:

(4) Dialectical materialism is emphatically a monistic system; it holds that every existent without exception is a manifestation of one underlying reality, i.e., matter. All explanation, therefore, is ultimately in terms of matter and its properties. If there were two fundamental principles in the universe—for instance, mind and matter, then there could not be a single principle which could explain everything. A philosophy which held that would be dualism.

The dialectical approach follows logically from a monistic system. If all is ultimately one and one is ultimately all, then any particular element could not be considered except apart from the whole; and more than that, any supposed opposite would contain within itself elements in common with that which it opposed. The best illustration of a dialectical system would be a magnet. The north and south fields come into existence simultaneously; if one were wiped out, the other would also vanish. They are of opposite polarity and anything attracted to the north pole would be repelled by the south, and *vice versa*. At one end of a bar magnet, the lines of force are concentrated at the pole; at the other end, the lines are also concentrated. In between, the lines of force separate and go toward one end or the other; anything equally pulled from both ends would remain motionless. This gives us a clue to what is meant by the Marxist idea of the unity of opposites: what appears to be opposition is actually part of the same system and is merely an action of one part of the totality upon another part. In a dualistic system, the two opponents would be unalike.

Objectivism is not officially monistic, but leans that way.[17] Peikoff, it will be recalled, condemns dualism but thinks that monism makes assumptions which have not yet been proved; he is even open under certain conditions to the idea of consciousness being finally reduced to physical nature. We have seen how Rand attempted to bridge the gap between the subject and the object by locating objectivity in the relationship between the two. In his recent study of the founder of this philosophy, Chris Matthew Sciabarra, declares that "Rand accepted the dialectical revolt against formal dualism."[18] In his book, Sciabarra shows where she attempted to remove several dichotomies from philosophy, such as "individual verses community," "morality-practicality", "logic-experience," and, of course, "fact-value," explaining in several instances that the ideas being disputed were but two sides of the same coin, and not fundamental opposites.[19]

Rand affirmed that consciousness was itself a form of existence—that "the axiom 'existence exists' is wider than the concept of the external world. It includes everything, as I indicated, including your mental states, mental processes, and such phenomena as ideas or feelings, which are not in the same category as physical reality, but they exist."[20] Yet, she denied the dualism of mind and body. That would open the way to supernaturalism; Rand, being an atheist, could not allow it. Objectivism is close to materialism but never quite reaches it, resting on some future deliverance from the special sciences to answer the question once and for all.

Dialectical Materialism rejects the vulgar materialism which held that the brain produces thought as the liver produces bile, but it gives no place to any dualism. Dialectical materialism holds that thought and extension are both attributes of an underlying matter; they are supposed to have this unity even though they are completely incommensurable and contradict each other. This is not the position of Rand, but her's is a neighbor of that one.

(5) Objectivism holds that knowledge is contextual. So,

with a different terminology does dialectical materialism. In the words of Lenin: "1) Things exist independently of our consciousness, independently of our perceptions, outside of us, for it is beyond doubt that alizarin existed in coal tar yesterday and it is equally beyond doubt that yesterday we knew nothing of the existence of this alizarin and received no sensations from it. 2) There is definitely no difference in principle between the phenomenon and the thing-in-itself.... The only difference is between what is known and what is not yet known.... 3) In the theory of knowledge, as in every other branch of science, we must think dialectically, that is, we must not regard our knowledge as ready-made and unalterable, but must determine how *knowledge* emerges from *ignorance*, and how incomplete, inexact knowledge becomes more complete and more exact."[21]

(6) Objectivism holds that essences are not metaphysical or final, but epistemological, or dependent on the state of man's knowledge. But so does Dialectical Materialism. As Lenin said: "The 'essence' of things, or 'substance' is *also* relative; it expresses only the degree of profundity of man's knowledge of objects; and while yesterday the profundity of this knowledge did not go beyond the atom, and today does not go beyond the electron or ether, dialectical materialism insists on the temporary, relative, approximate character of all these *milestones* in the knowledge of nature gained by the progressing science of man. The electron is as inexhaustible as the atom, nature is infinite, but it infinitely *exists*. And it is this sole categorical, this sole unconditional recognition of nature's *existence* outside the mind and perception of man that distinguishes dialectical materialism from relativist agnosticism and idealism."[22] Since the idea that essences are epistemological rather than metaphysical is a Randian notion that we did not refute, the importance of its probable origin in Rand's thought can hardly be overestimated.

(7) Objectivism holds that man perceives reality, not directly, but in a certain form; this is in contrast to what is called "naive realism," which holds that man perceives reality in

its intrinsic form. (Our realism differs from this kind of realism only in that we hold that the primary qualities are perceived directly and the secondary through their effect on our sense organs.) Marxism-Leninism proclaims that the mind copies or reflects reality; but, although this may seem at first hearing to be a variety of naive realism, it is not. The *reflection* which the advocates of Dialectical Materialism speak of is not a straightforward representation of an external reality, but a relationship between external reality and our internal organs. In the words of Lenin: "The sensation of red reflects ether vibrations of a frequency of approximately 450 trillions per second. The sensation of blue reflects ether vibrations of a frequency of approximately 620 trillions per second. The vibrations of the ether exist independently of our sensations of light. Our sensations of light depend on the action of the vibrations of the ether on the human organ of vision. Our sensations reflect objective reality, *i.e.*, something that exists independently of human sensations. This is how science views it."[23]

And, of course, the critics ask, if what we perceive as "red" exists in objective reality as ether vibrations of a definite frequency, why is the resemblance between two representations so discordant? The answers given by the Marxist-Leninists are like Objectivism's in a certain respects: "The resemblance between reflection and object is not a simple mechanical similarity, but a complex, contradictory resemblance. The sensory material, the living organism, reflects the operation of external objects and processes in its own fashion, on the basis of its own peculiar properties (the inner laws of its nature)."[24] "The objective quality of the light-wave is reflected in subjective form, in the form of sensation. The colour resembles the objective process consisting in the action of light which produces it, but only in a relative fashion."[25]

Here, as with Rand's argument from context, objective relativism is supposed to supply the answer: we perceive it, but in a different form. The difference between the two is first, that whereas Dialectical Materialism, in harmony with normal speech, teaches that the term "objective" belongs to the object alone and "subjective" only to the subject, Rand held that the term "objective" belongs to a special relationship between subject and object ; and second, Rand rejected the notion that reality is contradictory.

(8) Another area of agreement concerns the partisan character of philosophy. Marxism-Leninism's stand on that point is militant. Philosophy must not be neutral but must reflect the interests of the working class, as defined by that philosophy. Objectivism heralds the individual, rather than the collective, but its spokesmen must be completely consistent in their adherence to its teachings. Objectivist meetings are not debating societies in which the outer fringes of the movement are given their voice. Spokesmen who deviate and do not reform after their incongruent ideas or actions are pointed out to them, are dropped. This happened to several of Rand's principal lieutenants while she was alive. After she passed away, the leadership was assumed by her intellectual heir. Several years later, formal exclusion happened to a certain academic who had earlier published a book defending an important aspect of Objectivist epistemology. This gentleman had given a speech before a group of libertarians, showing how their own movement was, in part, made possible by Objectivism. He was criticized for giving this speech, the reason being that while the two movements do agree on economic theory and many points of political theory, still, the libertarians have mixed premises and there should be no latitudinarian meetings with them. He refused to recant and so the official Objectivists withdrew from him. Subsequently, this gentleman established a neo-Objectivist group of his own.

That is the end of my report.

Doxa: It should be emphasized that Ayn Rand was a staunch enemy of Marxism. Barbara Brandon states that the character, "Dr. Robert Stadler," perhaps the greatest villain in *Atlas Shrugged*, was based on Robert Oppenheimer, the atomic physicist, whom Ayn Rand had met.[26] Recently, it was shown that he was a traitor in behalf of Stalin's Russia.[27] Were she secretly on the side of the Kremlin, the character modeled after him would have been portrayed as a great scientist who was misunderstood by the Lilliputians whom he was trying to help, instead of symbolizing the betrayal of the free mind.

Penelope: Of course. I will make my summary after the close of the discussion.

Philosophus: The points from which Rand breaks off from Dialectical Materialism can be seen best in comparison and contrast with the ideas of Lenin. This is found primarily in Lenin's *Materialism and Empirio-Criticism*.[28] This book was quoted many times in the excellent report which we just heard. Lenin penned this book on the eve of Einstein's world fame. It was first printed in 1908. The old mechanical theory that physical reality could ultimately be analyzed in terms of pushes, pulls, and rotations seemed to be an over-simplification. It was known that radioactivity could alter the mass of an atom; the electron was a puzzle.

Lenin combated three ideas that were taking hold among scientists; (1) Straight out idealism, which taught that the world was ultimately mental in nature—that the separation between thought and external reality is a separation in thought only; (2) Kantianism, which taught that the thing in-itself could never be known, that we were stuck with the world of appearances; (3) agnosticism, especially as taught by Mach, a predecessor of Einstein, who held that we do not know anything but our sensations and our ideas of nature are simply an order which we impose upon the maze of experience, and that what we call "reality" is nothing more than a product of our own subjectivity. Lenin was not aware of Einstein, but he understood the attraction that the idea of relativity was having among the younger scientists of that day. "Another cause which bred 'physical' idealism is the principle of *relativism*, the relativity of our knowledge, a principle which, in a period of breakdown of the old theories, is taking a firm hold upon the physicists, and which, *if the latter are ignorant of dialectics*, is bound to lead to idealism."[29]

Rand also disagreed with these three groups, although her attack was concentrated mostly on the Kantians and the third group, which she called, the "positivists," yet her public remarks about Einstein were complimentary. The idealists were not much of a social factor at the time that she wrote.

Lenin believed matter to be infinite not only in extent, but also, as he put it, in depth. Motion for Lenin is change of all kinds. And this motion, he held, following Marx and Engels, to be contradictory. Matter for Lenin consisted not only of entities with attributes such as solidity and shape, but also mind; consciousness then, for Lenin, was not an irreducible axiom, but a form of Matter. Lenin's Matter contained two kinds of existence which he regarded to be contradictory: extension and consciousness.

But there are certain things which this matter could not be. Lenin completely rejected the idea that motion could exist without matter—that all one could say was *it moves*, while there was nothing moving, only a motion in a total void, a wave without a waver. "What is essential," he wrote, "is the point of departure. What is essential is that the attempt to *think* of motion without matter smuggles in *thought* divorced from matter—and that is philosophical idealism."[30] So, neither matter without motion nor thought without matter is possible. There, Rand was in agreement as far as the present context of knowledge is concerned.

Where the two differed most was in Lenin's teaching of fundamental contradiction at the root of things. It should be said that Dialectical Materialism does not teach contradiction at every point; if it did it would have to admit matter without motion. What it does teach is contradiction of attributes. In teaching that thought is a form of matter, Dialectical Materialism does not mean that thought is subordinate to matter. For this philosophy, as for the Hegelian, subject and object cannot be two incommensurable imponderables, cut off from each other; from the perspective of that theory, if they were totally different, the Marxist would argue that nothing could bridge the abyss.[31] Dialectical Materialism has its own kind of order.

To Lenin, sensation and thought were not anything separate from matter, but reflections of matter upon itself. This is the basis of the principle of the identity of opposites, a principle which was enunciated by Hegel when he taught that thinking and being are the same and yet different.[32] Dialectical Materialism is sometimes criticized because it does not have any notion of substance, i.e., that it does not hold anything to be fundamental and not dependent on anything else. But it does have such a notion. This is clearly shown in Lenin's rejection of the idea that motion can exist without matter; for this philosophy, matter and matter alone is self sufficient. It is precisely because this self-sufficient substance is held to be internally self-contradictory that motion is believed by holders of this philosophy to be possible. Motion and change exist because of internal contradictions; if there were no inherent conflict there would be no action. Without conflict, no motion would be possible. Everything would be at absolute zero, a final equilibrium which was not held together by tension. This is the basis for Marxism's claim to be inherently dynamic.[33] (Rand, as we have seen, holds that motion is not contradictory, that it follows from the specific nature of particular entities; with her, the law of identity holds always).

What does it mean to say that motion is contradictory? As Engels explained: "...even the most simple mechanical movement from place to place can only be accomplished by a body being in one and the same moment of time at one place and simultaneously at another place, at one and the same place and yet not at it. And motion is just the continuous setting up and simultaneous solution of this contradiction."[34] To use the bird in flight to illustrate their theory: At any given time along its trajectory, the bird occupies a particular space. A moment later, it occupies a slightly different place, partly overlapping the space it had occupied the moment before. But if at any specific point in time the bird occupies a definite place, then it is at rest. Yet, despite the contradiction, motion exists. Instead of attempting to resolve the ancient paradox of Zeno against motion, Dialectical Materialism embraces it. Lenin proclaimed: "We must grant the old dialecticians the contradictions which they prove in motion; but what follows is not that there is no motion, but rather that motion is *existent* Contradiction itself."[35]

At our last meeting, we argued that there is actually no contradiction; that not only can the distance traversed be divided infinitely, but also the time—not only the time but also the movement itself. At any moment a point on the bird corresponds to a point on the ground. Lenin was familiar with an idea similar to the one just expressed: "Movement is the presence of a body in a definite place at a given moment and in another place at another, subsequent moment—such is the objection which Chernov repeats... in the wake of *all* the 'metaphysical' opponents of Hegel." Then Lenin answered: "This objection is *incorrect* (1) it describes the *result* of motion, but not motion *itself*; (2) it does not show, it does not contain in itself the *possibility* of motion; 3) it depicts motion as a sum, as a concatenation of states of *rest*, that is to say, the (dialectical) contradiction is not removed by it, but only concealed, shifted, screened, covered over."[36]

My answer to Lenin and dialectics in general: It is a fallacy to suppose that one must show its possibility, for that implies that it arises out of the non-moving, in other words, that it is standing still at the same time and in the same place that it is in motion, which would indeed be a contradiction. The truth is that motion and rest are fundamental opposites, and neither can be reduced to the other. It is correct to characterize motion as the presence of a moving body at one point in space at one moment and then its presence at another point at a different time. In a way, it is also true that this is a result, since it is expressed in terms of where and when—which are not the same things as movement. But there is a subtle error in saying that the essence of motion is somehow being missed when it is so described. The implication is that a proper description would characterize it out of reference to space and time. But this would be impossible, since motion cannot exist when and where they are not—(Lenin himself rejected the idea of motion without matter).

Motion is a fundamental fact; and as such, cannot be explained to anyone who does not already understand it. Motion occurs through space during a specific amount of time. Space and time do not accidentally accompany motion. When we see the bird in flight, a number of receptor cells in our optical system are fired; this helps give us the perception of flight, but it is not itself flight. The same is true with space and time. Together or separately they do not make up motion, but, because they exist independently of motion, we can measure it. Speed or velocity and acceleration are not ratios between space (distance) and time. But motion is measured by them. In the differential calculus, instantaneous velocity is defined as the rate of change of distance per instant of time. That is the rate at which the distance is altering at that point of time and at that point in space. Then and there, it is moving; stated quite simply—*it is not at rest*. Nowhere is there an equivalence of motion with the means by which it is measured. We do not even perceive every instant of motion; the receptor cells are not continuous. This is obvious when we examine a film strip and find that what we took to be continuous was really a series of stills moved quickly. But few would conclude from this that motion is but a series of states of rest; our intelligence informs us that to get this effect, the film **must move**. The essence of motion, stated negatively, is that there are no rest states while it is taking place. We also know that space and time exist, separately and independent of motion and of matter; as was explained last time. There is no contradiction, for all three, motion, distance (space), and time, are infinitely divisible in the same way, in other words, that there is a one-to-one correspondence of one to each. (Matter may not be infinitely divisible, for a minimum size to it may exist).

To sum it up: Dialectical Materialism is able to retain this paradox by surreptitiously fusing space and time to motion. Were they all the same thing, or some part of the same thing, no real measurement of motion could be accomplished, for the time and distance would move with the object and the moment would also go with it, leaving no passage of time at all. Putting it differently: Lenin wrote that "Motion is the union of continuity (of space and time) and discontinuity (of space and time). Motion is a contradiction, a union of contradictions."[37] My answer: consider the beginning and ending point of a line segment a foot long. The two points are not next to one another. If Lenin were right, then when I moved my hand across this short distance, I shall have united the two separated points into an amalgam by moving my wand-less hand over that space. But that would not have been what had taken place.

Rand agreed with Lenin that an actual infinity was a contradiction. But since she held that reality could not be contradictory, she concluded that infinity could not exist in actuality. She needed to do something with motion too. To prevent the non-finite, she made time but a part of motion. Every entity was to have a specific existence and could not be other than what it is without ceasing to be that entity. Identity became for her but another way of stating existence. Monism was not proclaimed as a principle, but the fact that her philosophy is a reaction to that of Marxism, an answer to it, suggests that there might be some traces of Dialectical Materialism left in it—as indeed there are.

"Motion," wrote Lenin, "is the essence of space and time."[38] Dialectical Materialism rejects both the Kantian notion that time and space are subjective modes of presenting phenomena and the realistic notion that they exist independent of matter; it holds that they are objective forms of matter in motion. To this, Rand would have given her adhesion. But Dialectical Materialism goes a little farther than this: it

teaches that while there is nothing in space but matter, neither is there any space without matter.[39] Rand would have
agreed to the latter half of this statement; to affirm the opposite would have been tantamount to declaring nothing to
have some form of existence; as to the first half of the statement, however, she would have preferred to leave that to be
decided by physics. Dialectical Materialism also teaches that
while there is nothing outside of time, there cannot be any
time without matter.[40] Once more, Rand would have agreed
with the latter part of that statement, but would have had
reservations about the first. To her, finitude was the fundamental fact, not time and space.

Gustav Wetter, the Jesuit priest who wrote a definitive
study of Dialectical Materialism for his Order, said that "the
dialectical materialist conception of space and time is basically in agreement with that of scholasticism, which considers them to be creations of the mind on a factual basis (*en
rationis cum fundamento in re*) and therefore as a combinations of subjective and objective."[41] By *factual basis*, Wetter
meant that material objects are presented to the senses as
existing in extension and time, the latter being a succession.
By *subjective*, he meant that these spacial temporal-represen-
tations do not exist on their own, independent of human
consciousness. This tribute actually fits Objectivism slightly
more than Dialectical Materialism, since the former holds
space and time to be products of a relationship between consciousness and existence. Dialectical Materialism, on the contrary, holds that space and time, like mind, are attributes
matter, there being nothing outside of matter.[42] Rand wo
also have dissented from Wetter's subjective- objective
minology, but she would have understand his meaning

The mind in Dialectical Materialism is pitch-black
pared to Objectivism. To Lenin, consciousness was
flection. By that, he did not mean the familiar
intellectual "reflection", wherein thought is compa
contrasted with thought, for that takes place fully
domain of consciousness. No, to the Dialectical M

the property of reflection was material, somewhat like in a mirror, although multi-faceted. It is true, as was stated in that excellent summary of the similarities of the two philosophies, that the reflection is supposed to be internal and dialectical, etc. but it is still has that hard quality.

Now, there is, of course, an element like consciousness in a mirror, the object is apprehended in the place where it is not;[43] and in consciousness, the subject can apprehend an object existing outside of it. But this is only a shallow similarity. Rand knew that no mirror, however multi-faceted, however multi-layered, however dialectical, could have any intelligence, whatsoever. Although her own solution was wrong, she did not try to reduce consciousness to what it was not; she wanted to enthrone it among her irreducible axioms. Not for her was the mind's action a groping after matter in a darkness so complete that even light is just another thing bouncing off other things in order to push men to do what they cannot resist.

Rand, we have seen, because of her love of finitude, could not give space and time quite the universal character that Lenin assigned to them, namely the status of being constant aspects of matter. Were she to have done so, however, she could not have kept consistently to her idea that reality does not contain contradictions. She did not want what Lenin found in motion, a basis for the unity of opposites.

Hegel also taught that reality was ultimately finite. But Rand did not want to return to him. He was an idealistic monist. It was from his philosophy that Marxism-Leninism was born. Hegel tried to deduce the principal facts of reality from concepts. When he came to nature, or the reality that lies outside of thought, he tried to deduce it from concepts by arguing that Nature was "otherness". (His supposition was that the thought of the Other would posit something besides thought, not simply another thought on the same level). Marx, who wished to be a materialist, took the Hegelian dialectic and turned it upside down. Instead of starting with the concept of indeterminate being and deriving its various determinations through reasoning, he started with Nature. Since, this was "otherness" in the Hegelian system, it is not difficult to understand how Marx could have arrived at the notion that matter or fundamental reality was inherently contradictory. One can also see the Marxist affection for the concept of "alienation."

Rand wanted to get away from all of this. She taught that motion proceeded from the identity of the entity. Rand kicked out contradiction, but she kept context, also a Hegelian idea. She did not see the value of recognizing Nothing as an absolute part of space.

There is also a similarity in the Marxist and Randian concepts of motion, parallel to their mutual rejection of both Kantianism and realism in regard to time and space. To understand this, one must turn to Aristotle. This philosopher taught that the only natural motion was circular, which he believed to be the case with the heavens, with the Sun and the planets traveling around a stationary Earth. Now, much of the action taking place on earth is not circular, but rectilinear, irregular, parabolic, or otherwise non-circular. Non-circular motion was held to be unnatural, and the result of things being out of their proper places. The implication from that is that if the things on earth were to return to the places in which they belonged there would be no non-circular action. In a not altogether different way, Dialectical Materialism holds that all motion, circular and otherwise, results from the internal contradictions inherent in matter. If, *impossible*, these contradictions were to end, so would all motion cease; of course, Dialectical Materialism denies that this is possible, since, for it, all matter is in motion and all motion is material, but the lineage from Aristotle is plain enough. Rand, of course, held that motion proceeded from the identity of entities, whose nature is always specific. But we have seen how, as a consequence of her denial of the reality of space and time, the Objectivist position gravitates to that of Einstein whose ideas end up in the destruction of the idea of motion as we know it. All four in the same way made that same denial.

Galileo, Descartes, Newton, Locke, and the giants of the 16th and 17th centuries denied that rest is the natural state of things, and motion is the result of some unnatural disturbance. In this century, the engineers and inventors carry this idea forward. But the anti-technologists in their guise as environmentalists are busy chopping up the roads to the future; and the theorists of the universities and the well-endowed foundations are largely incapable even of formulating the difficulty. That is all I care to say about this.

Penelope: We are now in a position to answer the question with which today's meeting, namely, is there a significant connection between Objectivism and Dialectical Materialism? The answer is resoundingly in the affirmative. Although Rand was a firm anti-Communist and, probably, the most eloquent defender of *laissez faire* capitalism in history, the facts speak for themselves. She retained certain tenets of the philosophy which she had rejected. Both held that all reality is interconnected; and although Rand denied infinity, she agreed with Lenin that an infinite universe would be a contradiction and that there can be no empty space or that space and time were independent of matter.

This similarity was part of her appeal. Although few on either side would admit it; it was thought that if Marxism-Leninism were to be refuted from a standpoint partially visible to its adherents, the latter would find it easier to get on the capitalist road.

And to the superficial observer, that is exactly what has happened. The Communists have torn down the wall; officially, the Soviet Union is no more. The leadership has aggregated toward capitalism. When Rand began her career in America, free enterprise was in retreat. The newspapers were full of praise for government planners. FDR had successfully blamed the Great Depression on individualism. By 1957, the year of the publication of *Atlas Shrugged*, there were few college-level teachers of economics who were not socialists to one degree or another. Without a doubt, Ayn Rand played a great part in the partial reversal that has resulted.

The Communists had to change something. Their tyranny was past denying. The whole world knew that they could not keep their promises of eventual material abundance. Even in war production, they fell short; their best airplane, the *Foxbat*, required a new engine after every long flight.

Yet, as the West is beginning to realize, the old leadership has remained. Some wise man compared it to what happens to a huge tree full of crows resting on its various branches when a gun is fired. The crows leave their branches, flying around in a furious whirl of activity. But after a while, they settle down in approximately the same positions they held before.

There is a danger, however, resulting from the affinity between Rand's philosophy and that of the rulers of Russia and many of the successor states to the Soviet Union and its satellites. The former Communists may have repudiated the idea of common ownership of property; but with Dialectical Materialism, they can explain it away as an earlier stage in the evolution of the social dialectic. Lenin taught that contradictions exist. The former Communists, being Hegelians, may look upon the old Communist states as the Thesis and the *laissez faire* capitalism as championed by Rand as the Anti-Thesis. They will view the former Soviet world, having been turned inside out, as bristling with contradictions. The answer: a Synthesis of the various features of both. Rand's Objectivism, having originally been created in part as a refutation of Marxism on the same atheistic level and with considerable replacement of parts, may be seen as a tempting vehicle for the transformation. One of the chief features of Diamat which Rand did not accept was the negation of the negation. This was the idea that the anti-thesis, having been presented as the negative of the original thesis, is itself negated. Or, in the words of Lenin, "the repetition at a higher stage of certain features, properties, etc. of the lower and...the apparent reversion to the old (negation of the negation).'"⁴⁴

Stalin reminds us, "The dogmatists and talmudists re-gard Marxism and separate conclusions and formulas of Marxism as a collection of dogmas, which 'never' change, notwithstanding changes in the conditions of the develop-ment of society.'"⁴⁵ A cheap victory indeed.

Stanford: I think you are right that the former Commu-nist leaders will remain dialecticians, probably monists—Hegelians of some stripe, even. I agree that the Soviet Union was only retired. I observe that they are already turning back from *laissez faire* capitalism. But I am not convinced that they are using Objectivism as a fulcrum. To think that is to sup-poses that they will remain atheists, for if both the thesis and the anti-thesis is atheistic, then so must be the synthesis. I think instead that they will move in the direction of religion. Atheism is getting to be out-of-date.

Penelope: I stand.

Philosophus: Dialectical Materialism was probably not the only philosophical burden from which Rand sought to escape with less than complete success. This other source would have been the Cabala, a certain tradition according to which, the Deity was completely unknowable; no attributes could describe this Being, not even their perfection. One could only say that it was "not-this," "not-that", "not-something else", etc. This was the "Unlimited." I think that it was against this as well as against Dialectical Materialism that she struggled in her polemics in behalf of the finite. The reason-ing is like this: If something were unlimited in all respects, all would be reduced to the same unit; and all would be the same. In the absence of no difference whatsoever, if no char-acteristic limited it in some respect, there would be only ho-mogeneity. Every part of it would be commensurable. Rand failed to see the intellectual legitimacy of an infinity that was limited in some respects but not in others. Not seeing the possibility of a space that had no element of time in it or a time that was not one side of an identity of which the other side was space, or of a matter that could not originate mind out of its own unassisted powers, she therefore held on to finitude as the anchor of reason.

Yet, even in her doctrine, there are traces of what she rejected: we have seen that Objectivism holds that one cannot speak of the universe as a whole having a beginning or no beginning in time because there is nothing outside of it with which to make a comparison. Although this tradition holds that no attributes can be attributed to the Unlimited, contradictorily, it also holds that it is like pure light and certain sparks have gotten away from the Unlimited, and the job of the good people is to rejoin them. In a way, the motor in *Atlas Shrugged* that converts static charges of electricity into current electricity is a conversion of random, useless sparks into integrated form, suitable for civilization. Atlantis is both the correlate of what it was before the sparks were lost and what it can be like when they are reunited. This tradition teaches that through certain emanations, intelligibility is supplied to a a chaotic world. Objectivism teaches that the axioms provide light by which the lesser concepts can be formed, validated, and used to organize the vast mass of data which otherwise could not be stored, even if retrievable. In this tradition, certain letters are held to be both signs of things and means by which the powers of nature can be controlled. This may have been *a* root for Rand's idea that perception reveals the object in a different form.

Penelope: I think we are ready for what you have to say about universals now.

Doxa: Let that be the subject of our next meeting then.

DAY X

FACTS AND UNIVERSALS

*T*hey are once more present at **Penelope**'s *luxurious apart ment on the twenty-first floor of a high rise overlooking Portland, Oregon. Below is the city, wrapped in fog. A few other towers stand up into the clear air. A gossamer cloud rolls by, strikes the side of another high rise, and is broken up.*

Stanford: A. R.'s attempt to solve the problem of universals through reference to similarity was unsuccessful. It was an attempt to explain intelligibility by resorting to something almost mechanical. Within any similarity, there has to be an element that is identical. This cannot be escaped by referring the problem to a + or -, a more or a less.

Doxa: Is there any answer to the problem?

Philosophus: Yes, there is. But first we have to ask what universals are.

Stanford: A universal is that which is the same throughout a group of particulars; it is the element that is not different in a variety. Even if we take an array of colors consisting of various hues of red, such as rose, pink, carmine, vermillion, etc., there must be something in that display that is the same. If one goes back to the range of light vibrations behind it, the frequency that is capable of producing some shade of red in us must be somewhere within that extent.

Penelope: True. And the same frequency will produce in the same person the same shade when the color surroundings are the same. A frequency which produces a ruby red when surrounded by a certain frequency producing yellow will produce that exact shade when the same conditions are reproduced. Similarity will not work as an explanation.

Doxa: Or, to use one of the artificial things preferred by Ayn Rand, all of the objects known as "chairs" possess the attribute of being a man-made object consisting of a flat level surface with supports. What all the diverse things possessing this attribute have in common is *chair-ness*.

Philosophus: This leads to a question. Redness, blueness, yellowness and the other universals of colour all have in common the fact that they are all colors. Likewise, chairs, tables, desks, and beds have their differences but they are all items of furniture. Colour is the genus of which the various universals of color are species. Similarly, the universals of chairness, deskness, and the like are species of the genus, furniture.

The question is this? Are the separate universals which are species of their respective genus, particulars of that genus? In other words, if all the red things—the sunsets, the flags, etc.—are particulars whereby the universal (redness) is exhibited, then is redness in turn a particular of the universal, colour?

Stanford: A. R. would deny that this could be so. She would argue that the individual chairs, tables, etc. are instances of furniture as well as particulars of the types of furniture to which they belong. For instance, "chair," "table," and the like have no meaning apart from the things to which they refer; the more general concept, "furniture," refers to the same individual objects, albeit in a less specialized way.

Philosophus: Rand was right. And this is the case with all universals. The separate universals which stand as species to some more comprehensive universal are not its particulars. To give another example, the universals of color, redness, greenness, yellowness, etc. are species of the universal, colour; they are not, however particulars of color. If one takes a particular for an example—say a blue sky on a clear day—such a sky possesses the universal of blueness. Yet, it also has characteristics other than colour—temperature, pressure, volume, chemical mixtures, etc. The universal, *blueness*, on the other hand, does not possess any other characteristic than colour. It does not possess the universal, *colour*; it is a color. It differs from the other universals only with regard to color. Various colored things, like the sky over Portland during the summer, are particulars of blueness; they are also particulars of colour, for they are of at least one hue. The particulars of any universal can only be particulars; they can never be universals. A species of colour other than blueness is not a particulars of the genus-universal, colour or color-ness. The particulars of this last is whatever object or part of an object exhibits the attribute of colour, regardless of whether it is blue, green, yellow, etc. The particulars of the species under a genus are also particulars of that genus. As John Cook Wilson put it, "Part of, elements of, do not express the relation, whereas kind of, species of, differentiation of, do express it, for it is a relation *sui generis*."[1]

The same for the man-made objects. The quality of being a chair (or a table or a bed) is not a particular of the quality of being a piece of furniture. The quality of being a chair is but one of the divisions of furniture. A particular chair is not only a particular of *chairness*, but also of *furniture-ness*. (In English, cumbersome words like these are often replaced by expressions, such as "quality of" or "characteristic of".)

Stanford: But I thought the theory of universals was that they had some kind of a special existence apart from objects, that they subsisted rather than existed.

Philosophus: This, we will come to at the proper time. I have another question. How is a class distinguished from a universal?

Penelope: A class has something to do with the particulars of a universal.

Philosophus: To be more exact, a class constitutes the totality of the particulars of a universal. If red-ness is the universal possessed by each of the particular things which have that color, then all of those together constitute the class of red things. Similarly, to return to Rand's preference for artificial things, all the chairs in the world are particulars of the universal, chair-ness, and the totality of all these particulars makes up the class of chairs. Once again: all the particular chairs, tables, shelves, etc. are particulars of the universal, furniture-ness, the totality of which constitutes the class of furniture.

Stanford: A class is not a subjective thing like a concept; it is simply all that possesses a certain universal.

Philosophus: Yes. For the moment, let us consider the question of class.

Not every group of things which are related to each other constitutes a class. An army is not a class; it is an organization. No enlisted man, no officer, no support person, possesses an attribute which makes the army as a whole the universal of that characteristic. A blue object possesses this characteristic regardless of whether or not any other objects with that color exist; the ocean is not blue because of its relationship to some sapphire worn on a woman's neck. It is blue for other causes. On the other hand, the members of an army are members only because of the relationship they bear to one another. They are not particulars of the universal, army; they are its components. The same thing with an organism. The fur on an animal is not a particular of the universal, *animality*. But the animal to which the fur belongs is a particular of that universal. The particulars of the universal, army, are not the soldiers of the various armies, but the separate armies of the respective nations, such as the U.S. Army, the British Army, etc. The various officers and enlisted men, commanders and commanded are only parts.

Stanford: Would the people of a nation be a class or an organization?

Philosophus: It depends upon whether the relations between the adults are all contractual. If they are, then the citizens of the country are a class, because each is not only a resident but has a contract with the government. Each one individually possesses the characteristic of having consented to the social contract.

Stanford: In a country like the recently suspended Soviet Union, the people were supposed to belong to each other, and anyone who seriously questioned the regime was either a "traitor' or "insane."

Philosophus: Also interesting is the situation in a mixed regime that is partly contractual and partly something else. In such a situation, there is always confusion. Suppose that Robinson Crusoe were on that island on which he was marooned, and while he was there, everyone then in England and every English person abroad had died (except himself). He would still have been born in England; he would still speak that language; he still might have the religion and culture that had once been a part of that people. But he would no longer have been a subject of its monarch. Since the England of the 17th century still had feudal ties, the destruction of those ties would end not only his relationship with the government but also his nationality. By himself, he could not be the nation of England, not even its king. In a purely contractual society, the class to which he had belonged would have dissolved. But there would be no metaphysical problem as to what he was. He would still be what he always was, a free man and not a subject.

Penelope: So a group of individuals do not necessarily constitute a class of which each of them is a particular. They are particulars of that universal only when each of them possesses the attribute(s) in question, separately. And if they are in a contractual situation, it is a contract with them and the respective institution, regardless of how many others have drawn up similar papers.

So, when the Marxists say they want to abolish class, what they really want to abolish is freedom. Privilege, there is plenty in their societies!

It would also be possible to be a subject of a monarch, providing that the ruler did not by law own the property and the lives of his subjects, but simply owned a monopoly over the government or had a contract with his subjects to operate that institution. "The king's business," so to speak.

Philosophus: Quite right. Under a social contract, any of the three legitimate forms of government—monarchy, aristocracy, or republic—might be reasonable—this last being the most probable and the second one being the least likely.

Penelope: I have often wondered why so many scientists used to be socialists. Could it be because of a failure to grasp the difference between a class and an organization? They felt that what was in the mind of scientist A, his opinions as well as his knowledge, added together with the professional knowledge and opinions of scientist B; that these conjoined to scientist C, and that the intellectual contents of the minds of these three, interconnected with that of all their colleagues, constituted a cosmion of knowledge, an intellectual entity made up of their collective intelligence. They overlooked the fact that they were individual members of the *class* "scientist" and imagined that they were but vessels of an *organization*—in this case, an "organized body of knowledge."

Philosophus: That is just what too many of them think. Of course, such an idea is absurd, since what one scientist knows is not automatically transferred to some colleague who does not know simply by virtue of their both being part of some imagined super-sensible scientific community. The ignorant one must overcome his lack of knowledge through learning. Having the "right credentials" does not change the cognitive situation at all. That would be like saying that the head librarian of a large collection of books knows their contents simply because she has a million or so volumes about her. This fallacy may be behind some of the current hype about the internet.

Stanford: Would it be correct to say that a class is just the inverse of a universal? Instead of focusing attention on the universal, attention is shifted to whomever or whatever possesses it.

Philosophus: In a manner of speaking, that is correct. It is important that the two be distinguished so that this subject be properly understood.

And now we are ready to discuss a major fallacy. This is the contention that particulars have the quality of particularness, that this last is a universal.

Particularity is not an attribute of a particular like the redness of a rose or the roundness of a wheel. Such attributes can apply to more than one. Particulars are not what they are because they possess the attribute of particularity. They are simply *that*.

Stanford: What you just said is similar to what Rand had said about existence not being an attribute which the existents have in addition to their other characteristics. A similar point was made by Kant when he said that existence is not a predicate.

Philosophus: Not quite. Rand's axiom of existence does not refer simply to the *that* of things but also to *what* they are. Witness her contention that existence and identity are two different ways of referring to the same facts. "Particular" refers to only one.

And now let us consider more deeply what the universal is and is not.

The chief problem with the word, "universal," is the implicit requirement that there be more than one. A "universal" characteristic is supposed to be one which various instances of a certain kind of thing have in common. Hence, Rand's need to explain it in terms of her doctrine on similarity. But a characteristic, if it is real, should still hold even if there were only one example of it in the entire universe. Suppose first, *impossible*, there was only one round object: it would still be the case that this singular thing would exhibit the characteristic of roundness. If it did not, then it would not qualify as *round*. Take another example: suppose, as have many, that there was at onetime only one man in the whole world and none other, not even a woman. That being premised: it would still be the case that this man would exhibit the well known characteristics of his species, i.e., the shape, the form, the intelligence. Or suppose that it were the case that there were but one dinosaur left after a catastrophe had wiped out the others. Many specialists think this had actually happened. Would not this remaining giant possess for a while all the major characteristic of his species?

Penelope: That is why Rand insisted on that bizarre two or more instances, isn't it?

Philosophus: Yes. But this point was understood by John Cook Wilson, who may have had the best understanding of the nature of universals up until now. "The term we inherit from Aristotle is seriously misleading; in his own language it is a definition of a thing not by its essence but by an attribute which is not a property of a *given* universal. If we admit universals with only one particular, the designation 'universal' does not even apply to all universals."[2]

Stanford: Rand tried to get around the fact that the more-than-one is not necessary by trying to glue percepts together through the supposition that since similarity is a fact which implies plurality that, *voila*, she has solved the problem of universals.

Philosophus: Wilson's understanding of the phenomenon was loftier than Rand's in this respect, but he did not see over the thicket either. Wilson said things like the individual's being "is entirely comprised in the being of the universal; it is part of its whole being, not a part of its identical being, and the sum of the individuals, with the universal which is identical in them, is the complete being of that universal but not to be identified with the identical being of the universal."[3]

Penelope: What exactly does that mean?

Philosophus: By the "identical being" of the universal, he meant what it is about it that makes it what it is. For instance, with the universal *blueness*, the identical being is that very quality. Therefore, to say that blue things and blue lights are not part of the identical being of blueness is to say that while these things possess this attribute, they are not the attribute itself. The error he made is in supposing that these things were part of the universal anyway, that the complete being of the universal comprised both its identical being and the sum of its particulars.[4] This is a mistake which Rand would not have made. By making the universal include both its identical being and the being of its particulars, he also entered into the realm of contradiction.

There are certain other statements of his which are true when considered properly, but very puzzling when the problem of universals has not been solved. For instance, he said that the universal of motion has no velocity.[5] He also made some arguments which are wide of the mark- -for instance, that the universals of number are not themselves, addable.[6]

Doxa: How can that be? Common sense suggests that if a number cannot be added then it is not a number. If I have a "1" before me and a "2" and I cannot add them to produce a "3" then I have not got a number but some kind of a metaphysical imposter.

Philosophus: Right you are! What he lacked was a true account of the nature of universals.

And that is what is we are now ready for. It will be recalled that Wilson admitted that there could be a universal with only one particular. Wilson ended up saying that the universal is what it is not because it involves a plurality, but because there exists the possibility of there being more than one particular for each universal.

In this respect he is right. What has been called the universal is a situation in which there exists the potentiality of more than one application of an attribute or related group of attributes. This would be one type of fact. The other would be exactly the opposite, in other words, that in which there was something which was non-repeatable. Both are *facts*. Facts of the second category cannot be discounted. There are such facts. Any moment in past time, in fact, any period of time—even a millennium—is an absolute fact that belongs in the second category. The same with absolute space: although every part of this infinity is completely indistinguishable from any other—there being no center or periphery—each point in it is unique; it is unique even if we could never be able to know whether we had traversed the same point in absolute space again. Also action. Consider, for instance, an otherwise matter-less part of space in which a wheel is turning about itself, endlessly. Every turn after the first impulse would be like every other turn except for the moment itself. The hundredth revolution would differ from the hundred thousandth only in that they are not the same moment and therefore different. So the non-repeatable exists. This could also be the case with matter. Were the atomic hypothesis correct, and matter consists of identical bits of something, then every one of these would still be other than each other.

Stanford: Universals then are basically those facts which are repeatable. What about a repeatable action?

Philosophus: There are repeatable actions. Not only may the same attribute be found in various things and in various circumstances, but the same kind of action can be undertaken more than once by the very same entity. This is not often thought of as a part of the problem of universals, but it is.

Penelope: To glance back quickly at Objectivism, even the same kind of motion can differ from time to time in measure and degree.

Philosophus: Yes, indeed! Motion itself is a universal.

Stanford: Can the universal of motion move?

Philosophus: No. If the water in the river down below is moving downstream, then it is a fact that it is moving. If, at the same time the clouds above are moving, the universal of motion does not race up to the sky in order to superintend that effort. It is simply a fact that the river is moving and it is another fact that the air is moving. What exists is the fact of motion itself, whether it is fast or slow, regular or irregular, accelerated or uniform.

Doxa: Universals, then, are not ideas existing in some super-sensory world.

Philosophus: Universals are not mental at all. Suppose that the masses and their leaders agree to accept a lie. All the dissenters are killed or frightened into silence. Not one book proclaiming the correct notion is allowed, except for a few which in addition contain such obvious falsehoods as to make the correct statements in it laughable. It would still be the case that it was a lie, that the facts were different than what was considered acceptable opinion.

An attribute that had never been discovered would still be a fact; and if it were capable of being possessed by more than one particular, then it would be a universal. This would be the case even if for some reason men could never discover its existence. This has nothing to do with subjectivity. If there were no people or any other intelligent beings in existence, the fact it is or was or will be would still be the case.

Neither are universals physical. Let us go back to the hypothesis of a single round thing in reality and suppose that there were only two such in existence. Now, a universal is a fact that is repeatable. If both of these were smashed into jagged pieces which then repelled each other, there would never be a round thing again. But the fact would be that there once were two such things, even though trace-less. Neither are they the root out of which the mental and the physical evolve. They are facts which can have more than one application.

Penelope: Could a fact which can have more than one application be prevented and therefore fail to become a universal?

Philosophus: Please recall the earlier distinction between the necessary and the possible. It is only because of a being with free will that there are any options at all. With the man-made, it is possible that a universal have but one application, even if in a given case there is the potentiality of more. Within the realm of the necessary, if it only comes into existence once in eternity, then it never had the potentiality of more than one application. It never is, was, nor ever could be more than one. It is not a case of frustration; it is a case of what cannot be. Yet, for the reason given, universals are not mental.

Penelope: Is repeatability necessarily a part of the nature of an attribute or entity or action that is repeatable?

Philosophus: Not necessarily. If something has a round shape, we know in fact that there is more than one instance of this shape; but multiplicity is not part of its definition or of its properties. There are however instances where repeatability is involved in the nature of a thing. An example is a child. In order for this to happen, some of the genetic material which came from both the father and the mother would have to have existed more than once. Another would be the wonderful faculty of memory, whereby we become aware of something that happened earlier; this remembrance is not a replaying; were it only that, there would be no consciousness; it is a recognition that the event had taken place earlier. This recognition involved an element of repetition, a repetition of consciousness. It would be interesting to classify the sub-categories of repeatable and the non-repeatable, but we must move on.

Doxa: Your examples of the non-repeatable refer to the particular aspects of existence: a specific moment of time that went by which can never be repeated; a portion of absolute space which is uniquely itself. A material object which had once been destroyed could never be brought back, although copies which are identical in every respect could be recreated. To return to the language we have been using earlier, these examples all refer to the particular aspects of existents as distinct from the universal. My question is this: Is the non-repeatable the same as the particular?

Philosophus: Not necessarily. There may be attributes of which there can be no more than one instance.

Doxa: Can you think of any attributes which are not repeatable?

Philosophus: The only Being I can think that might have attributes like that would be God.

Stanford: A.R. argues that a *fact* is something we get later than that of an *existent*; she claims that the concept of fact is needed in order to recognize that human beings are capable of error.[7]

Philosophus: Rand said that her axioms of existence and identity are "not the abstraction of an attribute from a group of existents, but of a basic fact from all facts."[8] Since it is out of facts that her axiom of existence is derived, this gives the priority to the former. She also defined an axiom as "the identification of a primary fact of reality, which cannot be analyzed, i.e., reduced to other facts or broken into component parts."[9] In my language, this makes an axiom the subjective counterpart of a primary fact.

But let us not quibble. Both word "fact" and the word "existence" are so basic that they are used interchangeably by most people, as Rand herself stated. Many would regard my words as mere haggling over terminology. But they have different results, as will be increasingly obvious as we proceed. Observe the result when Fact is given first place and then decide! Here is the beginning:

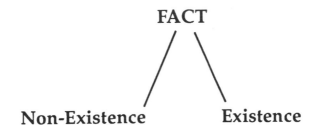

FACT

Non-Existence   **Existence**

Here, we see the resolution of the discussion that we had of the status of existence with respect to redness and roundness. Existence is a fact about them and they are facts about some existents.

Stanford: It would appear from this that A.R. was right in thinking that fact brought out what is real in contradistinction to what is a mistake. And if that is so, couldn't one argue perhaps she was right in supposing that existence is the more fundamental and "fact" is a mere specialized term?

Philosophus: So she thought. But non-existence does not mean error. An error is also a fact. It will be recalled that Rand had a lot of trouble with the existence of time and space—especially with accounting for the existence of empty space. During the course of our study of Rand, we have located four primary existents: Time and Space, Matter and Mind. (If there are more, it is outside the field of our inquiry.)

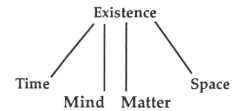

This *Time* is simply the instantaneous present, as we have discussed before. We are not directly conscious of it, although we know that it must exist. That of which we are directly conscious is the psychological present, which has elements of memory in it. Because apprehension takes time, there is a delay in our consciousness. Strictly speaking, there is no correspondence. The world apprehended is no more. Since the objective side of the act of consciousness is gone by the time that the subjective side completes its apprehension, there cannot be any dynamic, interactive relationship between the two, as hypothesized by philosophies like Objectivism. Recognition of this paradox has led to some interesting speculations. But we must go on!

Now, neither the past nor the future exist, but both are facts. There may be no record of something happening in the past, but nonetheless, it did happen; and that it did is a fact. Somewhere on a vacant planet, thousands of years ago, there may have been a flake of dust disturbed by a crashing meteorite, which came tumbling in from a vanquished world. But whether noticed or not, it took place.

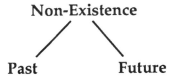

The present is the only time that exists. It is capable of being infinitely divided. The future is that which does not yet exist. The past is that which did but is no more. One way to divide the past is into repeated and non-repeated facts.

Doxa: Is that consistent with religion?

Philosophus: The non-existence of the past is recognized in the Bible. In the 22nd chapter of Matthew, there is the story of the Sadducees, men who did not believe in the Resurrection, coming to Jesus: He answered: "But concerning the resurrection of the dead, have you not read what was spoken to you by God, saying. I *am* the God of Abraham, the God of Isaac, and the God of Jacob. God is not the God of the dead, but of the living."

Now, let us look at that other great division of non-existence, the future:

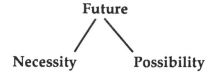

These could in turn be divided into repeating and non-repeating facts, as could the differentiations of Existence. But to show that would be tedious. What is past has no further possibilities. Expectation points toward the future, although it is not and cannot be there. Awareness of a necessity or of a possibility is a mental act. But they are still facts, whether or not they are identified by a consciousness.

Leftist revolutionaries like to remind us that we cannot return to the past; since they know that one cannot latch on to the future either, their recourse is to destroy possibilities.

Reserving the term non-existence for the past and the future enables us to escape the difficulties which Ayn Rand had gotten into. Interestingly enough, however, her characterization of it as standing in opposition to error has some truth to it. She has proved instructive even while we disagree with her so much.

Stanford: Why wasn't error presented as a third division of non-existence? What error purports to be does not exist.

Philosophus: The reason for this is that error is metaphysically different from the past, which once was but is no longer and also of the future which either must or may be. What is in these categories is non-existent, but not in the same way as a wrong answer. This is the case whether the person who is in error did it through his own or was the victim of a liar. Consider the latter, more complicated case. What is true of it is also true of the simpler case. The action of the liar himself comes under Fact through Existence and Non-Existence;

the same for the victim while he accepts the lie. This includes all the psychological paraphernalia which goes with it. As an act of imagination and will, it is a product of a mind. Its communication through some material means, such as the air or the written word, is included under Matter. It also takes place in Space and Time, etc.

Stanford: If it is not the committing of a fallacy or the acceptance of a lie that makes it a non- fact, these being completely within in the domain of fact, nor the mind's entertaining them as ideas or even as believing them (for states of consciousness too are facts), nor the content of the mistake or lie (these too existing in the mind), what then?

Philosophus: You yourself almost said it, earlier. What is not a fact is what the falsehood purports to be. What is it that it purports to be? A *fact*.

In short, error itself is a misapprehension. It comes under Mind. The non-fact is what it would be if it were *apprehended*.

Doxa: What if one were right for the wrong reasons?

Philosophus: It would be a mistake all the same. Knowledge is not the agreement of one's notion of something with that something. It consists in the apprehension of it. The same for true opinion. It is not simply the content of that opinion that counts, but the grounds on which it is based.

Stanford: Is error the only kind of non-fact?

Philosophus: Two other sets of phenomena constitute non-fact rather than non-existence. They are what the content of fiction and of dreams are taken to be while they are being believed—not the images, but the conviction that they are real. The intention of the author of a fiction differs from that of a liar in that there is no attempt to sabotage anyone's consciousness. Furthermore, the consumer has voluntarily placed himself under a temporary suspension of judgment. Much of what is coming into his mind in such a situation fits under Existence and Non-Existence. That which does not fit under these are what they would be if they were real. What has just been said about deliberate fiction would also be the case with those moments of dreaming, whether in sleep, or in listening to music, or when one "loses one's self " in a day dream. Error, dreams, and fiction, are species of imagination. But the act of imagining, the content, the images, the feelings, the believing, etc.—all these are facts. What is *not* a fact is that any of the three are, or were, or will be apprehendable. They are not facts.

Penelope: There is no mysterious essence of factuality standing behind facts: The only thing that facts have in common is either that they are, were, will be, or might be.

Doxa: Suppose that someone had concluded that in the late 1840's that Salem was the capital of the State of Oregon; at that time, it would have been a mistake. From 1849 to 1851, the capital was Oregon City. Later in 1851, the capital was moved to Salem. Would this not be the case that what was falsely reported as a fact eventually became a fact?

Philosophus: Yes, Salem eventually did become the capitol, but time is irrecoverable. There never would be a time when Salem was the capitol in the late 1840's, given the present meaning of these words.

Penelope: So far, you have spoken of time as if it were equated with the present, but the ordinary idea is that time has a triune structure—past, present, and future—isn't that also an apprehension?

Philosophus: Yes, we apprehend the triune structure of time: The present alone exists—that is a fact. But it is also a fact that what is past had once existed also. Then too, it is a fact that there will be a future. Two out of the three parts of the full apprehension of time refer to non-existence, but their necessary connection is known to the mind, even to that of a child. And there is no real understanding of this if one supposes that existence, not fact, is the most comprehensive notion, or that they are interchangeable, or that fact is only existence when considered in relation to error. People who attempt this either rule out time as an independent fact, as did Rand, or they become anti-intellectual, or they enmesh themselves in the poetry of subjectivity.

Yet the present continually changes; the past moves farther and farther back in duration; and the future, by immeasurably small steps goes forward. Matter and Mind are both in present time, and this Time is like nothing else.

Doxa: I think your drawing of mind, matter, space, and time as components of existence might need to be clarified as bit.

Philosophus: Your point is well taken. Here!
Note that the word "Present" is written down underneath "Time" rather than simply by itself. This is consistent with common language. In ordinary life, when we speak of "time," we usually mean the present. The other members of the triad are given by the special names "Past" and "Future."

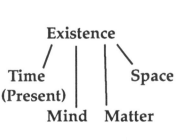

When one is discussing an extent of time, special words like "duration," "era," "period," "age", "year," "century," and the like are frequently used. But when we say "time," we usually are thinking of the present, even if it is only the psychological present that is on our minds, rather than philosophical time, which is instantaneous.

Stanford: Periods of a hundred years are repeatable. But the individual centuries are unique and incapable of occurring again. At any point in time before a century is over, only the most infinitesimal part of it is in existence. If the century has yet to begin, none of it exists. And if all of it is in the past, it neither exists, nor ever will again. Everybody easily runs through these facts, yet few really contemplate the vast meaning behind it.

Doxa: I have a question. So far, I have noticed two of Ayn Rand's basic axioms, "Existence" (in a greatly revised form) and "Consciousness" as Mind. But I have not discerned "Identity" Does it have a place?

Philosophus: My answer is two-fold. First, Existence and Mind are not axioms. Axioms are subjective: In Rand's philosophy, their task is to regulate all thought. Their use here is objective in the pre-Randian sense of that word. They exist as facts outside of and independent of human thought and will. In the realm of the subjective, the key duality is the act of apprehension and that which is apprehended. There is no need for axioms. It is just that some facts are of greater generality.

Second: In many cases, what Rand means by an "identity" is no different from a fact. Existence and Non-existence are identities. A fact about something that no longer exists is just that fact and none other. What error purports to be has no identity.

Doxa: Could "Identity" have been made the principal genus just as logically as "Fact"?

Philosophus: *Fact* is by far the better choice. First, using the other word in its place could bring practical confusion: As a principle of logic, identity belongs under Mind, a subdivision of Existence. As the basis for causality, it belongs under both Mind and Matter. Adding an even more abstract use on top of these could be confusing. Second, *Fact* is philosophically preferable because it does not refer more to logic and the operation of the mind that to anything else. It is just as applicable to the objective as to the subjective. It can be used to refer to either or even both together without any element of tendentiousness. Third, it can be used indifferently to refer to the general or the specific. For instance, in referring to a collection of entities, such as a crowd of men in a street or a cluster of stars, we would not normally ask, "what are the identities of these men?" or "What are the identities of this star cluster?" Instead, we would ask something like this: "What are the facts about this group of men?" or "What facts are known about these stars?" In this instance, the word "identity" aims at some sort of specificity.

Penelope: Thinking of universals as repeatable facts answers the formal problem. But it somehow lacks the grandeur of how the problem began—when Plato thought that universals were archetypes which were imposed on matter; while Aristotle, denying this, taught that universals existed only in matter and supplied the form to it.

Philosophus: Consider the non-repeatable. We have already spoken of a past which is absolutely unretrievable. The non-repeatable is the unique. This is not chaos, but it does pose some interesting questions.

When universals were first discussed in philosophy, there was a dimension to it that we have yet to consider; and that is the question of origins. Plato taught that the archetypes brought shape and direction to a formless matter, bringing into existence the concrete objects of the material world. Aristotle attempted to limit scientific discussion of this question by de-emphasizing the question of origins and concentrating on the dynamics of form and matter. But since his notion of a matter without form was incoherent and created all sorts of problems as to what sort of an identity an existent with no characteristics could have, his attempted solution invited many emendations. We have shown that a modern derivation of Aristotelianism which attempted to settle the issue through a theory of concepts consciously made by man out of percepts had failed. This opens up once more the cosmological question—which because of its vastness, we will confine to the issues generally raised by these two philosophers.

Stanford: Continue, please.

Philosophus: Let us abstract away all consideration of the question of the origin of Matter. Let us consider only the point at which God organizes it according to His design. This does not mean that Matter in itself is formless and has no characteristics of its own. It has its own nature. You all have seen that photograph which was taken by the Hubble Space Telescope showing what the scientists studying these matters claim to be the birth of stars about seven thousand years ago out of clouds of hydrogen and dust, trillions of miles long. The stars are being born out of pre-existent material.

Imposing His own archetypes upon the forms of matter, He makes stars and here on earth and perhaps elsewhere, beings which have a purpose of their own, that purpose being, as Rand would have it, "to live"—some of whom are conscious as well, and a few have free will. Locke suggested over three centuries ago that God can make matter think. In a way, men do something like this when they construct computers which think in limited ways once problems have been posed to them, although they are not conscious. And if men could make them conscious someday, it would only be because rational beings had constructed them in such a way that they could be made to think. The matter out of which it is composed could not, spontaneously, have been caught together. It would be something composed out of the minds of men and put together under the direction of a superintending intelligence. Adapting the famous illustration of William Paley: suppose one observed a modern computer lying in the sand of a beach; if through purely material laws, the silica had formed themselves into semi-conductors and the casing, whether of metal, plastic, or wood had arranged itself like the lying of sediment, then the skeptic could be speaking from experience. But if one were to suppose that matter has laws which allow for the arising of mind, autonomously out of itself when there is such a dearth of evidence in support of these laws, one would be believing primarily in the products of one's own imagination. At best, one would be betting on the merely conceivable. It would be like the Marxist who said that somehow Stalin or Mao or some genius would figure out how to make Communism work, even though the only thing it seems to be able to do is create trouble. The existing evidence supports the distinction between matter and mind. To believe otherwise is to embrace the side that is intellectually weaker. (The same difficulty exists for those who attempt dialectics).

Doxa: And if one insists on atheism, then one is being arbitrary.

Penelope: In the Bible, one reads about Moses being directed to make a tabernacle on Earth after a pattern made in Heaven.

Philosophus: Yes, and there is more of that in the Bible.
The matter being turned into life by God would have a form imposed upon it from Without. But, even so, there would be nothing in the red of a certain rose which made it any different than if it were the first and only one of its kind—with, perhaps, the root dying with the bloom and the seeds destroyed by a volcano—than if there were valleys filled with it. Universals would still refer just to the repeatable, and the only thing universal about an attribute would be that there could be more than one instance of it.
But with prototypes created by God, there would in many cases be an *intention* that there be more than one of a given

kind. And the material things formed in accordance with that intention would be expressions of the fact that there were to be more than one particular of certain kinds. Then both Plato and Aristotle each would have some truth on his side, Plato in his declaration that the prototypes exist, and Aristotle in supposing that the forms exist in the world only in the things that have them. And Rand would be right in concluding that Aristotle was closer to the truth. What the prototypes would be, however, is a plan or set of plans and the action required to realize them, not templates to be impressed upon a rude substratum—which was, I think, how Plato had imaged it. As Aristotle supposed it, our positive knowledge of forms is through the things which have them and which exhibit the regularities. It is only if we think that they are somehow incomplete that we would try to infer that there is something behind them. To refer to Raphael's great painting, both Plato, the man whose hand was directed upwards, and Aristotle, the man whose hand was pointed downwards, had a point— although the latter's claim to the intellectual territory which he had staked out was stronger.

But the prototypes do not enter into science of human origin; they are not direct elements of it. The universal is the repeatable.

Penelope: Are space and present time attributes of God?

Philosophus: That question is outside of our study of Rand. However, it should be said that in his address at Mars Hill, the Apostle Paul told the Athenians this about God, "For in him we live and move, and have our being...." These words are in the 17th Chapter of the book of Acts. Some think that these words were not meant to be taken literally; but there they are. Sir Isaac Newton thought that they are Divine attributes. Consider well.

Stanford: Was Kant wrong in thinking that man could not reason backwards from the phenomena to God?

Philosophus: This too is outside of our compass. Consider well.

Doxa: At our next meeting, we shall return to Ayn Rand's political discussions.

DAY XI

THE RATIONAL BASE OF ETHICS

The four are meeting this time at the restaurant. In front of each is a note pad. Books are also present. On one table near them is a boy and a girl on a date. On another table close by them are a couple of businessmen meeting over a possible merger. Across the room is a crowd discussing a coming basketball game involving the local professional team. Edged up against this crowd is an ugly politico and his flashy girl friend.

Doxa: With Lenin's position, anything is possible. Since matter (which, according to D. M., includes everything, even space and time and thought) is internally contradictory any action might be permitted; context would determine its application. A course which seems rational under one set of conditions might be completely inappropriate under another. It would all be a matter of which cards are dealt to you and what you can get by with.

By contrast, Ayn Rand's reliance on finitude made possible a morality. For her, existence allowed of no contradictions and any action inappropriate to the nature of man would be immoral, however much one might gain from it due to the irrationalities of others.

This puts Ayn Rand in direct conflict with the Marxists in the field of human action; moreover, she believed in free will, while the Marxists are iron determinists.

Ayn Rand's intent was to be romantic and rational all at once. She states that moral codes are systems of teleological measurement; that they position one's choices and one's actions in relation to the extent that they further or frustrate one's goals. "Teleological measurement deals, not with cardinal, but with *ordinal* numbers—and the standard serves to establish a graded relationship of means to end."[1] This means that when one is considering on which course to take, one grades each alternative in accordance to their conformity with a goal, i.e., "1st," "2nd", "3rd," etc.

This is only a partial truth. The ordinal theory of morality is incomplete. Overlooked is a choice that is so undesirable that it is not only last or nth choice, but rejected altogether. There is a case of that in *Atlas Shrugged*: John Galt, at one point states that if his heroine were captured by his mortal enemies, he would kill himself—the alternative of simply living with the loss and trying to make the best of it is rejected out of hand by her hero: "There will be no values for me to seek after that—and I do not care to exist without values."[2] By making the choice of suicide preferable, Ayn Rand removes the alternative from being even a last choice.

Philosophus: In addition, to this, it should also be said that ordinal measurement is not unique to the process of evaluation. For instance, LIFO, or last in, first out and FIFO, or first in, first out, are methods of making entries in accounting; they have nothing directly to do with ethics.

Doxa: During our second meeting, I made a presentation of Ayn Rand's attempt to break the dichotomy between facts and values by showing that many basic values owe their being to the *fact* of life. Her Objectivism, it must be repeated, did not argue simply that life is necessary as a condition for having values, but that rational values rest ultimately on the question of survival versus non-survival.

It will be recalled that she was unable to prove that human values were necessarily rooted in the alternatives of existence and non-existence. The proof that she used, namely the hypothecation of an indestructible robot, admitted too many exceptions to serve as a *reductio ad absurdum*.

Let us consider her contention that she has bridged the fact-value distinction. If someone should try to answer her by asking the question, "Is life good?" or the like, she would answer that they have committed the fallacy of the stolen concept, i.e., that they have questioned the value of life while either forgetting or being in ignorance of the dependence of the concept "value" on the concept "life."

A value is a fact. In that sense, there cannot be any distinction. But even when we make a distinction between facts and restrict the use of that term to those other than values, the two are still related. Values can sometimes be refuted by this kind of facts. An athlete may discover that alcohol or tobacco, which he enjoys, has a debilitating effect on his performance. He rejects these drugs both because of the fact which he has learned and because health and athletic performance are higher values to him. A value, on the other hand, cannot refute a fact, as is obvious, for facts are ultimate. Values might, however, be used to reject a false claim of fact; for instance, the claim that all anybody cares for is air, food, and sex is easily refuted by pointing to people who have rejected one or the other for some ideal. Values can also change facts. Because of what men have chosen, cities have been raised on plains and metals which were formerly imbedded in rock are being made into airplanes.

Penelope: But merely showing that some values follow from the facts of human life does not mean that all were drawn out of the alternatives of life or no-life on this earth. It could be that some have another source.

Philosophus: Rand defines "life" as "a process of self-sustaining and self-generated action."[3] There is of course, much truth in it. But even as it stands, it is not complete; for instance, no human being really generates itself; he or she must have progenitors. Neither is life always self-sustaining: it must be cared for in the body of the mother and is unable to sustain itself for some time after birth. Even

Romulus and Remus could not say that they always took care of themselves. The same is the case with very sick people.

Genesis 2:7 says that God formed man out of the dust of the earth and breathed life into him. Two actions are involved there: (1) The shaping of man from dust and (2) the introduction of life. Since merely breathing into a corpse would produce nothing of consequence, the breath spoken of must be a life principle.[4] If this is true, then life did not originate from the autonomous working of matter, as many have always believed. Not all values would necessarily be rooted in the preservation of this life; some may have come from that non-material Source.

Doxa: Suppose that this interpretation of this Biblical passage were correct, and man did not originate strictly though some earthly process. That would explain why, despite her brilliance and the plausibility of her argument, Rand was not able to completely close the difference between facts and values. The suture could not quite hold because man's life points to his Creator.

Philosophus: Rand was an atheist. "A concept," she wrote, "has to involve two or more similar concretes, and there is nothing like God. He is supposed to be unique. Therefore, by their own terms of setting up the problem, they have taken God out of the conceptual realm. And quite properly, because he is out of reality."[5] But, as has been shown, it does not take two instances.

Rand also objected to the attributes of omniscience and omnipotence, which she stated were "impossible, irrational characteristics which do not arise from reality...."[6] She did not attempt to explain what she meant by these two terms, so an answer would consume too much time; but one may suggest, that if these attributes were impossible in the way that she had understood them, then a God that exists would not have them.

In *Atlas Shrugged*, John Galt states: "To exist is to possess identity. What identity are they able to give to their superior realm? They keep telling you what it is *not*, but never tell you what it *is*. All their identifications consists of negating: God is that which no human mind can know, they say—and proceed to demand that you consider it knowledge—God is non-man, heaven is non-earth...."[7] The answer is that there are many believers who do not accept a God of negations either; who believe that they have had some experience of Him, who know Him through His effects, just as, in the realm of perception we know molecular motion through its effect on us as heat; that it is through the latter that we come to have knowledge of its cause. Strangely enough, there was a time in Rand's life when she was willing to consider the question of the existence of a God that was limited in some respect.[8] She chose instead her theory that there must be at least two of more examples of a type of fact to produce a rational cognition.

Rand's ideal of man's life is exemplified in her characters, John Galt and Howard Roark. She attempted to ground this ideal in her epistemology; but this has been shown to be fallacious in certain key respects. Her theory of concepts, especially that pertaining to the Conceptual Common Denominator and the requirement of commensurability have been found to be unnecessary; the same with her reliance on axioms. The case against the reality of time and space, as well as infinity has broken down, and the Randian concept of context has been shown to conceal more than it explained.

Doxa: Immediately after defining value as what one seeks to get or keep, Ayn Rand states: "The concept 'value' is not a primary; it presupposes an answer to the question: of value to *whom* and for *what*?"[9] This formulation is confusing. How can one talk about the value of something for whom or for what without first knowing what value means? Taken literally, that is a breach of logic. But I really think that she did not mean it that way. What she probably wanted to say is that no particular value means anything except by reference to these questions, not that the general term itself has no meaning apart from the answer to those questions.

Yet a slip of the pen from such an accomplished writer may signify something of significance. In their discussion of the nature of values, the Objectivists contrast their own idea with those who hold that values are valuable in and of themselves without respect to the beneficiary, or anything else.[10] A pure intrinsicist would say that beauty would still exist even if there were no being anywhere that could appreciate it and that virtue would exist even if there were no one who could either possess it. I do not agree with that position; *values are mental phenomena*. But there is another possibility: that there is a Being who had brought into existence the first man and woman, and that some of the springs from which flow human evaluation reflect the act of creation and the Creator Himself.

The issue is fundamental: either people like Ayn Rand are right when they teach that this present earthly existence of ours is all the life we can have, or they are wrong. If they are right, then all rational values can only be expressions of the life that we have on earth. If they are wrong, then hope in something else is rational. Men must think carefully before they decide.

Stanford: A.R.'s argument not only restricts one to existence on earth, but she contradicts herself when she has her hero, John Galt, announce that he will commit suicide if his enemies capture his beloved Dagny Taggart and try to use her as a hostage. (I know, I said this earlier. But now I am sure.) Strictly speaking, the only values that Rand's argument from facts to values can support are those founded upon the survival of a physical life.

Doxa: But Ayn Rand's whole point is that on top of physical survival, there is reason, the exercise of which is essential to man's survival, and what Galt was trying to accomplish was the triumph of all this and the final defeat of collectivism. To have accomplished that despite Dagny's destruction would have ruined everything, since she was his greatest value.

Stanford: The fact that he did not believe he could be happy was beside the point. The logical basis for values supplied by A.R.'s argument could only support physical survival and what rested upon it. If the failure of some great expectation of his mind would make him want to destroy his base, then protection of that base would require that the great dream be modified. The superstructure cannot be allowed to bend down and cut off the base. In terms of the base, to continue like that would be the same as the whim worshiping which A.R. denounced with such eloquence. It would be like growing a nail so long that one was in danger of stabbing oneself with it. The reason supplied by the argument based on her solution to the facts (other than values)-value dichotomy would recommend that he consider getting a new girl friend—that he think such thoughts as the following: "Dagny was wonderful; it is too bad she was caught; but that is the risk we all take. If I were caught, I would want her to go on without me; so does she."

Doxa: But what about his mental sanity? Since according to Objectivism, one's reason is the chief tool of survival, a crisis that might cause him to lose his mind could potentially damage his ability to reason.

Stanford: Exactly my point! To protect his reason and therefore his life, he would have to modify his values. Since they must be based on reason; and reason is, according to the Objectivist hypothesis, to be based on the survival of his life—his expectations and the "concepts" upon which they were based would have to be scaled down. Whatever gets in the way of the primary values would have to be eased aside.

Doxa: Your reasoning is good, but there seems to be something missing.

Philosophus: What is missing is the fact that Rand did not even prove her case for those values based on physical survival. A value is always a fact and a fact can sometimes be a value. We four know this. The fact-value distinction is a problem only for those who think that in order to have rational values, one must first have a fact with no ingredient of value in it and then must somehow deduce value from it. For such people, the problem really is getting an A from a non-A. Rand provided an answer to this requirement. Having noted that life is a fact, she can easily show that certain values are required for the maintenance of that life. Since life is an observable fact, she supposes she has drawn values out of a non-value type fact. In order to make her case, she must show that no value can claim to be rational unless it follows from her concept of life. But this, I contend, she cannot do. I will show that her real position is not only too narrow, but false.

We have already seen that her definition of life is incomplete. Standing by itself, however, this would not be enough to invalidate her position, since it is possible that the definition, incomplete as it may be, is adequate enough to cover the argument. But consider next how she tries to distinguish between life and non-life: "The existence of inanimate matter is unconditional, the existence of life is not: it depends on a specific course of action. Matter is indestructible, it changes its forms, but it cannot cease to exist."[11]

Is this the difference? Take a stone! In order to remain what it is, it must have the inertial capacity to withstand the forces which would disintegrate it. The same for the Grand Canyon; ditto the Empire State Building. Without specific molecular and physical ties existing between its parts, a stone object would soon be flattened like water. Take next a fast moving river! Imagine some small rocks dropping off an overhanging cliff. The action of these rocks is to disturb the flow. But the river moves on, dragging the pebbles along and also dropping them into the mud at the bottom. The water has momentum. *Inanimate existence, then, resists change of form also.* It undertakes specific courses of action. And the matter remains the same after the form supplied by a biological cell has been destroyed, just as when a rock is crushed or the water which normally went down a certain course has been re-channeled.

Doxa: Ayn Rand writes: "It is only the concept of 'Life' that makes the concept of 'Value' possible."[12]

Philosophus: It is true that one cannot value anything if one is not alive. The stone and the stream value nothing. It is also true that the thought of value cannot be extricated from at least a reference to life. But can it really be said that an unconscious thing like a plant has values when they probably don't even have percepts, let alone concepts? Rand says it does: "A plant must feed itself in order to live; the sunlight, the water, the chemicals it needs are the values its nature has set it to pursue; its life is the standard of value directing its actions. But a plant has no choice of action; there are alternatives in the conditions it encounters, but there is no alternative in its function: it acts automatically to further its life, it cannot act for its own destruction."[13] The last part is not true: a plant can indeed act against its own life. A tree which was forced to grow at an angle because of some obstruction might, nonetheless, fall because the ground could not support it. A straight tree might grow so much in a rich well-watered soil that during a period of heavy rains, its roots can no longer hold it up in the marshy soil against an a strong wind. If it escaped that, then in a dry spell, after it had dropped so many leaves year after year, a spontaneous combustion might result, killing it by fire. More importantly, the first part of Rand's statement is not true either. Inanimate objects, as we have seen, also operate to maintain themselves. An automobile that fills itself at the gasoline pump is possible now. It could even have a computer card giving the nearest stations as it tracks the automobile's movements.

Doxa: But autos are made by men. These machines have no values; they are created by intelligent beings who impress the material expression of their values into the machine.

Philosophus: Very true. And plants are made to respond. But to call this responsiveness "value" because it can be analogically compared with choice in men and desire and aversion in the case of both men and animals is preposterous. One might as well add together the automated car, the river, and the rock and call them "preceding stages in an evolutionary series." Rand defines value as "that which one acts to gain and keep."[14] We have seen that ordinary non-living phenomena act to keep being what they are; on her analogy, one could argue that the inertial resistence of a rock to being destroyed by a steam hammer is a "value." Machines exist which act to get as well as keep. So do some natural phenomena. By moving from higher to lower elevations, a stream acts both to acquire velocity and also to collect some water that may be found at lesser altitudes. By breaking through the outer crust of the earth, a volcano acts both to get a lower pressure and to facilitate the hardening of its lava. A plant may have been designed to accomplish certain objectives, the existence of which it does not have a clue. The same is manifestly the case with machinery.

Stanford: Why didn't she deduce value from conscious life?

Philosophus: Because she would have to accept as legitimate many of the questions that she wanted to rule out—questions, such as Kant's God, Freedom, and Immortality. Freedom, she could admit. The other two, she wanted to obviate. Hence, the attempt to predicate it all on physical survival.

Penelope: Now, I know that Rand had accepted the Marxist notion of the transformation of quality out of quantity.

Stanford: Value cannot be reduced to something non-mental without torturing its meaning. By attempting to distinguish the living from the non-living in terms of conditionality, she gave the whole thing away. Even if it were the case, as some investigators believe, that plants have a tiny degree of consciousness, Rand would still be wrong because she held that they have none. Values require consciousness.

Philosophus: The solution was really given by Miss Doxa when she stated that values are also facts, but because of the newness of this knowledge to her, she did not understand the full implications of what she said. Literally speaking, an attempt to deduce values from facts which have nothing to do with values would be an impossibility. If there were a fact that had no relation at all to any one—say a star which was so far away it would never be discovered by men—then by definition no argument we might make could link its properties to any value. In that sense, the fact-value people have to be right.

Rand's basic procedure is correct: answer them by showing that *value* as such is dependent upon some basic facts. Her attempt to do so was not successful.

What she really meant by "value" was not what one wants to get or keep, but that which is required for the maintenance or enhancement of life, regardless of whether one is conscious of it or not. This, of course, would allow her to say that plants have values.

But let us consider people. If a person was ill and was not aware of his state of health; and furthermore the cure for that disease had not yet been found, then the undiscovered cure would have to be considered his "value," even though he was unaware of all of the above. Suppose next that a man values something which was not good for him—cigarettes, for instance. This pastime, it will be recalled, is eulogized in *Atlas Shrugged:* Yet, in terms of the revised definition just given, smoking cigarettes could not be classified as a "value." It would not even be an irrational one, since the revision stipulated that it be *required* for the benefit of life. It would simply be something which was taken for a value when it was not. (To return to her actual definition would bring back all the old problems).

She really meant what one *ought* to get or *want*. If her metaphysics had been correct, the only argument would have been over details. But that was not the case, and so it is over essentials.

Doxa: I think we now understand that point. Let us move on.

Penelope: Rand sometimes tries to stack the deck by redefining familiar words. An example of this is her handling of the word, "selfishness." The most common meaning is seeking money and pleasure at the expense of others. This is what people mean when they say that "covetousness is selfishness." This meaning, I will call "selfishness I." The next most common meaning is that a selfish person acts consistently with his understanding of what is his best interest. This meaning, I call "selfishness II." Under this term, a man who believed in a God who could grant him immortality, would find it in his interest as he conceives it to act in a manner pleasing to this Being. That, of course, Rand would rule out. She considered religious people to be irrational, and a person not acting in conformity with her real interest is not rational. Rand's own meaning, I call "selfishness III." It means acting in accordance with the requirements of the Objectivist philosophy, or, if one has not heard of it, being the kind of person who would have accepted it if it had been presented. But, as we have shown, the Objectivist theory of knowledge and the metaphysics implied by it are both false. Selfishness III, therefore, is impossible, since it claims to be rational while being irrational.

What gives Rand her superficial plausibility is the existence of the Marxist movement, which is often presented as an altruistic effort to help people in need. Here, both kinds of selfishness have been at work. Selfishness I is exemplified in the envy of the masses and the cupidity of some wealthy few. Selfishness II, by the belief that the Communists might win and should, therefore, be appeased.

In The USA, collectivism has taken the form of the welfare state, instead of Communism. Yet, it is doubtful that it could ever have grown to such a size if the only reason for voting for it decade after decade was the dubious claim that it served the greatest number. In the Great Depression of the 1930's, the people who used it were either out of work or in fear of losing their jobs. Franklin Roosevelt came forth offering with a lot of other people's money in exchange for their votes. Plenty accepted. They were acting on a combination of Selfishness I and Selfishness II; the first, in that they were desperate people who felt that they needed the money, and so they took it; the second that they thought that it was only an emergency, and that it was needed in order for them to recover, given the circumstances. It is true that most did not see that they were being prepared for a 2nd World War; but it is also the case that in accepting Roosevelt, they had made their commitment to "change."

Beginning in the 1960's, the welfare state grew many times. Non-whites were told that the Whites were behind their slow progress and that they had a right to take from them. The fact that so many Whites had been brought up by teachers who had imbibed the attitudes of the New Deal to think that this was true only made the Blacks and their White supporters more bold. Again, the motives were also a mixture of Selfishness I and Selfishness II.

Doxa: Objectivism does have a point, however. There is little question that neither Marxism- Leninism nor the welfare state would have gotten very far without a lot of well-wishing people buying all or part of some big sob story.

Penelope: But there were lots of people whom Rand would have described as "altruists" who were resolutely opposed to modern collectivism. At the same time, there have been many people of the types that have been known to have liked some of her books who were either taken in by confidence schemes or who participated in disastrous sexual alliances. Rand's analysis was widely publicized during this period, yet the welfare state grew despite it. Was it too late, or was there something missing in her work?

Selfishness verses unselfishness is not the issue. One man can oppose communism because of what he takes to be his self interest; another can assist it for what he conceives to be *his*. As we have seen, Rand tries to give body to her position by equating unselfishness with sacrificing a higher value for a lesser one. No question about it, she is right in saying that people do this. For instance, a drunk might injure someone in a fight so badly that he ends up in jail or loses much of his wealth in a law suit; this drunk would still be selfish under the first meaning, but unselfish under the second, since he had not have taken sufficient account of his long term interests. A man who wanted to keep his wife but decided to have a quick affair in secret might be acting selfishly in both senses if he was able to keep it a secret.

Doxa: He would have to lie to his wife and in that sense not have a fully honest marriage.

Penelope: But if a fully honest marriage, not to mention fidelity, was less important to him than the adventure, he would, in terms of his code of values, be acting selfishly.

An older dictionary defines "selfishness" as "caring only for self; influenced solely or chiefly by motives of private pleasure or advantage."[15] This is like Selfishness I. Selfishness II simply refers to self-consistency in thought and action—in one word, "integrity."

Selfishness is not a philosophical primary; it is an in-between word. Instead of trying to redefine selfishness so that:

(1) it must be rational; (2) can only be rational if it is in agreement with Rand's philosophy or of a sense of life which she would have approved of, she would have done better to have merely concentrated on *reason*, instead.

Doxa: I beg to differ. Rand's concept of selfishness is very simple. It is not so much a question as to whether or not a person is acting in accordance with their values that determines it, although her own words certainly gave that impression. Rather, a selfish person is one who does not think that he has to go through someone else to determine what is right or wrong. If you think that you must follow the commandments of your God, you are *unselfish*, for you are allowing what you believe to be another entity, or those who claim to be the representatives of that entity, or the writings in a book which you hold to be sacred to be a determinant of your thought and actions. A selfish person does not allow such an intervention in his judgment. A selfish person is answerable to no one except himself for his decisions.

A selfish person can impose obligations on himself. He can establish a family and by so doing incur immense commitments. He can sign an employment contract which may involve penalties if he fails to perform.

Penelope: Why can't it be said that a religious person is also selfish when he or she has volunteered to enter into a system of values through his own free will?

Doxa: The person who does that is no longer boss. It is as simple as that. The employee in a common work contract can quit.

Penelope: So can a religious person. He or she too can quit.

Doxa: Yes. And be regarded as a traitor by those inside. That is different. I admit that it is small in some cases, but it is still there as a principle. If you think you have to ask for permission to live in any way, you are not selfish. The same for those with the nation, the race, or humanity. If you think you owe them anything above the contractual and its like, you are unselfish. This is what Ayn Rand means by selfishness.

Stanford: What if an ugly person should lie naked in their front yard and do certain other things in full view of their neighbors?

Doxa: Ayn Rand would not allow a few bad people to ruin freedom. An Objectivist might say to us, "This is selfishness! Take it or leave it!"

Philosophus: But if a man can enter into a labor contract which binds him for years, or establish a family, which could do the same thing for the remainder of his life, why cannot he enter into a contract with a Higher Being that would in exchange for eternal life, grant him many blessings? In so doing, he would be subordinating himself, although for an indefinitely longer time—and receiving in return constant replenishing, as with the Tree of Life in the Bible. The same for those who have hope.

Doxa: I suppose they would. Rand's selfishness is for atheists, agnostics, and those who have not made any such agreement, etc.

Philosophus: That explains "selfishness." But there is still a problem with her position on altruism. We have seen that Rand's attempt to explain altruistic sacrifice as an attempt at the substitution of the less valued in place of the greater value is that it is circular. A Stella Dallas who scrimped and saved in order to send her daughter, Laurel, to exclusive finishing schools so that she might enter into finer society may well have valued that daughter's success more than the years of labor that it cost her—may even have wanted it if she would not live to see her achievement; Stephen, the first martyr for Christianity valued the prospect of eternal life higher than his temporal existence. Even the unknown person who bit off his nose in order to spite his face would not necessarily fit the definition, since he might have been a deep believer in egalitarianism and therefore might have deemed it unfair that he should have had a handsome face.

Still, it cannot be denied that altruism exists. Altruism does involve placing the good of others above one's own. It does not mean substituting what one values less for what one values more. Were that the case, an altruist would be someone who did what he did not want to do even though no one had forced him, or who did what he knew he should not have done, or who did what he believed to be wrong. Such people may be irrational or immoral, but they are not all altruists. It would have been less misleading had Rand merely stated that altruism involves placing what one *ought* to regard as lower in a more elevated rank with respect to that which one *ought* to regard as higher. That would have made it simply a term referring to that which is irrational in the realm of values, which would in turn have made it depend upon the correctness of her philosophy. But then it would have been inconsistent with common usage. And, of course, Rand's Atlas, as we have seen, cannot lift the world.

Stanford: Yet, for all this, Rand has a point. As a practical matter, it is easy to see that the policies of the modern welfare state have brought a lot of suffering to the people who have had to pay for it. Right from the beginning of this system, critics were pointing out that it would ruin the country; that the policy of allowing people to take public money like that without ever being required to pay it back was ruinous.

Let us then look at the motives of those who willingly paid for it. Altruism was not the only motive. Many who felt themselves slipping saw it as a safety net which might catch them should they fall down; others who were better fixed thought that it might stand as a break against revolutionary forces. That they or their sons or sweethearts would soon be collected for a war which would exceed WWI, few of them had foreseen.

Yet, even with all that, the system did not have to be so stupid. Programs of public assistance could have been designed in which the recipients were expected to pay it back and had to take the first real job offered. This would have prevented the scandal of whole generations of indolent people electing politicians dedicated to maintaining and increasing the public largesse. It may well be that the original programs had been designed to have these flaws so as to elect and elect and elect.

Later on, when the consequences were known to them, many taxpayers may have been afraid of having to fight their way out. So they may have taken comfort from some altruistic catch-phrases, hoping that the pretense of a moral stance would magically transform their cowardice into something better.

Doxa: What then does altruism mean, if it does not mean putting the lower value in place of the higher one?

Philosophus: The facts were known to Rand, but, as we shall see, she apparently failed to grasp its exact meaning. The term "Altruism" was originally coined by Auguste Compte, a 19th century French philosopher who also invented the term, "positivism." It simply means to live for others, "vivre pour autrui." This is not the same as treating others as we would have them treat us; that involves calculation and so is a form of egotism. Neither is it the same as Kant's categorical imperative; acting in such a way that the principle behind that action could be a universal law would not really be living for others. A consistent altruist could not love himself except through others. Kant's ethics could be practiced by the sole resident of a desert island: he could ask himself whether his actions that day could have been an instance of a universal principle.

How is it possible to be an altruist? The answer given by Compte is unity, a "state of complete unity which distinguishes our existence, at once personal and social, when all its parts, both moral and physical, converge habitually to a common destination.... Such a harmony, individual and collective, being incapable of complete realization in an existence so complicated as ours, this definition of religion characterizes the immovable type toward which tends more and more the aggregate of human efforts."[16] What this means is that the individual is to see himself as a part and not as a whole. He is to imagine himself as becoming a whole only by merging himself first with the rest of humanity and finally with nature itself. Compte envisioned a new religion of humanity , one in which all men (living, dead, and to be born) who have not, are not, or will not do so much wrong as to disgrace the collective were to be deified as part of a goddess, the Grande Etre. When a man or a woman dies, what Compte termed their "objective existence" would be over—he did not believe in personal immortality—but if their life was judged worthy by the positivist authorities, they were—in a manner of speaking— to live in the memories of humanity; from that point forward, they would be entitled to "subjective existence." Even animals which have proven useful to humans, like the dog, for instance were to be included in the collectivist abstraction. The intellect was to be cultivated only to the extent that it serves humanity. Individualism of any kind was to be forbidden. To a great extent, Compte modeled his new religion on the Roman Catholic Church and extreme Calvinism. Divorce was forbidden, except for one reason— that reason being not adultery, but that one of the partners had been ostracized by society, i.e, had become a non-person. There were even to be prayers.

A consistent altruist, then, puts his highest values first. These values rest upon a conception of reality. To be consistent, the altruist must regard himself as a part of a greater whole, whether it be humanity, nature, or even God. The popular phrase "All is one and one is all!" is a declaration of certain of its metaphysicians.

The Marxist Communist is clearly an altruist; so is the member of a religious order who regards his actions as the property of his superior. But there are some frequently misunderstood cases. The soldier who yields his life in defense of his country is not necessarily an altruist. He may not see himself primarily as a piece of his country; he may prefer to die in battle rather than see it looted by strangers; such a soldier is little different from a man who leaves his property after his death to others, since he cannot take it with him. Rand was aware of the case of this soldier, but her theory of sacrifice may have prevented her from seeing more. For instance, even a person who accepts the military draft may not be an altruist. Far from imagining himself a tiny piece of his country, he may think of a political order as a kind of a contract which he and a number of other people enter into for private advantages. But he may also believe that since life has its risks, these must figure into the social contract. War is a threat to the good things which his society offers. And should it happen while he is fit and able to fight, his number is called by the draft board, then he may have to fight, just as a farmer may in the turn of events lose his crops in a flood. "You pays you' money and takes you' chances!" is what this man thinks. Such an attitude would be anathema to a conscious altruist.

An Ebenezer Scrooge type who always attends to the bottom line and who hires and fires strictly with regard to experience and expected capability could be an altruist. He could conceive himself as providing the most efficient production for society. At the same time, an employer who would willingly forgo some profit by hiring someone whom he liked in preference to a better worker whom he disliked would not have to be an altruist. Such an employer discriminates on some basis other than prospective monetary return.

Religious people may or may not be altruists. A person who literally thinks that he "belongs" to a church would be an altruist. On the other hand, a person who saw himself as only a church member and would quit if he came to disagree with the Minister's theology enough or if he did not like some of the members would probably not be an altruist. An individualist might be after eternal life. "By faith Moses, when he became of age, refused to be called the son of Pharaoh's daughter, choosing rather to suffer affliction with the people of God than to enjoy the passing pleasures of sin, esteeming the reproach of Christ greater riches than the treasure in Egypt, for he looked to the reward." (Hebrews 11:23-26). Conversely, a person like the singer John Lennon who (if the report of his son is true) thought that after death he would become part of the Divinity would have had to have been an altruist.

In short, an altruist is someone who regards himself, morally, as a part—whether of a nation, a church, a race, humanity, the earth, or whatever. To see the issue more clearly, let us consider the proposition: " All A is B." In logic, this simply means that A possesses the characteristic of B, regardless of how many A's there are or whether or not the various A's have any other relations besides that one. To put it differently, if there were only one A, it would still be true that All A is B. This is how the individualist differs from the altruist. The altruist is concerned with the lateral relationship between all the A's which possess a certain attribute. To him, the A's are not separate beings so much as parts of a super being. If the latter were characterized by the symbol C, then for the altruist the correct formula will be: C is B. The "All" would be superfluous, since the A's are not members of a class but portions of an organism, replaceable like the worn out cells of the body. We have already discussed this as "class" vs. "organization".

Two seeming exceptions to this are race and sex: Consider the possibility that not only did Robinson Crusoe discover that all the other English were dead, but also that a contagion had carried off the entire White race, leaving only himself. It would still make sense to speak of him as the last of his race. He would still have the same genetic material he could have passed on before the catastrophe.

Doxa: Yet, in another respect one could say that the race was incomplete, in that a female was not present.

Philosophus: That is true. Part of the race would have died out. But this one male would have remained. The death of all the females of his race did not change his sex. He would, however, be the last. But Robinson Crusoe was not a cell in a super body. Even if there had remained one female besides him, this does not mean that the race would continue. They might hate each other: "Not if you were the last on earth...." Furthermore—and this is the main point—sexual congress does not ever unite the two individuals into some sort of a hermaphrodite. The result, when successful, is the birth of a child. It is some genetic material that is combined, not the two individuals. When one of the parties dies, the survivor can still live without remarrying; if together they had made a type of organism, then, without a new cell with which to join, the survivor would soon die.

Doxa: What of the statement that marriage partners are "of one flesh"?

Philosophus: That is, I think, a figure of speech, indicating moral inviolability, dating back to the creation of Eve out of Adam, when it was physical. They were to serve as a type for future marriages. And even if there is link beyond the moral and intellectual ones, a physical link beyond that implied by mutual promises and heredity-prospects—a corresponding physical change in both parties—this cannot be used as a model for everybody in all aspects of life, as altruism would wish. To borrow the analogy would be like embracing something beyond polygamy, beyond free love—*indiscriminate bisexual sex on demand.*

And now, back to Rand and altruism. That she did not grasp the essential simplicity of altruism, and instead tried to show that sacrifice was the substitution of the lower for the higher, may have been due, in part, to her theory that concept formation requires two or more instances of that type of entity being comprehended under it. Her concepts were to be the product of a blending—and so is collectivism,

Penelope: As I said before, this is the root of their attack against class. They do not see people as isolated individuals with certain important characteristics the same. They see them as part of a super entity, the Grand Etre. It is surprising that with the current fixation many of these people have for what they call "The Goddess," there is not more talk among the literati about old Compte. Perhaps there is a common source—but that is another subject.

Doxa: Unless any one has anything else to add, our next meeting will be on free will.

DAY XII

FREE WILL

*T*he four meet again at the restaurant. Their circum
stances are the same. The management has brought
in a home entertainment center so that the patrons can
watch the basketball game. It sits on the opposite side of the large
room. In a semi-circle about it are some small tables for people who
want to watch it. Outside is the storm.

Doxa: Ayn Rand's metaphysics are not true; but there
are times when she rises very high indeed. One example is
in her case for free will. As part of her rejection of Lenin and
Dialectical Materialism, she holds that man is not determined;
that there exists for him an element of freedom. The Marxist-Leninists teach that man is simply a product of material
forces and every one of his actions are totally determined in
every respect. This view holds that the universe itself is completely monistic, that no human action is really initiated, that
everything is acting in response to everything else always, if
not in all ways.

Ayn Rand asked: how it would be possible for any man
to even make a rational decision? If every action, including
the smallest dilation of thought, is determined by what went
on before, then there is no place in it for rational thought.
What would be the point of thought? Sensations would take
place, setting in motion nerve impulses which would then
trigger the flexing and unflexing of muscles, which would
in turn move limbs. There would be no need for any such

thing as a guide to thought like logic, since any thought one had would be completely a product of what had gone on before. Irrationality would not exist. The decision would simply follow from what went on before—not just from the preceding moment either, as it in its turn inexorably followed that which went on before it. What need would there be of proof in a deterministic universe? Whatever would happen would happen.

The key term here is "irrational." As Dr. Peikoff ably puts it: "The concept of 'volition' is one of the roots of the concept of 'validation' (and of its subdivisions, such as 'proof'). A validation of ideas is necessary and possible only because man's consciousness is volitional. This applies to any idea, including the advocacy of free will: to ask for its proof is to presuppose the reality of free will."[1]

Stanford: In upholding free will, Objectivism never denies the law of causality; to this philosophy, an action by an entity must be consistent with the nature of an entity; and if that entity has freedom, then consistency requires that some of its actions be free.[2] If an entity is constructed in such a way that it has the freedom to choose, then *by necessity*, it has it, though it may fail to exercise that capacity from time to time. Peikoff himself recognizes the role of necessity in freedom: "The law of causality affirms a necessary connection between entities and their actions. It does not, however, specify any particular kind of entity or of action. The law does not say that only mechanistic relationships can occur, the kind that apply when one billiard ball strikes another; this is one common form of causation, but it does not preempt the field."[3] Necessity and freedom are reconcilable because the aspects of human nature that are free and those that are determined are not the same. The material parts which go into its making a being with free will like man are themselves fully determined to be what they are; but once the structure that makes free will possible is in place, the exercise of that power to choose is not determined. This is unusual, but we are acquainted already with the paradoxical fact that most of that which is encompassed in the triune structure of time, namely the past and the future, does not exist. I suspect that there are elements in free will that will always remain a mystery to us on this side of life.

Doxa: Peikoff's argument that free will is consistent with the law of causality is the opposite of Kant's argument for free will. According to Kant, the unknown thing-in-itself may be *free*—but only because the unknown realm of the noumenon may be hypothesized to not operate in accordance with cause and effect.

It is at the next point that Ayn Rand's original genius really shines through: The run-of-the-mill theory of freedom of the will teaches that man has the power to choose groundlessly in favor of one belief or another, the reward coming when he chooses correctly, in the same manner as is commonly believed to be done by those who win the lottery. But this would be a leap into the dark every time.

Ayn Rand holds instead that this choice consists in the decision to think or not to think, to focus or not to focus with respect to any problem that comes along. The rest of the time, one is on automatic. When something happens which we have already long since known how to handle, we do so; it is only when the new comes forth in some form, large or small, that a fresh act of thinking is required. It is like driving a car; once this has been well-learned—has become second nature, we automatically react to the changes that occur along the way—the too slow car ahead, the person who is legally passing on the left. But if someone were to come around us on the right, then we suddenly pay attention and initiate the process of new thought.

Penelope: Rand's theory is not unique. In the middle of the 19th century, something similar was proposed by the French intellectual, Charles Renouvier. This theory was brought to the attention of Americans by William James, who modified it. Rand knew of James. There is, however, an important difference between the two. Renouvier's idea was that free will consists of "the sustaining of thought *because I choose to* when I might have other thoughts."[4] Renouvier fixed upon the choice to think about X instead of Y. Rand thought in terms of the decision to think X instead of not thinking about it. Her's might have been more comprehensive, but he had the root idea ahead of her.

Doxa: Then Ayn Rand was an advancement over Renouvier.

It may be asked, is our freedom limited merely to the choice to think? Cannot we freely choose to act as well? A man who thought through to the correct answer to a problem and even figured how to bring the answer into fruition but did not do it would be not necessarily be remiss; he might also have figured that it was not worth doing, that the net return would be too low. But if he decided that it was worth doing and did not do it, he would be irrational. He would have failed to think it through to its base. Refusing to do what he knows he ought might introduce the kind of contradictions which would ruin his judgement.

The decision to think, which consists of the act of focusing, is not itself a process of thinking; it is the decision to exercise it.

This theory has not been without its critics. In the words of Professor Robert Hollinger of Iowa State: "Indeed, according to the view Rand accepts, the ideally rational person (i.e., one with all the relevant information) would not have any freedom—save the freedom to be irrational, since he would see that reason, knowledge, and truth force the right view upon him; for the freedom to decide is, in this view, directly proportional to the amount of ignorance one is under at the time! It is thus no coincidence that Rand, despite all her talk of freedom in the ethical, political, and epistemological realm, claims that a rational person has only one choice: to think or not to think! So much for freedom *and* reason!"[5]

First, that is a strange way to put it, especially by a college professor who is supposed to be in favor of people putting the search for truth first. Ayn Rand, of course, would agree that a person who was rational all the time would find life easier going. But this person could still decide to rest on his laurels and become lazy. He might decide to indulge in some of the things which he had already decided were wrong, and then come up to the surface before the bad consequences started rolling in.

Second, Professor Hollinger should recall that all questions are not of high pitch. Sometimes, we can focus just enough to see that the answer to the question before us is not important enough to go to the trouble of obtaining it.

Yet, is lethargy at the root of the difference between the good and the bad? We all have known or heard of some people who are *bad*—bad even from the perspective of Ayn Rand; yet, who work very hard and are very successful on their own terms. In order for her to be right, these people would have had to have blanked out every time the question of what had turned them toward evil came up but remained fully conscious and in control about everything else.—that they went along the path of evil because they were too lazy to think it through.

Is this really all there is to it? Let us go back to the religious hypothesis. Adam and Eve were told that they could eat anything in the Garden of Eden, except for the tree of the knowledge of good and evil. Now, to know evil, one must either do it oneself or experience it, either as a witness or as a victim. By taking the fruit, Adam and Eve had chosen to undergo this.

It would appear that Ayn Rand's idea is consistent with this account. Adam and Eve had failed to consider closely enough. Instead of focusing sharply on the question before them, they had allowed powerful emotions to guide them.

It should also be recalled that when a person becomes inured to the protests of his conscience, he becomes hardened. Eventually, he may lose the capacity to resist further temptation. In fact, the thought of turning himself around might seem like a temptation to be resisted—"Tomorrow's soon enough!". This is my third answer to Professor Hollinger: the young person in his ignorance may have more before him than the older but wiser one; but the person who has lost moral capacity has much less.

The key is the choice to focus. As Dr. Peikoff expresses it: "The choice to focus, I have said, is man's primary choice. 'Primary' here means: presupposed by all other choices and itself irreducible."[6]

And now my fourth and final answer to Professor Hollinger: sustained rationality is not dull. Sometimes a long-term course of action cannot be set simply on the basis of a single act of contemplation. During WWII, General MacArthur used to go into the front lines and expose himself to enemy fire, even though he was in his sixties. Sometimes, he would take his generals with him; and those who did not respond very well were relieved of battle-command. He wanted commanders who would move forward. One time there were two Japanese machine gunners outside his window. He stared at them and they stared back; then, after he had left the scene they started firing. This was not teeth gritting bravery on his part, which is common among mere fanatics. Rather, it was a calculated risk taken on the basis both of contemplation and also by a will that kept moving forward. When his aid-de-camp, Dr. Roger Egeberg, asked him why he took such chances, the answer he gave was that there were various reasons, some hard to explain. The risks were not as great as one might think; he had received a tremendous amount of combat experience in World War I when he was on the front—more than any one else who was later to become an American general officer. In WWI, he had received seven silver stars. There he learned when the situation was dangerous and when it was reassuring. Doing this gave him a sense of timing. He also said that he received strength from sharing some of the risks undertaken by the men. It was not a conviction that he could never be hit.[7] That sense of timing could not have been acquired simply by contemplation; constant checking was also required. Seeing what was really happening rather than relying on reports put forth by others; observing how the young men were handling it—all these things were important in order to gauge what his army was capable of doing, how fast they would go forward; how well they would handle a determined counter-attack by enemy soldiers. It had nothing to do with hatred of the enemy. It was the work of a forward driving will—one that takes action and then reflects upon what was learned.

Philosophus: Rand held that the operation of free will is confined to the decision to think or not to think, the latter amounting to continuing on with the automatic. Even this restriction means that there must be a will—that it is this and not some overarching axiom that makes the decision. The question is this? Is free will simply a matter of the choice to think as Rand taught? I can see another use of it besides deliberation. It can also involve a choice to persist at a certain course of action—to exercise one's will in behalf of an objective or a goal. One does not have to turn off one's active mind in order to do something. One can determine oneself to be an overcomer. With that, men have done wonderful things. We all know how the body can effect the mind; of the havoc that a brain injury can do. But there are the less common cases where mind affects body. There are instances of sick people who have made themselves well through determination after have been told by their physicians that the illness will triumph over them. It was not that they thought about the various ways that the bodily organs worked and then obtained relief through self-administered treatment. It was rather that they ordered the cells to move. They may have been ignorant of the physiology involved, but they acted anyway.

Penelope: Before we leave this subject, there is one epistemological possibility which I would like to mention. We have already discussed the class covered by Renouvier and Rand; mention has also been made of how one can exercise one's free will in moving matter. But suppose that there are some men who are inclined to evil anyway. They would still have the capacity to stop and think; they could even follow imaginatively the reasoning of those who are cogitating about what course would be the good one. But they would have their proclivities.

Doxa: Haven't we covered this with our discussion of Adam and Eve?

Penelope: Adam and Eve were originally good. The unwillingness to think through, yielding to recklessness explains their behavior to my satisfaction. But it does not cover what I am discussing. The Bible talks about how the sins of the fathers are visited on the sons, which is usually taken to mean that certain defects are transmitted across the generations. Just as through sustained thought a man can cure himself of disease, so it may be the case that the sins of the very bad produce tiny changes in the genetic material they carry, and that across generations of bad people, someone is born depraved. In the more civilized era which preceded this one, French police psychologists used to keep records on criminal families. Such individuals would still have freedom to choose to think, to sustain action, but about the final things, they would have no inkling toward betterment.

Philosophus: But then, they would not be responsible.

Penelope: Clearly, they would be responsible for less. They would have no real possibility of goodness. They would serve only as obstacles through which those with greater potentiality would be tested. They would be moral werewolves.

Philosophus: This is a new subject to me.

Penelope: It is to me, also. I do not have any more to say about it at this time. It is just a sudden realization that I mention so that I will not forget. I think we should go on.....

Stanford: What is it that we know about free will? First, we know that we have it; we know this because we use it. We know it both in the way characterized by Rand and we also know it in the manner characterized by Mr. Philosophus.

We experience this feeling over and over again. An error? The errors of the senses are occasional and detectable. We *know* we have free will; we experience it in the depth of our being. Yet, it defies explanation in terms of what we know about Matter. And it does not make sense in terms of the animal world either. But men, unlike beavers, can question their own desires. This is a *power*, not a specific determination. The beaver can check to see if this or that piece of wood will work for the dam. He is bound strictly by his surroundings. His questioning is nothing more than a checking out.

Doxa: Second, if we did not have it, the whole process of consciously using logic in order to direct our thought would be incognizable; it would take pages and pages of rationalization to make it seem intelligible in deterministic language. And after we have convinced ourselves of this hypothesis, we would go back to acting as if we had free will as soon as we have left our study, just as David Hume would have had to treat nature as full of necessity, whenever he was operating in the ordinary work-a-day world.

Stanford: The value of truth—that is what the squirrels miss. How can one be determined to seek the truth? Let us explore this hypothesis. Suppose someone is so determined: It is still possible that he will fail. This would mean that he was determined not to realize the very goal which he was just as determined to seek. But if he is determined to fail, why the presence of a motivating desire which cannot be fulfilled in the case of the one doomed? Whence comes the built-in illusion? Futility would be built into it.

Then there is the objection that the effort of the squirrel to finish his dam may be squelched by a fire; and since that would be fully determined, why should it be any different for a man?

The answer is that the squirrel instinctively does this. He does not set a goal consciously for himself. It is set by his nature. He is firmly locked within his context. The determinist would answer, of course, that there is an innate prompting in the form of an illusion which carries the man who is going to fail "impotently on," to borrow a phrase from the *Rubaiyat*.

Suppose a man were determined to think that it is all a joke put on us by a causality so stupid it doesn't know what a joke was—that fate was Charlie McCarthy without Edger Bergen. If such a person tried to contemplate his fate, he would tend to be stone cold inside—perhaps a grim fanatic, or become a mad chaser after pleasure. Consider the endless variations on this theme. The one that was fated to grasp the truth about determinism would be a resolute pessimist. The optimist would be the one fated to take the wrong course of believing in free will. This would denature the old impulse-gratification scheme so beloved by behaviorists. To hold to determinism, one would have to suppose that wisdom on this subject is different from any other, in that it brings as its reward, restlessness, misery. In the instance of the fanatic, dullness with respect to the richness of the lives of his intended victims would be taken as a sign of brilliance. Joy would belong to fools. And the wise would end up cherishing deceit. A man would have to be crazy to believe that.

Philosophus: The phenomenon of error is inexplicable on the grounds of determinism; if a mistake were purely the result of uncontrollable antecedents, it could be one only from the standpoint of a chain of causality which was impossible anyway. Some animals know that they must keep quiet when a stronger enemy is near them; they are afraid; they tremble. A deer jumping over a log and then falling because its leap was too short might be able to realize that it didn't jump far enough. But they cannot rise to the idea of error itself, an idea which is rooted in the recognition that *alternatives exist*—that in any given situation, one is right and the others, however favored by feeling, are wrong. Error cannot be reduced to its corresponding positive, and the two stand before us like the two doors in that great short story, "The Lady Or the Tiger."

More than intellectual ability to contemplate error or even alternatives is involved. The beaver may be able to experience responsibility, but he does not rise to the idea of moral responsibility itself, an idea which is unintelligible apart from free will. Those who accept determinism suffer from despondency. The flabby type has already been mentioned. The other is the man of iron—one who has refashioned himself so as to be consistent with the Destiny which he regards as unchosen anyway. This dying country has had its fill of Lenins and Nietzsches.

Stanford: Third, we know that is compatible with the law of causality. But a mere lack of incompatibility is not a definitive identification. There is nothing like it to which a comparison can be made. An explanation is an account of the unknown in terms of something familiar with which it can be connected.[8] But no explanation of free will can be given strictly in terms of determined events because the former and the latter are dichotomies; their dissimilarities are too great for full intelligibility; it is like infinity. Yet, we can know that all metaphysical possibilities exist because of free will. Without it, everything would be bound by an unyielding necessity. That is why deterministic writers sometimes introduce the idea of contingency, i.e., the idea that events can happen randomly. Having disowned free will, they know that there is something in their thinking that does not cohere. And so they hypothesize about a breach in causality, which is a weak form of saying that contradictions can exist, a conclusion which the timid professorial type with his posits and inverted commas cannot quite bring himself to make, but which bold barbarians like Lenin, Stalin, and Mao could and did.

Penelope: Sounds can be discriminated by contrasting them with colors; heat can be differentiated from solidity. But with free will, the contrast is to the rest of existence, including the animal world of sight, smell, taste, touch, and hearing. This points to that which we do not understand. The atheist can only <u>underscore</u> what she is trying to hold onto.

Stanford: Let us assume for the sake of the argument that evolution were correct. Under that hypothesis, a creature with free will would have to come out of a mindless fate. It could not have been based on some need of an evolving organism, as many evolutionists imagine. For that would mean that a being which did not yet exist could bring itself into existence because of what it would require in order to exist. It would be like saying that non-existence causes existence.

Doxa: One other point to consider is that those who simultaneously deny that values can be the logical result of facts and who also deny free will would be contradicting themselves. If all was the inexorable product of what went on before, then an evaluation would be the direct result of that which had preceded it—the production of values from facts destitute of values. Since we have already shown that validation has no place in such a scheme, a value would itself be, not a moral fact of independent metaphysical status, but a twinge, a step in a relentless process.

Penelope: Why isn't the need for morality enough evidence? Or to put it more exactly, why is it that the reduction of the mental to the mere urges and urges to prompting and that to push and pulls has such psychological power? I think it is the lure of monism, the attractiveness of the notion that if all could be reduced to a single principle, a comprehensive explanation would then exist. That is why the college trained have so much trouble with free will.

Philosophus: What the existence of free will in man suggests is that matter, which cannot think, was, in the case of man, endowed with a mind by another Being. And that would be God. Computers are given certain of the attributes of consciousness, although they are not themselves conscious. They are given this by man, a being which can choose. The same thing in a much grander way may well be the case for man himself.

Penelope: Pure mind determines what it will think about. Just as mixed creatures like us can move matter through mental activity, so can Pure Mind.

Philosophus: This returns us to a problem with Rand's concept of value. It will be recalled that Rand had asserted that the fundamental alternative in the universe is existence or nonexistence. Then she argued that this alternative pertained only to living organisms, since matter cannot be destroyed and can only alter its forms. "It is only a living organism that faces a constant alternative: the issue of life or death."[9] But we just stated that alternatives exist only for those with free will. Rand defined values in such a way as to include even unconscious plants. But if values require this alternative, then plants cannot have values, for their actions are totally determined. If a root reaches a rock, it will attempt to get around it, but this is not because it is aware of the fact that it must not allow the rock to prevent it from reaching more water; it is merely the result of its heredity, of "how it is programmed," to use the contemporary argot. They are not trying to stay alive; they are merely living.

Yet, the plant has been made to keep on living as long as it can. Whether it is able to get around the rock may be completely determined by the size of the obstacle and the growth capabilities of a plant—the blind unalterability of it all. It is not confronted with a set of alternatives; if it is unable to get the water and other nutrients, then it simply dies. Put differently: it is true that if the plant stopped doing this it would begin to wither, but *not doing this* can never an alternative; the plant simply continues going on like that as long as it can. In the deep sense that we have been using the term "alternative", it has none. For it, there is no Either-Or. Only if there were a being intelligent enough to conceive of removing the rock so that the root could continue downward would there be any metaphysical possibility of any alternative. An earthquake or a falling meteor could also remove the obstacle, but they would be fully locked within the deterministic order. No alternative there.

The same is the case with an animal. Unlike the plant, when confronted with a foe, an animal is aware that there is an obstacle and in some cases of the nature of the threat. It experiences fear. This triggers the fight—flight syndrome. Whichever is stronger prevails. Its response would be determined by its heredity, its experience, the terrain, etc. If the animal fought and fell, then it would have failed. But there could not have been any metaphysical possibility of any other outcome. It would not have been the result of a choice between alternatives.

Sometimes, it will be moved to do two things at once. We once had a small dog that would sometimes run off to a certain neighbor's place. When we would come after him, the little fellow would walk very, very slowly toward us. He would obey both his desire to stay and have fun and also would do as summoned. Obeying both together, he would go in the direction of the stronger impulse, but slowed down by the other one. He did not choose; he did not weigh alternatives; to some extent, he was behaving like a figure being formed on a Cartesian coordinate grid by the simultaneous placement of the x-y or horizontal-vertical coordinates—except that he was conscious of both impulses and was acting in response to both. This dog would also behave that way when he was being led to bed after he had been having an exciting evening of play. The animal is conscious, but does not really experience the choice between alternatives. What was true with this pet is also true of the wild carnivore which bites its foot off to get out of the hunter's trap.

In war, men must sometimes act faster than the time it takes to deliberate; they are, therefore, trained to make their action less deliberative, and more like a conditioned response. The same with race car drivers; they save their thinking for novel or tricky situations. As do we all.

As far as I know, animals do not have moral codes—not even the loyal dog. Many of these creatures are more than mere perceptual beings as supposed by Rand; they sense both the trees and the forest. But they are strictly reactive. Within a limited range, they are able to think, but only in response to explicit need; thus the beaver will find a substitute for a log. But they do not initiate; and they do not envision possibilities. If the beaver selects a certain place to build his dam, he is fully determined by the circumstances which surround him and his felt needs. It is only from the standpoint of an intelligence greater than theirs' that the phenomenon of alternatives arises. Even if some professor comes up with the notion of a breach in causality, a cosmic contingency, it would not change this situation; all there would be is some indeterminate fuzziness, no sharp alternatives.

To the thinking determinist, there can be no such thing as an alternative in a metaphysical sense. There are no possibilities. *"Qui Sera, Sera. Whatever will be, will be. The future's not ours you see. What will be, will be!"*[10] To this type of person, to talk about an alternative is to either commit a plain falsehood, to indulge in an engaging exaggeration, or to confess one's ignorance. With plants and animals, this is how it is. Rand, therefore, cannot define life in terms of facing the alternatives between existence and non-existence. Life cannot be defined in terms of anything else, only described.

It is the presence of beings with free will that enable possibilities to exist. When men survey other life, they see that there is indeed something about it which is distinguished from inanimate life, even though in both cases the action is unconditional. In the coming-into-being and passing-out-of-being of the various forms of life is evidence that some intention, some organization was impressed. Outside of free will, there is no either-or in nature, but there is evidence in it of a plan which in its forming did involve choices. And what we by mistake call "alternatives in nature" are the faint traces of the choices made by the One that designed it and arranged it—something the atheist Rand noted without understanding when she spoke of a plant having "values."

The Objectivist cannot fully understand possibility, whether metaphysical or epistemological, for another reason. The reason is that when some theory is fully consistent with all the evidence, it is identified by them as a "contextual absolute," an earlier form of what will almost certainly take on a different and higher form, later on. For all these people know, the same thing could be the case with the distinction between possibility and necessity. Since they place their minds under the veil of context, they do not see what the radical difference that free will makes.

Penelope: What is the metaphysical status of an extinct possibility, of what was once an alternative but is not one any longer?

Philosophus: If it is simply the case that the possibility has not been realized, then it is a fact about the future, one of its possible outcomes as distinct from one of its necessary kind. This would be the case even if it were never realized. An artist may botch a work of art—may fail to bring out its higher possibilities. The artist may die. What that work could have been would still be a fact, even if it were never taken up again. If, on the other hand, that possibility has been ruined and can never come back again, then it is a fact about the past.

Penelope: What kind of a fact about the past would it be?

Philosophus: It would be a negative fact about the past. In that respect, it would be like any other historical fact. We all know of some ruined possibilities. To cite a couple of famous examples: Would Napoleon would have been able to stay on the throne if he had won the battle of Waterloo? Would the Confederacy been able to prevail, had General Lee succeeded at Gettysburg? Even their negativity is not particularly remarkable; it is also a fact that the Earth is not in the same place in space as it was a minute ago.

Each fact about the past, whether positive or negative, is distinct. As the present moment—so to speak—*recedes* from us, each of the past events, including the ruined possibilities, become more distant. There is a change here in terms of how far they are in the past. But it is not a material change—not a mental change either. The change is simply metaphysical—a change of fact.

Because there is at least one free will in the universe, facts are different than they would have been if there were none. Its existence does not by that fact alter any thing else. For that, it needs to be exercised in some way. But the mere fact that it exists makes a profound metaphysical difference. If there is such a thing as action at a distance, the implications are enormous.

Stanford: In short, we know we have free will, that we can judge between alternatives, that we can discern possibilities. But we cannot account for it in terms of the laws of matter. It would be arbitrary to assume some material law when we have none, when it cannot be found anywhere in matter and its workings. We are led to a Source Outside of Matter. Free will is ultimate omphalos for us.

Philosophus: And that takes us far beyond the hopeless philosophy of Objectivism.

Doxa: Our next meeting is either our last or next to the last one. At that meeting we will discuss Ayn Rand's reflections on money.

DAY XIII

MONEY

O nce again the intrepid four are meeting at the res taurant. In front of them are books and notes. This day, the sports crowd is not in evidence; the huge TV set is blank. At the nearby tables are business people and bureaucrats.

Doxa: There are many ways in which Ayn Rand was undoubtedly right. From the time of FDR's New Deal until the middle of the 1960's, government planning was toasted as the great achievement of modern political science. In *Atlas Shrugged* and in subsequent writings, she ridiculed this whole idea, arguing that, in the end, it would destroy the industrial system on which most of us depend for our existence. The professors sputtered and fumed about this, claiming that her indictment of their beliefs was an oversimplification. Today, many government planners openly boast that they are trying to de-industrialize America. Few ordinary taxpayers regard that as benevolent.

In 1957, the year that she published that novel, American academics were characterizing the welfare state as the most scientific and humane social system yet conceived; its advocates spoke of it as a great social net which would prevent anyone from falling beneath a certain level; they also said that it constituted an intelligent redistribution of wealth that would in the long run outpace the old private property system as goads for progress. Today, nobody talks that way. Everyone knows that it has proven an enormous expenditure, ruinous to the American middle class. Hardly anyone

listens now to the politician's claim that through some jug-
gling with work requirements or through some new "self-
help" program paid for by the taxpayers, the problem will
be brought under control.

Around the time that *Atlas Shrugged* was published, the civil
rights movement was calling not only for the end of laws
mandating racial segregation (which then existed in but a few
Southern states) but also that white owned businesses engaged
in such public accommodations as hotels, restaurants,
and barber shops be forbidden to choose whom they might
wish to do business with. This assault against freedom of
association was made part of the 1964 civil rights act. At the
time, its advocates vociferously denied that it would lead to
affirmative action hiring and other racist practices in favor
of non-Whites. One of the law's two sponsors, Senator (later
Vice President) Hubert Humphrey said he would eat his hat
if that happened; he died before he was called upon to honor
his pledge.

Ayn Rand was opposed to racism in principle; she up-
held the rights of personal choice and private property. (Interestingly enough, the proponents of the collectivist version
of anti-racism have ended up attacking it only when it is
employed on behalf of Whites). Ayn Rand regarded the policies of the civil rights movement to be disastrous for all
peoples. Today, hardly anyone thinks that compulsory integration has been the kind of a success that its promoters had
publicly claimed it would be.

And, of course, socialism as an intellectual doctrine is
not defended nearly as much as it was in 1957. The Soviet
leadership has officially dropped the ideal of abolishing private property, torn down the Berlin wall, dismantled the
USSR, and has, instead, concentrated on other power plays.

Ayn Rand is one of the most important advocates of private property. Her case for capitalism, however, is not much
different from any other advocate of laissez faire capitalism,
such as Ludwig von Mises or Henry Hazlitt. Their procedure was either to show the inherent contradictions in the

claims of their opponents, or that the reforms suggested by those opponents actually ended up helping certain favored groups at the expense of the rest of society.

Since Ayn Rand's views on the details of capitalism are little different from that of these other advocates, only one aspect of her economic teachings will be investigated.

This is the gold standard. In it may be found the quintessential Randian paradigm for the concept: a standard that serves as a unit and a unit that serves for a standard.

Money, for Ayn Rand, should be gold.[1] Gold is a commodity. It has use in jewelry, architectural ornamentation, and even in industry. That is to say, it is bought and sold quite independently of its potential use as money. As money, it would be a commodity in terms of which the value of other commodities could be stated. With it the inconveniences of barter could be left behind. Instead of directly exchanging goods on a one for one basis, prices could be stated as so many units of some standard commodity. Thus the price of a wagon load of apples would be exchangeable for so many bushels per ounce of gold; the price of shoes for a certain fraction of an ounce; a particular horse for some other amount of the yellow metal, etc.

Note the similarity between Ayn Rand's analysis of the concept and the characteristics of a gold standard:

A product of a volitional consciousness. It is central to her purpose that the monetary unit be something that has been freely chosen by the market. Otherwise, its selection would be arbitrary. Gold fulfills this; the metal "is a tangible value in itself."[2] The antithesis of gold would be a paper currency which would not have existed without the decision of government authorities and which could not be converted into any precious metals. In this regard, gold would be like Objectivism's notion of the concept as a mental construct which cannot come into being until a man has chosen to make the effort.

At least two or more instances. Let us take the case of two traders, each which with different goods to offer: one with wheat, the other with leather. They could simply swap, which would obviate the use of money. But suppose that the one with the leather did not want the wheat. In order for an exchange to take place, something else would be required. The wheat farmer might have some gold. If this metal were used as money, then the leather maker could accept this in exchange even though he might not have some practical use for it, because he knew that another party would exchange something he did want for the gold money. Now, in order for this to happen, there must be more than one unit of gold available in the trading community. If there were not, then gold could not be used as a common means of exchange. It would simply be a rare item, like a one-of-a kind postage stamp. The use of the money device is called "indirect" exchange, in contrast to direct exchange or barter where a certain quantity of goods of a given kind are exchanged for a specific quantity of some other kind.

Unit. The monetary unit would be defined in terms of the attribute of weight, usually ounces or grams. Any good or service could be exchanged for so much gold; soon everything held for trade would be thought of in terms of how much gold it will bring. Blocks of gold of a certain purity are similar, although they may differ in quantity; various blocks can also differ in degree of fineness. It is differentiated from that which it is not and integrated on the principle that each block of gold is similar, although they may differ in quantity and degree of fineness.

Conceptual Common Denominator. A note or money substitute would be possible, but these could only be exactly that. Since they are stated in terms of units of some commodity used as money, they are unintelligible apart from it. They are therefore defined as a species or sub-species under money, which must be a commodity, of which gold is the most practical.

Context: Prices are relative, but behind them lies that unchangeable reality, the monetary unit, or gold.

Freedom: Anything is for sale but only a fool would sell himself; thereafter, he would be unable to trade on his own account without permission.

For Ayn Rand, a new concept is just like a coin which allows entry into some new experience of reality; creating concepts is just like making money, and intellectual progress is like increasing wealth. It is here that her theory of the concept seems to work; there appear to be no inconvenient incommensurables. Neither are there any truths which require only one instance to comprehend. In this particular place, finitude in the forms of scarcity and precision are guaranteed; contextually, the human situation absorbs all considerations of time and space.

Penelope: If her theory of the concept were perfectly consistent with commodity money, there could be no aesthetic love of nature at all. The *Fountainhead* opens with Howard Roark standing naked above a cliff, looking down at a lake far below while considering his future. "These rocks, he thought, are here for me; waiting for the drill, the dynamite and my voice; waiting to be split, ripped, pounded, reborn; waiting for the shape my hands will give them." [3]

From that standpoint, enjoyment of the mere contemplation of nature would evidence a lack of seriousness which would have to be justified—perhaps thought of as a change of scene so that one can more clearly discern one's prospects.

Stanford: Perhaps! But, on the other hand, the scene may have been written as a modern analogue to Michelangelo's contemplating the potentiality inherent in a block of marble.

Doxa: The pragmatists used to talk about the "exchange value of ideas," but Ayn Rand was so much more literal. When she spoke of America as *"a country of money,"*[4] she meant it.

There are certain attributes that money should possess: among the most important are portability, uniformity, scarcity, initial demand. These, gold certainly has; it is not easy to find—it is a natural element and so is, at least, theoretically uniform. Even when it is not used as money there is always a demand for it—gold is the metal of the sun. Although heavier than most metals, a great amount of value can easily be transported in a small space, unlike cattle (which have from time to time been used as money).

Philosophus: But if gold has these attributes, so does silver. Why should gold be chosen as a commodity money to the exclusion of silver?

Rand and writers like her imply that the 19th century was the hallmark of the gold standard. But this is untrue. Until 1873, the only major country on a monometallic gold standard was Great Britain. Until that year, the German states were for the most part on a silver standard. France and a few other European countries were on a bimetallic system of gold and silver. The Latin Monetary Union was formed to promote bimetallism. The U.S.A. was on an inoperative bimetallic system inclined toward gold but vastly augmented by all sorts of paper money. In the Far East, China and India were on a monometallic silver standard.

The great switch from silver to gold was due to government fiat more than it was to autonomous market forces. In 1873, the newly constituted German Reich switched from silver to gold for reasons which were largely political rather than economic.[5] Next, the Scandinavian countries decided to go on the gold standard. Holland prohibited the coining of silver and authorized that of gold. The U.S. followed suit. France and her partners in the Latin Monetary Union started vacillating; and the scene was set for the era of an international monometallic gold standard. Within the next twenty-one years (1871-1895), silver's price would drop in half.[6]

But gold's triumph was short lived. The demonetization of silver that took place throughout the Western world left gold with the double duty of filling in for the work that silver used to do when it too was used as an international monetary medium. The result was deflation. It was an era of industrial progress; and the demand for gold increased at a faster pace than its supply, causing gold's unit value to rise and the general level of prices to fall. During that 1874-1895 period, the prices of the 45 leading commodities in Great Britain fell about as much as the price of silver had: 40 index points as distinct from 46.8 index points, respectively. This led Alfred Marshall, the famous English economist, to proclaim in 1888 that silver had not depreciated "in the sense of having less purchasing power. I think it has appreciated, and has now a higher purchasing power as regards commodities than it had before."[7]

According to a conjecture by Milton Friedman and Anna Jacobson Schwartz in their famous book: if the U.S. had not demonetized silver in the 1870's; if instead it had adopted silver, deflationary tendencies would have loosened—perhaps even been broken—on a worldwide as well as a domestic basis. The reduced U.S. demand for gold might have encouraged other countries to keep, maybe even convert to silver, thereby lifting part of the load off the world's gold stocks. "For the period before 1897, therefore, the choice between silver and gold hinges on one's judgment about desirable price trends. If one regards the deflationary price trend as an evil...silver would on this account and for that period have been preferable to gold. The only other effect of any importance for the period was on the system of international exchange rates. The adoption of silver by the U.S. would have meant rigid exchange rates between it and other silver countries, but flexible rates between that group and the gold standard countries. This effect too we are inclined to regard an advantage of silver rather than a disadvantage. A striking, more recent, example of how much of an advantage it can be is furnished by China's experience from 1929 to 1931. Because it was on a silver standard, it avoided almost entirely the adverse consequences of the first two years of the world wide depression, which began in 1929"[8]

After 1896, the gold discoveries of the Klondike came in, increasing world monetary stocks enough to raise prices. The gold production of the following year nearly doubled that of 1890.[9] Silver continued to fall until 1903 when it took a great rise.[10] The result was inflation. Take the period between 1890 and 1914: as a result of the gold discoveries in the Klondike, in South Africa, and in Colorado, world gold stocks probably doubled; between 1897 and 1914, U.S. prices rose between forty and fifty per cent.[11] Nor was this the first time in American history that there was a gold-induced inflation. Take the decade or so after 1851—a period less than half as long as that between 1890 and 1914: as a result of the Californian and Australian mining discoveries, world gold stocks also doubled; according to Friedman and Schwartz, it is probable that U.S. prices increased even faster than they did during the later period for which better statistics are available.[12]

The international gold standard lasted until some time during World War I. Hardly much of an era.

It was the very instability of the period—an instability due in part to the too rapid official demonetization of silver, in part to the vicissitudes of mining, in part to the fractional reserve banking system (which I will explain later)—that made it possible for the Federal Reserve scheme to come into being.

Actually, the system which preceded the international gold standard was more stable. This was a system in which some countries were on the gold standard, some were on the silver, and a certain number of key countries were bimetallic.

A bimetallic standard is one where two metals, usually gold and silver, are allowed to exchange with each other according to some specific legally defined ratio. Thus 19th century France coined gold and silver freely and made them indifferently legal tender at a ratio of 1:15 1/2. (In other words, one gram of gold could be exchanged at any time for 15 1/2 grams of silver.)

Doxa: I think that at this point the Objectivist would answer that in accordance with Gresham's law, the bad money would drive out the good. What the law means is that when the aggregate amount of two or more kinds of money in circulation becomes excessive, people begin to pay their debts or make their purchases with the least valuable currency while sending the more valuable one abroad where it will command a premium over its official price. One of these metals, the opponents of bimetallism assert, will at any given time be overvalued and the other undervalued in terms of the former. If the official ratio were fixed at 15 1/2:1 and the world price should climb to 15 5/8:1, people would start to accumulate gold or send it abroad while dumping their silver on the market, thereby sending the ratio farther out of joint with reality.

Philosophus: Were this argument simply valid, one would expect the French ratio to have been in effect but a short time. But this did not happen. Historically, the French were able to maintain the ratio from 1803 to 1874, a period which included such unsettling crises for France as the Napoleonic wars, the successful revolutions of 1830 and 1848, the Mexican and Crimean fiascos, and the catastrophic Franco-Prussian War.

The French maintained their ratio during the Californian and Australian gold discoveries. In 1857, production of gold compared to silver had increased five-fold over 1851, and over a period of forty years, fifteen-fold.[13] During the course of the several international panics which disturbed finance in those years, it seems that the bank of France was able to hold up much better than did the gold's champion, the Bank of England.[14] In 1871, the year after France's defeat by Prussia and her allies, the market ratio of gold to silver was still close to the legal one, averaging 15.57:1. In 1872, after Germany had passed its provisional demonetization act, the market ratio was still 15.63:1. Even in 1873, the year France announced that she would go off the bimetallic standard, it was still 15.92:1. Only in 1874 did it slip to 16.91:1.

The explanation, fully consistent with Gresham's law, was given by the great 19th Century American economist, Francis Amasa Walker:

> If, at any time, either of the two metals became less valuable than by the legal ratio, every debtor instinctively sought coin of that metal, with which to meet his obligations, in preference to coin of the other metal. This increased the demand for the cheaper metal; and, by that very act, decreased the demand for the metal which was becoming dearer in the market. Now, to increase demand is, other things equal, to raise price; while to decrease demand is, other things equal, to lower price. Thus, through its power to regulate the payment of indebtedness, the government practically threw its weight upon that one of the two metals which tended to rise, and kept it down. No one wanted the dearer metal to pay debts with; every one wanted the cheaper metal for that purpose; and, since the volume of indebtedness coming due every day in any commercial country is very large, the force thus invoked was sufficient to produce an enormous economic effect. It was not at all because the French government declared that one part of gold should be worth 15 1/2 parts of silver that this result took place; but because the French government set in motion competent economic forces to that end.[15]

Doxa: The Objectivists would, of course, remind us that the act of the French government to freeze the ratio was one of force—but then, as you have shown , so were the forces that created the international gold standard of the late 19th and early 20th centuries. As were the forces that broke that standard.

Philosophus: But the point is that the standard based on a duality of two metals which did not always work in harmony with each other seemed to do better than the monometallic one that Rand favored. Because of this, one is entitled to wonder if her theory of the concept is even adequate to the phenomenon from which it may have drawn some of its inspiration. Since the market forces dictating the two major monetary metals are not always commensurate, would there not be less distortion through a mixed system, in that each of the two contestants would handle part of the traffic rather than be stuck with all of it?

I think that bimetallism could work without the governmentally fixed ratio. In today's world with its omnipresent personal calculators, the latest price of gold in terms or silver, or vice versa, could be calculated almost instantly. A woman who was operating on the gold standard could stride into a silver-based supermarket, pick up a ticket with the latest conversion ratio stamped on it while she was gliding through the turnstile, and have the prices converted without perceptible delay at the check stand.

Penelope: Without any legal ratio to tie them together, the two systems would operate in parallel. If one became too dear, there would be a rush toward the other, producing a countervailing effect. Although this might, at first, bring some confusion to the marketplace, it would soon die down. With the availability of modern electronic calculators, a price that was stated in terms of the inconvertible currency could quickly be translated into its equivalent in gold and silver. What would have been a an insurmountable problem in the 19th century is not one today. *I can see that.*

Can you foresee any set of circumstances in which this might be of great assistance to what is left of America?

Philosophus: Having two quite different systems in place at the same time would be of value, should the United States be surrounded by enemies. The two largest known gold deposits exist in Russia and South Africa; both are under the control of the successors and allies of the Bolsheviks. The third is Australia, which is a weak country, easily subject to intimidation by a resurgent Asia; furthermore, much of this wealth does not seem to be in the hands of people who value general liberty. Not only that, but my information is that Australia is disarming at the same time that Indonesia is arming itself to the hilt.

Having two standards would make it more difficult for enemy forces to cause havoc.

Doxa: How, concretely would gold and silver enter into the monetary system as money?

Philosophus: This type of money could either be supplied by the market, or people could bring their metal to the government, which would test it for fineness, refine it if necessary, and then coin it for them into units of weight, certified by government seal. For this service, the government would charge a fee called "seignorage." The government could also coin the supplies which they had in their possession. Private companies would also be allowed to coin gold and silver, although in order to compete successfully with the government coins, they would also have to state the proper weight and fineness and be able to stand behind their work; moreover, they would have to convince the public of their trustworthiness.

Gold and silver would trade against each other without a fixed legal ratio. The legal ratio was appropriate to a world of sea voyages by trading ships where the trader would prize any port which would exchange so much gold for his Indian silver, so much silver for his Californian bullion. But today, with radio communications and computers, a nearly instantaneous result can be obtained.

Doxa: Would this be like providing an element of incommensurability and by so doing complete the requirements of money?

Philosophus: That would be the ideal. But one should remember that while parallel standards are not commensurable from a physical standpoint, the exchange ratios in which they are expressed in a particular transaction are. At any given point in the market, an ounce of silver would sell for so much gold. But having different but parallel standards will tend to prevent instability. This will rest on the relative quantities involved, the status of the government, and the monetary media themselves.

Stanford: A full discussion of the merits of a bi-metallic system would be beyond our compass, but enough has been given to show the inadequacy of Rand's theory of the concept to account even for money, which may have served as a model for part of her system.

Philosophus: Let us turn to the question of convertible money. There are two kinds, certificates and notes. A certificate is simply a form of paper currency which states that it may be redeemed by its maker for a certain equivalent amount of the monetary metal. Until the mid-sixties, the U.S. Treasury used to issue silver certificates from $1.00 on up. Anybody could present them for redemption for a like value in silver. To each certificate, there corresponded in the treasury a specific amount of silver. Up until the 1930's, there also existed gold certificates, but FDR confiscated all them.

The second type of convertible currency is a note, which is a form stating an amount of indebtedness.

Notes increase the amount of currency in circulation; certificates do not; the latter are simply substitutes: there is a one-to-one correspondence between the monetary base and the paper which certifies its existence.

The difficulties with the note is its use in fractional reserve banking.

The fractional reserve bank is best understood by contrast with its logical opposite, the full reserve bank—although the latter may not even exist today apart from memory or imagination. If A were to deposit his money in a full reserve bank, the bank might lend B the full amount of A's deposits. But while this money were out on loan, A could not make any withdrawals from his account. The date on which the bank's obligations to A fall due must not precede the date on which the bank's corresponding claims on B mature. This is because the same money must be in the same place at the same time. Needless to say, the full-reserve bank would have to pay interest on deposits to entice A. The nearest equivalent to a full reserve bank is a "C.D."

A fractional reserve bank works like this. It may lend part of A's deposit but while the money is on loan A may withdraw up to the full amount of his and/or her account. This creates a net increase in the money supply. To obviate conflict, the bank keeps on hand a fraction of its deposits; hence its name. A bank with 20% reserves would be one which could not lend out more than four fifths of its deposits at any given time. This would handle all normal situations and a minor run on the bank as well.[16]

Penelope: Putting this in concrete terms: if A had deposited $100 in a fractional reserve bank with a 20% reserve ratio, that would mean that the bank could loan out $80 of this money—all the while A still had the right to withdraw the full amount. If the borrower then took this $80 and redeposited it in the this very bank or another bank with the same reserve requirement, then 80% of the amount deposited, or $64, could be placed on loan.. If this too were redeposited, then the bank could loan out 80% of that, or $51.20. What is the maximum possible exposure of a banking system with a twenty percent reserve requirement?

Philosophus: Given a 20% reserve, it is theoretically possible for the banking system to create four additional dollars for every dollar deposited in a demand account. Should the bank miscalculate and have withdrawals exceeding reserves, the result would be insolvency. Should the banker be unable to cover through additional sources, there is the potential for a panic. (The implications of all this have been drawn out by the distinguished economist, Murray Rothbard.)

Penelope: That is fraud.[17] More money claims are issued than the bank can meet. The banker simply hopes that he or she can keep up the front of affluence well enough that not very many will demand their money back. In a commodity money system, it also increases the money supply and is inherently inflationary.

Philosophus: In Rand's book, *Capitalism: The Unknown Ideal*, there is a chapter written by Alan Greenspan, entitled "Gold and Economic Freedom." This was published approximately twenty years before his accession to the Chairmanship of the Federal Reserve System. In his essay, Greenspan admits that a gold standard banker will sometimes loan out more than his gold deposits on hand. But Greenspan defends this policy:

> ...when the business ventures financed by bank credits are less profitable and slow to pay off, bankers soon find that their loans outstanding are excessive relative to their gold reserves, and they begin to curtail new lending, usually by charging higher interest rates. This tends to restrict the financing of new ventures and requires the existing borrowers to improve their profitability before they can obtain credit for further expansion. Thus, under the gold standard, a free banking system stands as the protector of an economy's stability and growth.[18]

But does the height of the interest rate make the system self-regulating in the way that Greenspan (and, by implication Rand) envisioned? "Wild cat" banking was very popular in 19th century America. Strings of banks took whole regions down with them when their inflationary boom was followed by a bust.[19]

Doxa: Were not such abuses inevitable for a young nation, struggling to tame the West?

Philosophus: Consider, then, these figures from the decade *after* the official closing of the frontier: From 1890-1900, nearly 400 National banks plus 1400 State Banks, private banks, and trust companies were closed out of insolvency.[20] Doubtless the system is self-regulating, but then so is an airplane weathercocked into the ever-tightening turns of a spiral dive.

This scandal, as well as the economic troubles of the first decade of the new century, provided all the excuse that the manipulators needed to hatch their plans for what became the Federal Reserve Act in 1913. The nation entered this new system after first experiencing fractional reserve banking and the monometallic gold standard. And so in a different way did Greenspan, decades later—after first championing that standard and that form of banking. (The dollar is now worth about 1/15th of what it was in 1913.)

Penelope: By counting fractional reserve currency as money, Rand contradicted her claim that "the words 'to make money' hold the essence of human morality."[21]

Doxa: Corresponding to the banker's promise to pay, there is nothing except his calculation. Ayn Rand should have denounced the practice; paradoxically, she actually approved of it. I believe that she got into this trap because she considered approximations to be a perfectly acceptable way to handle the incommensurable. She thought that a banker who knew how much he could get away with was all that was needed.

Penelope: What is to be done about the huge quantity of paper money that has been issued by our government?

Philosophus: There are various ways. In an interesting proposal offered made in 1974 and revised in 1975 by Peter Erickson, called "the Tripartite System,"[22] no convertible money could be issued as legal tender. Since the notes could not enter the market as money substitutes, they would be incapable of expanding the money supply. The instrument of signifying debt would stipulate principal, interest, and due dates; there is no way it could pass as the same thing as legal money.

In his interesting proposal, there are three independent monetary systems, all operating as parallel standards. The first two are gold and silver. The third consists of a way to handle the huge quantities of dollars which have been issued in the past without either repudiating them, allowing them to increase any further, or mixing them up with the gold and silver systems—which should be kept pure, lest the errors of the past will creep in again. Sir Isaac Newton is reported to have challenged the inflationists with the declaration that in applied mathematics, you must describe your unit.[23] In the case of all three parallel standards, the appropriate unit is adequately described. But to discuss this would take us far afield. Here, I have brought three copies of his proposal. Perhaps, we can meet some other time to discuss them.

Stanford: Yes, I will take one.

Penelope: So will I.

Doxa: And I too. I believe that we have discussed in sufficient detail Ayn Rand's defense of the gold standard and of fractional reserve banking. Since I think we now have sufficient understanding of the strengths and weakness of Objectivism, our next meeting will be our last.

DAY XIV

CONCLUSION

*F*or the last time, the four are meeting to discuss Objectivism. The place is the same restaurant. Half of the tables have
been arranged in a semi-circle around the entertainment
center, the people seated at them watching an important game being played against the team that has emerged as their greatest rival. They are stopping off for a snack before they go to the Colosseum
to witness their favorites in action. Outside, the wind and the rain
are attacking the pennants tied to the street lamps.

Doxa: There is no need for a summary of the tenets of
Ayn Rand's philosophy. We all understand them very well—
the strengths and the weaknesses. But it would be good to
determine where it stands with respect to present day American culture.

Stanford: Let us begin by looking at American history:
The old American Constitutional order is decrepit. Students
in school hear about the bicameral Congress and the division of powers, but they do not learn of the type of person
who originated that order. It was largely based upon the
white Protestant Englishmen who founded it. *Those who came
from elsewhere were expected to adjust to it, or go back to where
they came from.* The observations of Alexis de Tocqueville, a
young French aristocrat who visited the United States in the
eighteen thirties, are frequently quoted even today. Remarking on the difference between American and French newspapers of that day, he closed with these words: "In America...

it is only from time to time that one finds a corner devoted to passionate discussions like those with which the journalists of France are wont to indulge their readers."[1]

In 1839, another Frenchman, the economist Michael Chevalier, wrote a book about the United States, after having paid it a long visit. Here is one of his observations: "There must be harmony between the political and religious schemes that are suited to any one people. Protestantism is republican; puritanism is absolute self-government in religion and begets it in politics. The United Provinces (Holland) were Protestant; the United States are Protestant."[2]

But the country did not exclude non-Protestants. Henry Ford, America's premier industrialist, was a Roman Catholic. John Phillip Sousa, certainly one of the country's greatest composers of music, was of Jewish extraction. Throughout its history, it received the support of men and women of all races. Booker T. Washington, a champion of self-help, opposed the collectivism and elitism of W.E.B. Du Bois, founder of the NAACP and later member of the U.S. Communist Party.

The American Constitution served as the model for several Latin American countries, shortly after it was adopted here; yet after the passage of a few years, many of them were suspended in one way or another. Within a decade or so after Mexico had been established as an independent country from various Spanish colonies, she abandoned her own republican constitution in favor of the dictatorship of Santa Anna. A few years later, Texas won its Independence. So great was the agreement of the United States in the first half of the 19th century that in the Mexican war they won every battle against an enemy that was as well armed, in which that enemy's army was three times as great, and on territory which the enemy knew better.[3] Robert E. Lee and Ulysses S. Grant fought on the same side. That was the high point of internal morale. Less than twenty years later, the lives of a half a million young America males would be taken in the Civil War when the population was only thirty million. From

1865 onwards, the literature of New England began to lose its excellence.[4] Economically, the South did not recover from war and reconstruction until nearly a century later. But American science and invention raised a colossus that overshadowed any feelings of loss. Yet, there were warnings. Toward the century's close, the sociologist, William Graham Sumner characterized the outwardly successful Spanish-American war as Spain's conquest of the United States.

Sentiments like that became more common as the years advanced, although they did not become general until late in the next century.

A.R.'s great fame began at about 1960. This was a time when that order had been seriously weakened by World Wars I & II, by the social legislation of Wilson and FDR, and by the religious, moral, and intellectual drift that preceded and accompanied them. An effort to recover was made after WWII. Patriots like General MacArthur, Senator Robert Taft, and Senator Joseph McCarthy enjoyed considerable popularity for a time. But, by the late fifties, it was becoming clear that America's strength was starting to slip away. Everything was intact, but an inner emptiness could be discerned. The movie actor, James Dean, who expressed this inarticulate dissatisfaction so well, became immensely famous—even though he had died before his third successful picture was released. The young were ready to listen to strange voices.

Since then, several collectivist groups have won power in America, the most noted being the Civil Rights movement which took away freedom of association from whites through the "public accommodation" clause of the 1964 Civil Rights Act, justified racial violence when instituted by blacks against whites, instituted affirmative action, and did other things of the same ilk.

Doxa: Ayn Rand cannot be blamed for this. She was critical of the Civil Rights movement. She challenged the Left by supplying an alternative to an old order that was rapidly losing its strength. Her's was to be the aristocracy of honest money. The socialist New Deal and its successors were to be abandoned; the same with any other laws that infringed on individual rights. The idea was that private property would be kept, but the religious base on which the country was founded would simply be discarded. What was then called "the sexual revolution" would not be stopped and those who demurred would be allowed their opinion, but the competition of ideas would dictate the outcome. The socialist demand that their attitudes be financed by the taxpayers and made mandatory in the schools would be rejected. Legal segregation, such as existed in a few Southern states at that time, would be ended; but nobody would be forced to integrate either. The idea that white people could resort to a legal separation of the races in order to prevent miscegenation would be denied; but so would government programs approving race-mixing. The Welfare state created by the Federal government would be ended, and so would more modest programs involving local government.

More clearly than many of those who stepped into the vacuum and tried to put on the shoes of the old order, she saw that a mere economic case for laissez faire capitalism would not be enough; that the legislation of FDR was passed despite the trenchant refutations of some of the most learned people in America. Eloquence, too, fell short. She believed that it would have to be built upon an intellectual foundation that was rock solid. Otherwise the enemy would win. In the universities, for instance, the irrationalists were in charge of the philosophy departments. It would not be long before this would adversely affect America's optimistic sense of life. A man who lost confidence in his mind is exactly the kind of person who would be intimidated by ambitious thugs. Her new philosophy must be rational through and through.

She made her case, and it was immensely influential. When the Nathaniel Brandon Institute was founded in the early sixties for the purpose of spreading her philosophy through the sale of lectures, tapes, and books, there were very few educational groups handling intellectual subjects independent of the educational establishment or of organized religion. Today, there are many. A number of today's successful publicists have been influenced by her. The same type of person who would have been a Hippie dreamer twenty five or thirty years ago now wants to be an entrepreneur.

Stanford: But behind the return of the capitalist, the socialists have cast some dark shadows. The business heros in *Atlas Shrugged* made their living though an honest capitalism. They were either self-starters who had made their fortunes by long struggle like Hank Rearden or were maintaining and enhancing inherited wealth like Dagny Taggart. Yet, many great fortunes are also made through contact with government—especially projects connected with those activities which she and other advocates of individual liberty had denounced.

Doxa: Once certain bad laws have been taken off the books, new fortunes will take their rise and the influence of the welfare state profiteers will start diminishing.

Even with legitimate capitalism, the fortunes which were once so prominent tend to lose their importance over time; their heirs multiply; competition increases. What sort of influence do the Astors, the Vanderbilts, or the Morgans have today in America? Their palatial mansions are now museums. Yet certain 19th century writers complained that they would end up owning everything. Today, people talk about Microsoft taking and destroying the competition; twenty-five years ago, they said the same thing about James Ling and his now defunct LTV.

Penelope: Another threat is the environmental movement, which when considered in depth, calls for either the end of industrial society or a great reduction of the population. Corporations and wealthy individuals provide much of the financing for its propaganda. With socialism, it was relatively easy for an intelligent student to spend a few months reading and thinking about some books to be able to refute each and every pretension. What the socialists talked about concerned matters which nearly every adult and many juveniles knew quite a bit about simply by living in a modern society. But environmentalists make claims allegedly based on chemistry and advanced biology. There are experts who have offered refutations, but these books are not easy reading, since they concern matters which cannot be verified so easily through introspection upon the familiar. On top of this, most scientific research is now funded by government or Leftist foundations; and the committees that approve research usually consists of politically correct people. University trained writers on philosophy routinely denigrate objectivity, and so there is encouragement for ambitious people who were trained as scientists to fudge the facts when doing so will advance their careers.

Doxa: Ayn Rand cannot be blamed for this in any way; she was one of the first to denounce political environmentalism.

Stanford: At present, the country is being flooded with immigrants, both legal and illegal. The legal number alone is at present about one million a year. Too many have come in to be successfully Americanized. The border with Mexico has turned into a sieve. Immigrants from that country celebrate the 5th of May instead of the 4th of July; many of them refuse to learn English. Organizations have been formed calling for union of the American South-West with Mexico or the formation of a new country called, "Azatland." Then there are the terrorists who come to harm us.

Doxa: Ayn Rand would have opposed extending welfare benefits to such people, as her principles demand. She would have favored honest investigations into terrorist groups, not the phony stuff they are doing today, where honest dissenters are set up and framed.

Stanford: But what about laws restricting the numbers of legal immigrants? On her principles, it is hard to see how she could have prevented the flood. To her mind, a government is just an institution with a legal monopoly of force operating over a specific territory. She could stipulate that every one of these people have the means to take care of themselves. But that would be consistent with unscrupulous employers bringing droves of low-paid people across the border to work for practically nothing and through their actions, drive down the living standards. It would also be consistent with terrorist sympathizers setting up dummy corporations as shells for bringing their bad friends into this country.

Doxa: One remedy that the people who did not like it would have is to refuse to trade with those doing this.

Stanford: That might work; but then again, it might not. Under capitalism, people could make a profit by secretly trading with the people on the blacklist, making it possible for the latter to win.

The only sure way to prevent that or a similar scenario is to legally lower the immigration gates. This can be done under the old social contract theory of John Locke which the founders of the country generally accepted. According to this theory, the people who formed the government would collectively own all the public property. The use of this type of property would be left to the care and protection of the government. In terms of this theory, it would be possible to declare that the borders of the country be public property. The few private properties touching the borders would have an easement across them, stipulating that no one could cross who was not a citizen. Given the above, it would be perfectly legal for such a government to cut down or even stop any future immigration.

The social contract theory could allow for eminent domain and easements like that; A.R.'s theory could not. Under her theory, it would be totally a matter of what two or more individuals or firms had agreed to. Since no force or fraud was involved in bringing foreigners across to work, the law would have to protect this agreement.

Philosophus: Let it also be remembered that the social contract theory as applied to the United States led in about a hundred and fifty years to a welfare state; the patriots who wanted to follow George Washington's advice were ridiculed as "isolationists." Under a social contract, each generation, once it is of age, has the right to confirm or deny it. They also have the right to revise it, which they now do continuously through legislation and by accepting left-wing judicial rulings. The social contract can degenerate into mere community standards without much more than a lack of attention.

But a social contract could be written which would explicitly embody individual rights and which could call for its dissolution in the event that certain carefully defined principles had been compromised—Ayn Rand once suggested that there be a Constitutional amendment along these lines. In the final analysis, however, no arrangement among men can continue unless a sizable number of its participants are willing that it should. Men laugh at the stone boasts of Shelley's Ozymandias.

Stanford: And in the meantime the immigration crisis mounts.

Philosophus: Suppose that the cry against additional immigration should result in new legislation forbidding it. This would, of course, require that the majority of those interested in politics are behind it and that they are willing to push through with enough effort to win. To succeed, they will have to overcome legal delays (as in California), lobbying by such foreign governments as Mexico, the trendy internationalism which the leadership of both parties have championed—and even violence from those on the other side.

This, of course, is possible. But it would take years to accomplish. Let us agree that the present immigration laws are a disgrace. Even so—would it not be the case that the same effort required to muster public opinion behind the proposed change in the laws could simply be used to get people to change their minds about the value of new immigration? And that mental change would induce free men and women to perform the appropriate actions in their private lives without requiring the assistance of additional legislation?

I will explain. Suppose that instead of agitating for political action, those who wanted the new restrictive laws had simply decided to support only those businesses that did not hire new immigrants, that did not endorse in one way or another the internationalism that would savage our borders—in other words, that these advocates of change confined themselves strictly to the weapons of freedom: namely, acceptance, support, or withdraw. Suppose further that instead of acting like an angry mob, the opposing side quietly supported business interests that favored immigrants, endorsed its artists, stood behind the positive values which the idea of open borders engenders—in short, behaved in the dignified manner that once characterized believers in liberal causes like the late Adlai Stevenson. Then each side would follow its own way in an atmosphere of mutual toleration. (True toleration, remember, does not imply approval. It simply means that one will not attempt to prevent the other side through coercive action.) The probable result would be that there would be less immigration and that which took place would mostly be of the kind that was beneficial.

Penelope: But that could not be done because it would be against the anti-discrimination laws.

Philosophus: Exactly! Where reason is not allowed to have its way, the road ahead is full of pitfalls and boulders. And that, unfortunately, is how it is so often in politics. So instead of the two sides acting separately to get individuals to apply their ideas in their private lives, it will be a contest between the politicians and their supporters.

Doxa: At least, Ayn Rand tried to rescue this country from all that. In the 1940's, while some of the direct descendants of the very Puritans that landed at Plymouth Rock were denouncing Congressional investigations of Communism in government and in the entertainment industry, this Russian immigrant penned these luminous lines:

> Now if the Hollywood Ten claim that a public revelation of their communist ideas damages them because it will cost them their Hollywood jobs—then this means that they are holding these jobs by fraud, that their employers, their co-workers and their public do not know the nature of their ideas and would not want to deal with them if such knowledge were made available. If so, then the communists, in effect, are asking that the government protect them in the perpetuation of a fraud. They are demanding protection for their right to practice deceit upon others. They are saying, in effect: I am cheating those with whom I am dealing and if you reveal this, you will cause me to lose my racket—which is interference with my freedom of speech and belief.[5]

Some will complain that Ayn Rand had weakened what was left of the old order that the English Protestants had founded. In a way, she did. But, for her defense, one should recall the reply that Napoleon once made to some critics: that he had not stolen the crown of France, but found it lying in a gutter.

Penelope: Yes. She was like a good Sadducee.

Doxa: It wasn't the hardline anti-Communists in the United States and Western Europe that finally caused the Reds to abandon their system. That movement shored up America during the late forties and early fifties, but it went into a slow decline after the fall of Senator Joseph McCarthy in 1954. It was intellectuals like Ayn Rand; it was economists, like Ludwig Von Mises, Henry Hazlitt, F. A. Hayek, Murray Rothbard, and Milton Friedman who brought about the great change. They exposed the intellectual fallacies in socialism. The Marxist-Leninists were what is fashionably called today, "secular humanists;." despite all their well documented crimes, they accepted science. This is not to say that they quit because they were truth-seekers; quite to the contrary. But when the verdict of science turned against them, they knew that they must either knock off the West in a hurry or give it up. They huffed and they puffed, but the West was still intact. They undermined it, but so deep were the foundations that the walls crumbled only a little. The second option had to be tried. The Soviet bosses calculated that if their retreat were constructed in a certain manner, they could remain in power almost everywhere, even after they had abandoned the very *raison d'etre* for their might. It was a dangerous gamble. Apparently they won.

Now, it may be that Ayn Rand and these economists do not have all the answers for the crisis looming before us. But they should be saluted.

Penelope: No question about it. Their work in bringing about the retirement of Communism was great. But the former Red rulers are still in positions of power where they can plot our downfall.

Stanford: How sad it is that the country is in mortal danger, and all that these people here in this restaurant seem to be concerned with is a basketball game.

Philosophus: Modern life is dangerous.

Doxa: *(To Philosophus).* You came to your own philosophy after confronting Objectivism, didn't you?

Philosophus: Yes. Ayn Rand must be counted, prominently, among my philosophical antecedents.

Penelope: *(To Philosophus)* What do you call your new philosophy?

Philosophus: *"Factivity."*

ENDNOTES

DAY I - To America with Love

[1] William Buckley, Jr., "A Tribute To Barry Goldwater," *National Review #1*—331/3 RPM High Fidelity Record, (New York: National Review, Inc., 1960). "...the conservative spirit of America, a wasting battery perhaps, but one which like none other can still light up the world with incandescent flashes of courage and spirit and faith."

[2] Claudia Roth Pierpont, "Twilight Of The Goddess," *The New Yorker*, (July 24, 1995), p. 70. "As late as 1991, the Library of Congress found that a majority of Americans surveyed named 'Atlas Shrugged' as the book that had the most influenced their lives, after the Bible."

[3] Ayn Rand, *The Virtue Of Selfishness: A New Concept of Egoism With Additional Articles by Nathaniel Brandon*, (New York: Signet, 1964), p. 51.

[4] Barbara Brandon, *The Passion Of Ayn Rand*, (Garden City, New York: Doubleday, 1986), pp. 415-22.

DAY II - Ayn Rand's Philosophy of Objectivism

[1] Ayn Rand, *Ibid.*, p. 34.

[2] *Ibid.*, p. 16.

[3] *Ibid.*

[4] *Ibid.*, p. 50.

[5] *Ibid.*, p. 18.

[6] *Ibid.*, p. 16.

[7] *Ibid.*, p. 27.

[8] Ayn Rand, *Atlas Shrugged*, (New York: Random House, 1957), p. 210.

9 Rand, *The Virtue Of Selfishness*, p. 16.

10 *Ibid.*, p. 19. "The best illustration of this can be seen in the rare, freak cases of children who are born without the capacity to experience pain; such children do not survive for long; they have no means of discovering what can injure them, no warning signals,..."

11 Leonard Peikoff, *Objectivism: The Philosophy Of Ayn Rand*, (New York, NY: Duton, 1991), p. 210.

12 *Ibid.*

13 *Ibid.*

14 *Ibid.*, p. 36.

15 *Ibid.*, p. 18.

16 Ayn Rand, *For The New Intellectual*, (New York: New American Library, 1961), p. 22.

17 Rand, *Atlas Shrugged*, p. 942.

18 Wallace Matson, "Rand On Concepts," *The Philosophic Thought of Ayn Rand*, ed. by Douglas J. Den Uyl and Douglas B Rasmussen, (Urban and Chicago, Ill: University of Illinois Press, 1986), p. 33.

19 Peikoff, *op. cit.*, p. 35.

20 V.I. Lenin, *Materialism And Empirio-Criticism: Critical Comments On A Reactionary Philosophy*, (Moscow: Progress Publishers, 1968), p. 359.

21 Gustave Wetter, *Dialectical Materialism: A Historical and Systematic Survey of Philosophy in the Soviet Union*, tr. Peter Heath, (New York: Frederick A. Praeger, 1958), pp. 281-6. Wetter gives a number of quotations from Marxist-Leninist classics to show these two aspects of their theory. Typical of these are from Stalin: "That the world is by its nature *material*, that the multifold phenomena of the world constitute different forms of 'matter in motion', that 'the world develops in accordance with the laws of movements of matter' and therefore 'stands in no need of a 'universal spirit,'to explain it.'" (p. 283). Stalin also asserted that dialectical materialism is "contrary to idealism, which denies the possibility of knowing the world and its laws, which does not believe

in the authenticity of our knowledge, does not recognize objective truth, and holds that the world is full of 'things-in-themselves' that can never be known to science....(pp. 283-84).

[22] Frederick Engels, *Ludwig Feuerbach and the Outcome of Classical German Philosophy*, ed. by C.P. Dutt, (New York, NY: International Publishers, 1941), p. 21.

[23] Brandon, *op. cit.*, pp. 200-3.

DAY III - Perception

[1] Peikoff, *op. cit.*, p. 38.

[2] Ayn Rand, *Introduction To Objectivist Epistemology, With An Additional Essay by Leonard Peikoff, Expanded 2nd Edition*, ed. By Harry Binswanger and Leonard Peikoff, (New York: Meridian, 1990), p. 5.

[3] Rand, *Ibid.*

[4] *Ibid.*

[5] *Ibid.*

[6] Ayn Rand, *Philosophy: Who Needs It*, (New York: Bobbs-Merrill, 1982), p.6.

[7] Ayn Rand, *Introduction To Objectivist Epistemology*, p. 6.

[8] *Ibid.*, p. 7.

[9] *Ibid.*, p. 6.

[10] Peikoff, *op. cit.*, p. 75.

[11] Rand, *op. cit.*, pp. 62-3.

[12] John W. Robbins, *Answer To Ayn Rand: A Critique of the Philosophy of Objectivism*, (Washington, D.C.: Mount Vernon Publishing Co., 1974), p. 3. "The point is that such experiments do not (and cannot) measure perceptual as opposed to conceptual ability: adult human beings cannot observe without implicitly (or subconsciously) counting.... Rand's experiment simply measures how fast persons can count. The concepts are there inescapably. So it is with the crows. Just as a person can count only so far in a split second, so a crow

can count only so far in a much longer time. Just as a person inevitably loses track of his counting after a certain number of units have been counted, so a crow loses track—after only three units have been counted. The fact Rand says the crows discriminated three *units* obviously implies that crows have limited conceptual ability, not that they have none at all."

13 Peikoff, *op. cit.*, p. 76.

14 *Ibid.*, p. 78.

15 *Ibid.*

16 Ayn Rand, *For The New Intellectual*, (New York: Signet, 1961), pp. 29-30.

17 James L. Gould and Grant Gould, *The Animal Mind*, (New York: Scientific American Library, 1994), 129.

18 Peikoff, *op. cit.*, p. 79.

19 Rand, *op. cit.*, 170.

20 *Ibid.*, p. 16.

21 *Ibid.*, p. 169.

22 Sir William Hamilton, quoted by Robert Perceval Graves, M.A., in *Life Of Sir William Rowan Hamilton, Vol. I*, (Dublin, Hodges, Figgis, & Col, 1882), p. 643. Reprinted, New York: Arno Press, Inc., 1975.

23 Rand, *op. cit.*, p. 31.

24 *Ibid.*, p. 29.

25 John Cook Wilson, *Statement and Inference, With Other Philosophical Papers*, (Oxford At The Clarendon Press: 1926), pp. 324-25. "It is of the essence of the perception of melody as opposed to that of harmony that a relation should be perceived or apprehended between successive sounds as successive. For this it is necessary that a past sound should be in some sense retained: it must be in some sense remembered, for clearly without memory we should only be conscious of the sound at the particular moment and not of its relations to the sound which was in the past and has ceased. Now, if the retention were the retention of the memory-image of the sound and this last were an actual present sensation of sound, the comparison and memory necessary to melody, or rather the perception of melody by a series of sounds, would result

in the simultaneous presence to consciousness of the sounds constituting the series, or rather of actual sounds equivalent to them. This, of course, would yield the perception of harmony, if the interval between successive notes were constant, and of discord, if they were not; it would not yield a consciousness of melody."

[26] John Stuart Mill, editorial note no. 38 in James Mill's *Analysis Of The Phenomena Of The Human Mind, Ed. With Additional Notes By John Stuart Mill, Vol. I*, (London: Longmans, Green, Reader, and Dyer, 1878), pp. 413-423.

[27] Rand, *op. cit.*, p. 159.

[28] *Ibid.*, p. 260.

[29] Peikoff, *op. cit.*, p. 20.

[30] John Stuart Mill, editorial note no. 38, *Ibid., Vol. II*, pp. 198-9.

[31] Wilson, *Ibid.*, p. 516.

DAY IV - Forms of Perception vs. Perception

[1] Peikoff, *op. cit.*, pp. 39.

[2] Rand, *Introduction to Objectivist Epistemology*, p. 6

[3] Peikoff, *op. cit.*, pp. 41-42.

[4] *Ibid.*, p. 42.

[5] *Ibid.*

[6] *Ibid.*, p. 45.

[7] *Ibid.*, p. 46.

[8] *Ibid.*, pp. 46-47.

[9] *Ibid.*, p. 117. "To be 'objective' in one's conceptual activities is volitionally to adhere to reality by following certain rules of method, a method based on facts *and* appropriate to man's form of cognition."

[10] *Ibid.*

[11] Arthur O. Lovejoy, *The Revolt Against Dualism: An Inquiry Concerning the Existence of Ideas*, (La Salle,

Illinois, 1960, Second edition), p. 120. "'Intrinsic character' here seem to be characters not conditioned by the
functioning of a percipient organism."

[12] Peikoff, *op. cit.*, p. 149.

[13] *Ibid.*, p. 24.

[14] *Ibid.*, p. 112.

[15] Rand, *op. cit.*, p. 280.

[16] *Ibid.*

[17] Lovejoy, *op. cit.*, p. 152.

[18] Peikoff, *op. cit.*, p. 112.

[19] Lovejoy, *op. cit.*, pp. 122-123.

[20] Rand, *op. cit.*, p. 280. "You perceive the attribute
<of length> by means of your eyes, but you can also
perceive it by means of touch. And both these enter your
mind as certain sensations conveyed by certain kinds
of nerves and nerve endings in response to certain
stimuli. Therefore, if you say that taste is a 'secondary
quality' but length is a 'primary' one, you are open to
the same criticism."

[21] *Ibid.*, pp. 279-80.

[22] *Ibid.*, p. 280.

[23] Cf., Wilson, *op. cit.*, p. 803; also, p. 70, 74.

[24] Rand, *op. cit.*, pp. 280-1.

[25] Wilson, *op. cit.*, pp. 781-782.

[26] *Ibid.*, p. 780. "There could be no science of the 'extension in itself' any more than of the thing in itself.
Moreover, science assumes *not* that the extension of the
blot that I see is *like* the extension of the thing, or *represents* the extension, but that it *is* the actual extension in
the body. It is visual extension simply as real extension
seen."

DAY V - The Conceptual Level of Consciousness

[1] *Ibid.*, pp. 6, 14, 13.

[2] *Ibid.*, 14. "Similarity is grasped *perceptually*; in observing it, man is not and does not have to be aware of the fact that it involves a matter of measurement. It is the task of philosophy and of science to identify that fact."

[3] *Ibid.*, p. 6.

[4] Wallace Matson, "Rand On Concepts," *Ibid.*, p.24.

[5] Wilson, *op. cit.*, p. 41. "Nor should we seriously try to find out the meaning of a definition of a circle by examining various circles and asking what they had in common."

[6] Rand, *op. cit.*, p. 7.

[7] *Ibid.*

[8] *Ibid.*, p. 7.

[9] *Ibid.*, p. 9.

[10] *Ibid.*, p. 63

[11] *Ibid.*

[12] *Ibid.*, p. 13.

[13] *Ibid.*, p. 12.

[14] Peikoff, *op. cit.*, p. 85.

[15] Rand, *op. cit.*, 186.

[16] Euclid, *The Thirteen Books Of Euclid's Elements*, Tr. From the Text Of Heiberg with Introduction And Commentary by Sir Thomas Heath, 2nd Ed., (New York: Dover Publications, Inc., 1956), *Vol. 1.*, p. 154. "**Rectilinear figures** are those which are contained by straight lines, **trilateral** figures being those contained by three, **quadrilateral** those contained by four...."

[17] Wilson, *Ibid.*, p. 334; See also, *Ibid.*, pp. 307, 333-4.

[18] Rand, *op. cit.*, p. 7.

[19] Robbins, *Answer To Ayn Rand*, p. 31. "If the relationships exist they are not solely in the consciousness of the observer: they are external to the observer...."

[20] *Ibid.*, p. 6.

[21] Robbins, *op. cit.*, p. 31.

[22] Rand, *op. cit.*, p. 14.

[23] *Ibid.*, p. 15.

[24] *Ibid.*

[25] *Ibid.*, p. 13.

[26] *Ibid.*, p. 146.

[27] *Ibid.*

[28] Wilson, *Ibid.*, pp. 340-41. "Now, if we notice a particular A_1, we cannot apprehend it as a mere individual, but as having some distinctive quality A, this quality being individualized in A_1. To notice the quality as distinct we must distinguish it from some other quality; thus we need to notice at least two individuals A_1 and B_1, where A and B are distinct. We are *ex hypothesi* concerned with the case where A and B are noticed or apprehended for the first time. If A_1 is a particular colour, B_1 is not necessarily another colour; B_1 might be for instance a sound. Such distinction classifies the distinguished and involves the apprehension of a universal, as the being common to them, even if only the universal of something-in-general. Each as distinguished is apprehended as *a* being.... We recognize difference and identity of being in A_1 and B_1, because we have apprehended in them two different forms of being. But in thus noticing A in A_1 for the first time, we have *ex hypothesi* not more than one instance of A before us in apprehension."

[29] Rand, *op cit.*, p. 145.

[30] *Ibid.*, p. 11.

[31] *Ibid.*, p. 7. Unfortunately, a key term is rendered as "establishd" through a typographical error in my edition. I have quoted it as the author undoubtedly had it.

[32] *Ibid.*, p. 63.

[33] Augustus De Morgan, *The Connexion Of Number And Magnitude: An Attempt To Explain The Fifth Book Of Euclid,* (London: Taylor And Walton, 1836), p. 42.

[34] Robbins, *op. cit.*, p. 36.

[35] Rand, *Ibid.*, p. 198.

[36] John Cook Wilson, *On The Traversing of Geometrical Figures,* (Oxford At Clarendon Press, 1905), 153 pp., plus notes on reciprocating figures.

[37] Rand, *op. cit..*, p. 7.

[38] *Ibid..*

[39] *Ibid.*, p. 23.

[40] *Ibid..*

[41] *Ibid..*

[42] *Ibid.*, p. 12.

[43] *Ibid.*, pp. 31-32.

[44] *Ibid.*, p. 142.

[45] *Ibid.*, p. 36.

[46] *Ibid.*, p. 33.

[47] Joseph Stalin, "Dialectical and Historical Materialism," *Problems of Leninism*, (Moscow, English Version). P. 571.

[48] Sir William Hamilton, From "Poetry," Graves, *Ibid.*, p. 317.

[49] Rand, *op. cit.*, p. 15. " The first concepts man forms are concepts of entities—since entities are the only primary existents. (Attributes cannot exist by themselves, they are merely the characteristics of entities; motions are motions of entities; relationships are relationships among entities.)"

[50] Wilson, *Statement and Inference,*, p. 337. "Even if we have had but one experience of a given quality, when we recall it in memory we can think of other instances of it as possible. This, put merely in the strict form of entertaining the question whether there could be other instances of it would be impossible unless we apprehended it as more than merely individual. The same thing follows from our power of *imagining* different instances of it."

DAY VI - Definitions and Universals

[1] Rand, *op. cit.*, pp. 43-44.

[2] Douglas J. Den Uyl and Douglas B. Rasmussen, "Ayn Rand's Realism," *The Philosophic Thought of Ayn Rand*, p. 16. "It is important to realize that Rand does not consider a concept to signify all the characteristics of its referents in a Leibnizian way...."

[3] Wilson, *op. cit.*, p. 382.

[4] H. W. B. Joseph, *An Introduction To Logic, 2nd Edition, Revised*, (Oxford At The Clarendon Press, 1916), 608 pp, including index.

[5] Philipp Frank, *Einstein: His Life and Times*, tr. George Rosen, (New York: Alfred A. Knopf, 1953), pp. 165-6.

[6] Herbert Ives, "Derivation of the Mass-Energy Relation, " *Journal Of The Optical Society Of America, Vol 42, no.1* (August 1952), pp. 541-42; reprinted in *The Einstein Myth and the Ives Papers*, ed. with comments by Richard Hazelett and Dean Turner, (Old Greenwich, Conn: The Devin-Adair Company, 1979), pp. 182-85.

[7] Euclid, *Elements, Book 1*, Definition 2.

[8] Rand, *op. cit.*, p. 49.

[9] Ayn Rand, "The Nature of Government," *The Virtue Of Selfishness*, p. 125.

[10] *Ibid.*, p. 128.

[11] Justice Story, *Commentaries on the Constitution*, chap. 44, sec. 1897, quoted in George Anastaplo, *The Constitutionalist: Notes on the First Amendment*, (Dallas, Texas: Southern Methodist University Press, 1971), p. 672.

[12] Aristotle, *Politics*, Bk II, 1267-9. This point was made first made by a writer on gun control; but the name of that writer and the title of the book have been forgotten.

[13] Floyd Ratliff, "Contour And Contrast," *Scientific American*, Vo. 226, no.6, (June 1972), pp. 91-101.

[14] Rand, *Introduction To Objectivist Epistemology*, p. 47. "And for the very same reasons, a definition is false and worthless if it is not *contextually* absolute—if it does not specify the known relationships among existents (in terms of the known *essential* characteristics) or if it contradicts the known (by omission or evasion)."

[15] Peikoff, *op. cit.*, p. 173.

[16] *Ibid.*, p. 173-4.

[17] *Ibid.*, p. 176.

[18] *Ibid.*

[19] *Ibid.*

[20] Robbins, *op. cit.*, p. 42.

[21] Lovejoy, *op. cit.*, p. 123.

[22] Rand, *Introduction To The Objectivist Epistemology*, p. 239.

[23] *Ibid.*, p. 234.

[24] *Ibid.*, p. 24.

[25] *Ibid.*, p. 45. "When a given group of existents has more than one characteristic distinguishing it from other existents, man must observe the relationships among these various characteristics and discover the one on which all the others (or the greatest number of others) depend, i.e., the fundamental characteristics without which the others would not be possible."

[26] Wilson, *op. cit.*, p. 309. "So then the answer to the question 'what is the conception of X? would seem to be that is X, and therefore nugatory.... We might say that force is the cause of the body's state of rest or motion or to give some similar definition. Mathematicians like to say that force is that which changes, or tends to change, a body's existing state of rest or motion, but they would be very hard put to explain what they meant by *tends* to change. Or again one might say that cause is the necessitation of an event. But these expressions are only an explanation of the meaning of the words force and cause. Cause does not stand for anything different from necessitation of an event, and similarly for the answer given in the case of force. This shows that in the answer we are merely giving what is verbally different, in the form of a synonym for the word used in the question, to denote the object inquired about. Thus, it is really quite as nugatory to ask what is the conception of force or of cause as to ask what is our conception of blue."

[27] *Ibid.*, p. 586.

[28] *Ibid.*, p. 427.

[29] Leonard Peikoff, "The Analytic-Synthetic Dichotomy," in Ayn Rand's *Introduction To Objectivist Epistemology*, p. 110.

DAY VII - Axioms

[1] Rand, *op. cit.*, p. 60.

[2] *Ibid.*, p. 55.

[3] Lovejoy, *op. cit.*, pp. 390-91. "The notion of existence, which is so often treated as mysterious and incomprehensible, appears to be so only because it is fundamental in our thinking and irreducible; intelligence cannot take a single step without employing it. Those who think they have dispensed with it are transparently deceiving themselves. We are empirically acquainted with its meaning by ourselves being—and by the being, at any moment, of our present data. But we can, and must, and persistently do, extend it to objects and events to which we impute positions not our own in that order of temporal relations which we conceive as including and transcending our own position and that of our data."

[4] Rand, *op. cit.*, p. 58.

[5] *Ibid.*, p. 56.

[6] *Ibid.*, p. 55.

[7] Wilson, *op. cit.*, p. 458.

[8] Rand, *op. cit.*, p. 56.

[9] *Ibid.*

[10] Rev. James McCosh, L.L.D., *The Intuitions Of the Mind: Inductively Investigated*, 3rd ed., (New York: Robert Carter And Brothers, 1872), p. 178.

[11] Rand, *op. cit.*, p. 58.

[12]

Ibid., p. 58.

[13] Peikoff, *op. cit.*, p. 168.

[14] Wilson, *op. cit.*,p. 269. "The calculus can only show it is impossible that there should be such a quantity by conducting to an operation which we recognize as impossible, e.g. x = sin -1 a/b, where a/b is greater than unity and therefore x is determined to be an angle whose sine is greater than unity..... If we equated them to zero we should get a two-

fold false result. In the first place, to equate to zero does not show what we are seeking is impossible. Zero in the problem may refer to quantity measured in some definite way.... Secondly, if we equate impossibilities to zero, we thereby equate them to one another, and the result of these in algebra would be that all real quantities would have to be equated to one another."

[15] Harold Joachim, *The Nature of Truth: An Essay*, (Oxford At Clarendon, 1906), p. 130.

[16] Wilson, *op. cit.*, pp. 261-262. "Thus neither is a form of the other and neither is the general form of the statement or proposition. The general form itself cannot be symbolized by '(S)1 is B' or 'all A is B' or '(S)1A is B', or anything of that kind, any more than the universal of number can be expressed numerically, for such a universal cannot be odd or even. What then is the common form?

"From the side of apprehension or conception it is simply the idea of a general determination of the given conception, which is brought about by the act, whether of knowledge or opinion, which finds expression in the statement. Now, in seeking a new determination of the logical subject, we must have before us some positive conception of a kind of being in relation to which the determination is to be got, and this determination differentiates itself at once in two ways: either the being to which the positive conception refers belongs to the subject, or it does not. The assertion of the first is the affirmative statement, of the second is the negative.

"From the side of what is apprehended we may represent the matter thus. A given reality is definite and determinate, as opposed to having being in general or as opposed to some universal wider than itself, by having certain kinds of being and not having others. Its determinativeness therefore necessarily has these two aspects: the positive one, of the being which it has, and the negative one, of not having the other which it has, and the negative one, of not having the other kinds of being. An act of knowledge, whether judgment or not, is the apprehension of some determination which we have already apprehended in it. This is what determines the generic definition of statement of knowledge. As to the two special forms, the statement is affirmative if we apprehend another kind of being as possessed by the thing; that is, if we apprehend the positive determination, and negative if we apprehend some other kind of being as not possessed by it; in other words, if we apprehend the negative determination. Opinion and its statement are to be treated analogically."

[17] Rand, *op. cit.*, p. 241.

[18] Peikoff, *op. cit.*, p. 8. "The validation of axioms, however, is the simplest of all: sense perception."

[19] *Ibid.*, p. 13.

[20] *Ibid.*, p. 32.

[21] Friedrich Engels, *Herr Eugen Dühring's Revolution in Science: Anti-Dühring*, English translation, (Chicago: Charles H. Kerr & Co., 1935), p. p. 120. For Dühring's belief in the finiteness of the universe, Cf., pp. 47-49.

[22] Martha Hurst, "CAN THE LAW OF CONTRADICTION BE STATED WITHOUT REFERENCE TO TIME?", *Journal Of Philosophy*, Vol. XXXI,(Sept. 13, 1934), pp. 519-20.

[23] *Ibid.*, p. 520.

[24] Rand, *Atlas Shrugged*, p. 962. "The law of causality is the law of identity applied to action."

[25] Joseph, *op. cit.*, p. 420. {Joseph's book was sold and recommended by the Nathaniel Brandon Institute, an organization owned jointly by Ayn Rand and Nathaniel Brandon. It was authorized to market her philosophy throughout most of the 1960's.}

[26] Rand, *Introduction To Objectivist Epistemology*, p.242. "Prof. B: "Is 'fact' a concept like 'necessity' in the following respect? The referent of 'necessity' is the same in a sense as the referent of 'identity'; but 'necessity' is a concept which comes much later in the hierarchy and derives from our particular form of consciousness [i.e., from its volitional nature—see "The Metaphysical Versus the Manmade,' in *Philosophy: Who Needs It*]. It is a concept we need to distinguish things outside our control from things in our control."

"AR: 'Correct.'"

[27] Peikoff, *op. cit.*, p. 24.

[28] *Ibid.*.

[29] Rand, *op. cit.*, p. 6.

[30] Peikoff, *op. cit.*, p. 13. "In particular, the grasp of 'entity,' in conjunction with the closely following grasp of 'identity,' makes possible the discovery of the next important principle of metaphysics, the one that is the main subject of the present section: the law of causality."

[31] Rand, *Atlas Shrugged*, p. 962.

[32] Peikoff, *op. cit.* p. 31.

[33] Wilson, *op. cit.*, p. 630.

[34] Robbins, *op. cit.*, p. 52

[35] Rand, *Atlas Shrugged*, p. 942.

[36] Peikoff, *op. cit.*, p. 123.

[37] *Ibid.*, p. 35.

[38] *Ibid.*

[39] *Ibid.*

[40] Rand, *Introduction to Objectivist Epistemology*, p. 80.

[41] Lovejoy, *op. cit.*, p. 391.

[42] George V. Walsh, "Ayn Rand And The Metaphysics Of Kant," (Privately Printed: Delivered to the Ayn Rand Society of the American Philosophical Association, Eastern Division, Washington, D.C., Dec., 29, 1992), pp. 18-19. "There is a danger of not capturing Kant's meaning, therefore, if we interpret him as asserting that this world is a collective delusion, because collective delusions can be sorted out by empirical tests against a background of empirical reality. The *real difference* between Kant and Rand is accurately stated in her own words, interpreting *his metaphysics that* "reason [in his sense of the empirical understanding] and science are 'limited'...they are valid only so long as deal with this world...but they are impotent to deal with the fundamental issues of existence, which belong to the 'noumenal world.' She believes that the scientific method, keeping within the axiomatic concepts, is unlimited in its potential for knowledge; whereas, he believes that it is limited by the boundaries of

pure intuition. *This* is the fundamental metaphysical difference between them."

[43] Peikoff, *op. cit.*, 8.

[44] Rand, *Introduction To The Objectivist Epistemology*, p. 257.

DAY VIII - Time and Space

[1] Rand, *Introduction To Objectivist Epistemology*, p. 56.

[2] *Ibid.*, pp. 56-57.

[3] *Ibid.*, p. 257.

[4] *Ibid.*, p. 260.

[5] *Ibid.*, p. 259.

[6] Immanuel Kant, *Immanuel Kant's Critique Of Pure Reason*, tr. by F. Max Muller, 2nd ed. (London: The MacMillan Company, 1896), p. 24.

[7] Rand, *op. cit.*., p. 260.

[8] *Ibid.*, p. 259.

[9] Aristotle, *Physics*, Bk IV, line, 219. I accept the interpretation of John Stuart Mill on this difficult passage. J. S. Mill, Notes to James Mill's *Analysis, etc.*, II, pp. 136-7. "He then proceeds to exposition; and after remarking that Time is one and alike everywhere, amidst the greatest diversity of events succeeding each other—he says that it is not indeed identical with Motion, (as some theorists considered it), but that it is nevertheless inseparable from Motion being one of the aspects or appurtenances of Motion."

[10] After the meeting, **Miss Doxa** asked **Mr. Philosophus** the following question: Why would the non-universality of time destroy the syllogism.?

Philosophus: (A) The premises cannot be temporally conditioned. They must be valid at all times. For instance, the major and minor premises cannot be events preceding the conclusion. If they were, then they would have passed away by the time the conclusion was reached, destroying the necessary connections which make it valid. The conclusion would be left standing alone.[Cf., Wilson, *op. cit.*, p. 53.]

(B) However, as was already shown, in order that the syllogism not be a *petitio principii*, one of the premises must be known earlier than the other. The example of the minor premise being known earlier has already been given. There are also occasions knowledge of the major premise comes first. Given the standard syllogism, All A is B/ C is A/ *ergo*, C is B: It is possible that we might know that the major premise before we did the minor. To give a concrete example: Suppose we knew the major premise that *all poisons are dangerous*, but did not know whether a certain chemical was poisonous. Then it was proved to be such, producing the inevitable conclusion. [Cf., *Ibid.*, p. 464.]

With the syllogism, the argument must be independent of time, but one premise has to be known earlier than the other in order to remain an argument. If time were not a fact independent of all else but simply a nexus of some local relationships, then (A) could not hold because (B) would be radically immeshed in context; and this because there would be no universal time which transcended all the various contexts. *Before* and *after* would not the same everywhere. (Refer to the discussion at our last meeting of the attempt to reduce the eighteen year old boy's age to the number of times that the earth went around the sun without making reference to time.)

Doxa: Why couldn't the syllogism still be inviolate even though what was *earlier* to one nexus would be *later* to another and vise versa?

Philosophus: All categorical syllogisms involving time (especially causality) would lose their extension. They would have to be stated with the qualification that they apply only in a certain nexus. Either that, or they could be changed into hypothetical syllogisms, which have a lower, sometimes much lower claim to knowledge. Correspondingly, syllogisms involving time which are already hypothetical would become even more continent. Many disjunctive arguments would fail for similar reasons.

[11] Kant, *op. cit.*, p. 25.

[12] Lovejoy, *op. cit.*, p. 232.

[13] *Ibid.*, pp. 157, 163.

[14] Rand, *op. cit.*, p. 273.

[15] *Ibid.*, p. 148.

[16] *Ibid.*, p. 18.

[17] *Ibid.*, pp. 148-9.

[18] Rand, *Atlas Shrugged*, p. 275. "'...Hank, do you understand? Those men, long ago, tried to invent a motor that would draw static electricity from the atmosphere, convert it and create its own power as it went along. They couldn't do it. They gave it up.' She pointed at the broken shape. 'But there is.'"

[19] Harold Nordenson, *Relativity Time And Reality*, (London: George Allen and Unwin, Ltd., 1969), p. 17. "It is therefore primarily a physical theory, as has been clearly emphasized by Einstein himself. The same is declared by A.S. Eddington in his book: *The Mathematical Theory Of Relativity.*"

[20] Albert Einstein, *Relativity: The Special and the General Theory*, tr. Robert W. Lawson, (New York: Crown Publishers, Inc., 1960), p. 22.

[21] *Ibid.*, p. 26.

[22] P. Bridgman, The Logic Of Modern Physics, quoted by Arthur Lovejoy, "The Dialectical Argument Against Absolute Simultaneity," reprinted in Turner and Hazelett, *op. cit.*, p. 240.

[23] Lovejoy, *Ibid.*, p. 243.

[24] Nordenson, *op.* cit., pp. 53-66.

[25] Lovejoy, *op. cit.*, p. 244. "You can not say that while S moves to the right S' moves to the left, if there are in reality simply two distinct 'whiles,' one definable solely with reference to S and the other solely with reference to S'; for in that case, you will have isolated the two systems so completely from one another that the relation called 'motion' can no longer be conceived to subsist between them."

[26] Einstein, *op. cit.*, p. 155.

[27] *Ibid.*.

[28] *Ibid.* I am indebted to Gerhard Kraus, who makes this point in his book, *Has Hawking erred?* (London, England: Janus Publishing Co., 1993), pp. 55-56.

[29] Turner and Hazelett, *op.cit.*, p. 15.

[30] Peikoff, *op. cit.*, p. 148.

[31] Lillian R. Lieber (drawings by Hugh Gray Lieber), *The Einstein Theory Of Relativity*, (New York: Holt, Rinehart And Winston, 1945), p. 88.

DAY IX - Ayn Rand and V.I. Lenin

[1] V. I. Lenin, *Materialism And Empirio-Criticism: Critical Comments On A Reactionary Philosophy*, p. 119.

[2] Robbins, *op. cit.*, pp. 46, 100, 48, 49, 73, 82-83, 85, 87, 107.

[3] Chris Matthew Sciabarra, *Ayn Rand: The Russian Radical*, (University Park, Penn.: The Pennsylvania State University Press, 1995), p. 403 n. 6.

[4] Barbara Brandon, *op. cit.*, p. 3.

[5] *Ibid.*, p. 60.

[6] *Ibid.*, p. 42.

[7] *Ibid.*

[8] Sciabarra, *op. cit.*, pp. 87-88.

[9] *Ibid.*, pp. 85-86.

[10] *Ibid.*, p. 87. "Consequently, in 1921, Lossky—officially— taught no university courses." "Sorokin adds that those professors who were barred from teaching were also barred from organizing special alternative courses."

[11] Lenin, *op. cit.*, p. 255.

[12] Cf., DAY II.

[13] Joseph Stalin, *op. cit.*, p. 570.

[14] Peikoff, *op. cit.*, p. 123.

[15] Stalin, *op. cit.*, p. 570.

[16] Peikoff, *op. cit.*, p. 123.

[17] Cf., DAY II

[18] Sciabarra, *op. cit.* , p. 3

[19] *Ibid.*, pp. 10, 14, 24, 25, 68, 106, 158, 166, 221-22, 243, 247,

[20] Rand, *Introduction To Objectivist Epistemology*, p. 249.

[21] Lenin, *op. cit.*, p. 81.

[22] *Ibid.*, p. 271.

[23] *Ibid.*, p. 290.

[24] M. A. Leonov, quoted in Wetter, *op. cit.*, p. 504.

[25] M. B. Mitin, quoted in *Ibid.*

[26] Brandon, *op. cit.*, p. 293.

[27] Pavel Sudoplatov and Anatoli Sudoplatov, *Special Tasks: The Memoirs Of An Unwanted Witness—A Soviet Spymaster*, (Boston: Little, Brown and Company, 1994), pp. 3, 86. 172, 193-94. *National Review*, Vol. 46, no. 10 (May 30, 1994), p. 36.

[28] V. I. Lenin, *Materialism and Empirio-Criticism*, 392 pages with an index of names.

[29] *Ibid.*, p. 297.

[30] *Ibid.*, p. 256.

[31] W. T. Stace, *The Philosophy Of Hegel: A Systematic Exposition*, (New York: Dover Publications, 1955), p. 72. "If the object is something quite different from that which thought makes of it, then subject and object, knowing and being, are two incommensurable opposite realities, facing each other, cut off from each other by an impassable chasm. The object is unknowable." The difference between the Hegelian and the Marxist, of course, is the former regards thought as the primary while the latter takes the opposite position.

[32] *Ibid.*, p. 73. "This stone is certainly external to me. It is not-me. This is the separation of knowing and being. But the stone is still *within* the unity of thought. It is not external to me in the sense that it is something utterly *outside* thought, unknowable. This is the identity of knowing and being." Reverse this, putting matter first and you will understand the perspective of Dialectical Materialism.

[33] V. I. Lenin, "Philosophical Notebooks," *Collected Works*, Vol. 38, tr. by Clemens Dutt, (Moscow: Progress Publishers, 1968), p. 140.

[34] Engels, *op. cit.*, p. 121.

[35] Lenin, *op. cit.*, p. 140.

[36] *Ibid.*, p. 259. Cf, Wetter, *op. cit.* , p. 337. "Various 20th-century 'metaphysicians', such as P. Struve and V. Chernov, attempted to resolve this antimony by asserting that there is actually no contradiction at all; if one divides up the whole course traversed by the moving body into a series of minute sections, or points, the moving body occupies a point in space at each single point in time; at one moment it is at one point, at the next moment it is at the next point, and so on. Lenin repudiated this sort of argument; it derives motion, which is continuous, from a sum of states of rest."

[37] Lenin, *Ibid.*, p. 258.

[38] *Ibid.*

[39] Wetter, *op. cit.*, p. 304. Referring to the viewpoint of Dialectical Materialism, he writes: "There is nothing which is not spatially extended; but nor, on the other hand, is there any space which is not occupied with matter. 'All space is filled with matter.' The same applies to time. Nothing can be located out of time, nor yet, conversely, 'can there be any time with nothing in it.' Matter therefore exists in space and time as its modes of existence but is not on that account to be identified with them."

[40] *Ibid.*

[41] *Ibid.*, p. 308.

[42] *Ibid..*

[43] Wilson, *op. cit.*, pp. 794-6. Here, he brings out that in optical reflection, we perceive the object where it is not.

[44] Lenin, *op. cit.*, p. 222.

[45] Joseph Stalin, "Marxism and The Problem of Linguistics, "quoted in Wetter, *op. cit.*, p. 264

DAY X - Facts and Universals

[1] Wilson, *op. cit.*, p. 672.
[2] *Ibid.*, p. 711.
[3] *Ibid.*, p. 676.
[4] *Ibid.*
[5] *Ibid.*, p. 187.
[6] *Ibid.*, p. 352.
[7] Rand, *op. cit.*, p. 241-45.
[8] *Ibid.*, p. 56.
[9] *Ibid.*, p.55.

DAY XI - The Rational Base of Ethics

[1] Rand, *Introduction To Objectivist Epistemology*, p. 33.
[2] Rand, *Atlas Shrugged*, p. 1013.
[3] *Ibid.* , p. 939.
[4] Donald E. Mansell, *The Mystery Of Consciousness*, (Boise, Idaho, Pacific Press Publishing Association, 1988), p. 35. "It goes without saying that 'breath of life' is not simply the air we breathe. No amount of air pumped into a lifeless corpse can restore it to life and consciousness. But breath or breathing is an evidence that the life-principle is present. Hence the Bible uses breath to symbolize the life-principle."
[5] Rand, *Introduction To Objectivist Epistemology*, p.148.
[6] *Ibid.*
[7] Rand, *Atlas Shrugged*, p. 960.
[8] Rand, *Letters Of Ayn Rand*, (New York, Dutton, 1995), p. 185.
[9] Rand, *Virtue Of Selfishness*, p. 16.
[10] Peikoff, *op. cit.*, p. 245. "The intrinsicist school holds that values, like universals or essences, are features of reality independent of consciousness (and of life). The good, accordingly, is divorced from goals, consequences, and beneficiaries."

[11] Ayn Rand, *Atlas Shrugged*, p. 939.

[12] *Ibid.*

[13] *Ibid.*

[14] *Ibid.*

[15] *The Century Dictionary and Cyclopedia With A New Atlas Of The World: A Work Of General Reference In All Departments Of Knowledge, VIII*, (New York: The Century Co., 1911), p. 5478.

[16] Auguste Compte, quoted in translation from the French by John Stuart Mill, *Auguste Compte and Positivism*, (Ann Arbor, Michigan: Ann Arbor Paperbacks, The University Press, 1961), p. 140.

DAY XII - Free Will

[1] Peikoff, *op. cit.*, p. 70.

[2] *Ibid.*, p. 68.

[3] *Ibid.*

[4] Charles Renouvier, quoted in William James' *The Letters of William James*, ed. by Henry James, (Boston: Atlantic Monthly Press, 1920), p. 147.

[5] Robert Hollinger, "Ayn Rand's Epistemology in Historical Perspective," *The Philosophic Thought of Ayn Rand*, p. 47.

[6] Peikoff, *op. cit.*, p. 59.

[7] Roger Olaf Egeberg, *The General: Mac Arthur and the Man He Called 'Doc'*, (New York: Hippocrene Books, 1983), pp.156-57.

[8] Joseph, *op. cit.* p. 502. "We are said to **explain**, when a conjunction of elements or features in the real, whose connexion is not intelligible, from a consideration of themselves, is made clear through connexions shown between them and others."

[9] Rand, *Atlas Shrugged p. 939.*

[10] Jay Livingston and Ray Evans, "Qui Sera, Sera or Whatever will be will Be," (Artists Music, Inc., 1955).

DAY XIII - Money

[1] Rand, *Atlas Shrugged*, p. 387. "Those pieces of paper, which should have been gold, are a token of honor...."

[2] Ayn Rand, *Philosophy: Who Needs It*, p. 154.

[3] Ayn Rand, *The Fountainhead*, (Indianapolis: The Bobbs-Merrill Company, 1943), p. 10.

[4] Rand, *Atlas Shrugged*, p. 391

[5] Milton Friedman and Anna Jacobson Schwartz, *A Monetary History of the United States*, (Princeton, NJ: Princeton University, 1963), pp. 166-7; R.G. Hawtrey, *The Gold Standard in Theory and Practice*, (London: Longmans, Green, 1931), p. 74.

[6] F.A. Walker, *International Bimetallism*, (New York: Henry Holt and Company, 1896), p. 122.

[7] *Ibid.*, pp. 179-81.

[8] Friedman and Schwartz, *op. cit.*, p. 134.

[9] George H. Shibley, *Stable Money, New Freedom, and Safe Banking, Provided in the Democratic Banking and Currency Bill, with Three Exceptions*, 63rd Congress, 1st Session, Doc. NO. 135, p. 22.

[10] W. Kemmerer, "The Recent Rise in the Price of Silver," *Quarterly Journal of Economics*, Vo. XXVI (1912), p. 462.

[11] Friedman and Schwartz, *op. cit.*, p. 135.

[12] Walker, *op. cit.*, p. 122.

[13] *Ibid..*, pp. 122-23.

[14] *Ibid.*, pp. 196-97.

[15] *Ibid.*, pp. 94-95.

[16] Murray N. Rothbard, *What Has Government Done to Our Money?* (Auburn, Alabama: Praxeology Press, 1990, orig. 1963), pp. 47-52.

[17] *Ibid.*, p.50.

[18] Alan Greenspan, "Gold and Economic Freedom," in Ayn Rand's *Capitalism: The Unknown Ideal, With Additional Articles by Nathaniel Brandon, Alan Greenspan, and Robert Hessen*, (New York: New American Library, 1967), p. 98.

[19] Charles Holt Carroll, *Organization of Debt Into Currency and Other papers*, ed. by Edward C. Simmons, (Princeton, NJ: D. Van Nostrand Company, Inc., 1964), pp. 74-94; 136-175; 349-358.

[20] Thomas McClary, "Banking and Currency Reform. Its Necessity. Its Possibility." 62nd Congress, 2nd Session, *Document No. 295*.

[21] Rand, *Atlas Shrugged*, p. 391.

[22] Peter Erickson, *The New Introduction To THE TRIPARTITE SYSTEM: A Monetary Program for Americans*, (Portland, OR: Privately Printed, 1975), 50 pp.

[23] Isabel, Paterson, *The God Of The Machine*, (Caldwell, ID: Caxton Printers, 1943), p. 213.

DAY XIV - Conclusion

[1] Alexis De Tocqueville, *Democracy In America*, tr. Henry Reeve, Esq., (New York: Adlard And Saunders, 1838), p. 165. (Reprinted, New York: Classics Of Liberty Library, 1992).

[2] Michael Chevalier, *Society, Manners & Politics IN THE UNITED STATES: Being a SERIES OF LETTERS ON NORTH AMERICA*, tr. (Boston: Weeks, Jordan and Company, 1839), p. 368. (Reprinted, New York: Augustus Kelley, Publishers, 1966).

[3] N.C. Brooks, *A Complete History Of The Mexican War: Its Causes, Conduct, And Consequences: Comprising An account From Its Commencement To The Treaty Of Peace*, (Philadelphia: Grigg, Elliot & Co., 1849), 558 pp.

[4] Van Wyck Brooks, *New England: Indian Summer, 1865-1915*, (Chicago: University Of Chicago Press, 1950), 557 pp.

[5] Ayn Rand, "Notes on the Thomas Committee," *The Intellectual Activist*, Vo. 7, No. 6, November 1993), p. 5.

BIBLIOGRAPHY

BOOKS

Anastaplo, George, *The Constitutionalist: Notes on the First Amendment*, Dallas, Texas: Southern Methodist University Press, 1971.

Aristotle, *The Basic Works Of Aristotle*, Edited and with an introduction by Richard McKeon, New York: Random House, 1941.

Brandon, Barbara, *The Passion Of Ayn Rand*, Garden City, New York: Doubleday & Company, Inc., 1986.

Brooks, N.C., *A Complete History Of The Mexican War: Its Causes, Conduct, And Consequences: Comprising An Account Of The Various Military And Naval Operations, From Its Commencement To The Treaty Of Peace*, Philadelphia: Grigg, Elliot & Co., 1849.

Brooks, Van Wyck, *New England: Indian Summer, 1865-1915*, Chicago: University Of Chicago Press, 1950.

Carroll, Charles Holt, *Organization of Debt Into Currency and Other Papers*, edited by Edward C. Simmons, Princeton, NJ: D. Van Nostrand, Inc., 1964.

Chevalier, Michael, *Society, Manners And Politics In The UNITED STATES: BEING a SERIES OF LETTERS ON NORTH AMERICA, English translation*, Boston: Weeks, Jordan and Company, 1839.(Reprinted, New York: Augustus M. Kelly, Publishers, 1966).

De Morgan, Augustus, *The Connexion Of Number And Magnitude: An Attempt To Explain The Fifth Book Of Euclid*, London: Taylor And Walton, 1836.

De Tocqueville, Alexis, *Democracy In America*, translated by Henry Reeve, Esq., New York: Adlard And Saunders, 1838. (Reprinted, New York: Classics Of Liberty Library, 1992.)

Den Uyl, Douglas J. and Rasmussen, Douglas B., editors, *The Philosophic Thought of Ayn Rand*, Urbana, Illinois: University of Illinois Press, 1986.

Einstein, Albert, *Relativity: The Special and the General Theory*, translated by Robert W. Lawson, New York: Crown Publishers, 1960.

Erickson, Peter F., *The New Introduction to THE TRIPARTITE SYSTEM: A Monetary Program for Americans*, Portland, OR: Privately Printed

Engels, Friedrich, *Herr Eugen Dühring's Revolution in Science: Anti-Dühring*, translated, Chicago: Charles H. Kerr & CO., 1935.

Engels, Frederick, *Ludwig Feuerbach and the Outcome of Classical German Philosophy*, edited by C. P. Dutt, New York: International Publishers, 1941.

Euclid, *The Thirteen Books Of Euclid's Elements*, 2nd Ed., *Revised With Additions*, With Introduction And Commentary by Sir Thomas L. Heath, New York: Dover Publications, 1956.

Frank, Philipp, *Einstein: His Life And Times*, translated by George Rosen, edited by Shuichi Kusaka, New York: Alfred A. Knopf, Inc., 1953.

Friedman, Milton and Schwartz, Anna Jacobson, *A Monetary History of the United States*, Princeton, NJ: Princeton University, 1963.

Gould, James L. Gould, Grant, *The Animal Mind*, New York: N.Y.: Scientific American Library, 1994.

Graves, Robert Perceval, *Life Of Sir William Rowan Hamilton*, Dublin: Hodges, Figgis & Co., 1882, (Reprinted, New York: Arno Press, 1975).

Hawtry, R. G. *The Gold Standard in Theory and Practice*, London: Longmans, Green, 1931.

James, William, *The Letters of William James*, edited by Henry James, Boston: Atlantic Monthly Press, 1920.

Joachim, Harold, *The Nature Of Truth: An Essay*, Oxford At Clarendon, 1906.

Joseph, H. W. B., *An Introduction To Logic, 2nd Edition*, Oxford At Clarendon Press, 1916

Kant, Immanuel, *Immanuel Kant's Critique Of Pure Reason*, translated by F. Max Muller, 2nd ed., London: The MacMillan Company, 1896.

Kraus, Gerhard, *Has Hawking Erred? London:* Janus Publishing Co., 1993.

Lenin, V. I., *Materialism And Empirio-Criticism: Comments On A Reactionary Philosophy*, translated, Moscow: Progress Publishers, 1968.

Lenin, V. I., *Philosophical Notebooks, Collected Works, Vol. 38*, translated by Clemens Dutt, Moscow, Russia: Progress Publishers, 1968.

348

Lieber, Lillian and Hugh Gray, *The Einstein Theory Of Relativity*, New York: Holt, Rinehart and Winston, 1945.

Lovejoy, Arthur O., *The Revolt Against Dualism: An Inquiry Concerning the existence of Ideas*, 2nd *Ed.*, La Salle, Illinois, 1960.

McCosh, Rev. James, *The Intuitions Of The Mind: Inductively Investigated*, 3rd *Ed.*, New York: Robert Carter and Brothers, 1872.

Mansell, Donald E., *The Mystery of Consciousness*, Boise, ID: Pacific Press Publishing Association, 1988.

Mill, James, *Analysis Of The Phenomena Of The Human Mind*, edited with additional notes by John Stuart Mill, London: Longmans, Green, Reader, and Dyer, 1873.

Mill, John Stuart, *Auguste Compte and Positivism*, Ann Arbor, Michigan: The University Press, 1961.

Nordenson, Harold, *Relativity Time And Reality*, London: George Allen and Unwin, Ltd., 1969.

Paterson, Isabel, *The God Of The Machine*, Caldwell, ID: Caxton Printers, 1943.

Peikoff, Leonard, *Objectivism: The Philosophy Of Ayn Rand*, New York: Dutton, 1991.

Rand, Ayn, *Atlas Shrugged*, New York: Random House, 1957.

Rand, Ayn, *Capitalism: The Unknown Ideal, With additional articles by Nathaniel Brandon, Alan Greenspan, and Robert Hessen*, New York: The New American Library, 1967.

Rand, Ayn, *For The New Intellectual*, New York: Signet, N. Y.: Scientific American Library, 1994.

Rand, Ayn, *Introduction To the Objectivist Epistemology, With An Additional Essay by Leonard Peikoff, Expanded 2nd Edition*, edited by Harry Binswanger and Leonard Peikoff, New York: Meridian, 1990.

Rand, Ayn, *Letters Of Ayn Rand*, New York, NY: Dutton, 1995.

Rand, Ayn, *Philosophy: Who Needs It*, New York: Bobs-Merrill, 1982.

Rand, Ayn, *The Virtue Of Selfishness: A New Concept of Egoism With Additional Articles by Nathaniel Brandon*, New York: Signet, 1964.

Robbins, John W., *Answer To Ayn Rand: A Critique of the Philosophy of Objectivism*, Washington, DC: Mount Vernon Publishing Co., 1974.

Rothbard, Murray N., *What Has Government Done To Our Money?* Auburn, Alabama: Praxeology Press, 1990.

Sciabarra, Chris Matthew, *Ayn Rand: The Russian Radical*, University Park, Pennsylvania: The Pennsylvania State University Press, 1995.

Shibley, George H., *Stable Money, New Freedom, and Safe Banking, Providing in the Democratic Banking and Currency Bill, with Three Exceptions*, 63 rd Congress, 1st Session, Doc. No. 135.

W. T. Stace, *The Philosophy Of Hegel*, New York: Dover Publications, 1955.

Walker, Francis Amasa, *International Bimetallism*, New York: Henry Holt and Company, 1896.

Storey, Justice Joseph, *Commentaries on the Constitution, 2nd Ed.*, Boston: Little, Brown & Co., 1851. Cf., Anastaplo, etc.

Sudoplatov, Pavel and Anatoli, *Special Tasks: The Memoirs Of An Unwanted Witness—A Soviet Spymaster*, Boston: Little, Brown and Company, 1994.

Turner, Dean and Richard Hazelett, editors and commentators, *The Einstein Myth and the Ives Papers: A Counter-Revolution in Physics*, Old Greenwich, Connecticut: Devin-Adair Co., Publishers, 1993.

Wetter, Gustave, *Dialectical Materialism: A Historical and systematic Survey of Philosophy in the Soviet Union*, translated by Peter Heath, New York: Frederick A. Praeger, 1958.

Wilson, John Cook, *On The Traversing of Geometrical Figures*, Oxford At the Clarendon Press, 1905.

Wilson, John Cook, *Statement and Inference With Other Philosophical Papers*, Oxford At The Clarendon Press, 1926.

ARTICLES

Hurst, Martha, "CAN THE LAW OF CONTRADICTION BE STATED WITHOUT REFERENCE TO TIME?", *Journal OF Philosophy, Vol. XXXI*, (Sept. 13, 1934.

Ives, Herbert, "Derivation of the Mass-Energy Relation," *The Journal OF The Optical Society Of America, Vol. 42, No. 8*, (August, 1952); Cf., also Turner, etc.

McClary, Thomas, "Banking and Currency Reform. Its Necessity. Its Possibility" 62nd Congress, 2nd Session, *Document No. 295*.

Rand, Ayn, "The Fascist New Frontier," New York: The Nathaniel Brandon Institute, 1963.

Rand, Ayn "Notes on the Thomas Committee," *The Intellectual Activist*, Vol. 7, No. 6, November 1993.

Ratliff, Floyd, "Contour And Contrast," *Scientific American, Vol. 226, no. 6,* (June, 1972).

Walsh, George V., "Ayn Rand And The Metaphysics Of Kant," Privately Printed, 1992.

DICTIONARY

The New Century Dictionary and Cyclopedia With A New Atlas Of The World: A Work Of General Reference In All Departments Of Knowledge, Vol. VIII, New York, N.Y.:The Century CO., 1911.

SHEET MUSIC

Livingston, Jay & Evans, Ray, *Qui Sera, Sera or Whatever will be will be,* New York: Artists Music, Inc., 1955.

RECORDING

William F. Buckley, Jr., "A Tribute To Barry Goldwater," *National Review # 1*—33 1/3 RPM High Fidelity Record, New York: National Review, Inc., 1960.

PHOTOGRAPH

"Gaseous Pillars in M 16, Eagle Nebula, Hubble Space Telescope, WFPC2", Greenbelt, MD: NASA/Goddard Space Flight Center.

Index

A

absence 1, 13, 14, 29, 31, 34,
  37, 126, 140-142, 145, 146
absolute 4, 5, 38, 99, 102,
  103, 104, 108, 109, 110,
  113, 114, 143, 147, 152,
  162, 230, 233, 242, 286,
  308
abstraction 1, 30, 31, 33, 36,
  99, 132, 135, 146, 170,
  172, 234
algebra 122
altruism 7, 21, 262, 263,
  264, 268, 269
animals 1, 102, 116, 117, 118,
  120, 121, 128
anti-Communist 217, 317
apprehend 235, 238, 239, 241
apprehension 235, 236, 238-
  241
Aristotle 228, 242, 245
art 2, 3, 4, 5, 6, 308, 309,
  310, 311, 314, 315, 317
Atlas Shrugged 2, 6
attribute 71, 75, 79-81, 83-86,
  90, 93, 96, 100, 120, 122

B

Bible 2, 4, 5
bimetallism 294
Buckley, William F. 1

C

caloric 66
capitalism 3 6, 23, 310, 311,
  313
cardinal 52
Catholic 308
causality 30, 31, 53, 121,
  122, 126, 135, 148, 152,
  154, 158, 159, 161, 171,
  241, 272, 273, 280, 281,
  285
chair 222, 223, 224
Chevalier, Michael 308
circle 307
commensurable 219
Compte, Auguste 264, 265,
  269
conceivability 189
class 155, 166, 267, 269
color 18, 19, 43-45, 47, 48,
  57, 58, 60-64, 67, 68,
  70, 75, 76, 80-84, 90,
  100, 132-135, 138, 139,
  170
colour 72
concept 9, 10, 16-19, 27,
  29, 31-33, 36, 61, 71,
  72, 74-77, 79-86, 89, 90,
  94, 95, 100, 101, 106, 112,
  114-120, 127, 128, 131-133,
  135, 140, 141, 145, 147,
  148, 154, 157, 159, 160,
  168, 173-176, 184, 186,
  187, 191, 192, 201, 204,
  216, 222, 224, 234, 249-
  251, 254, 255, 261, 269,
  272, 283, 291, 293, 299,
  301

Conceptual Common Denominator 81, 82, 84, 88, 91, 92, 132, 145, 160, 251, 292

consciousness 8, 17-19, 22, 117, 118, 120, 121, 125, 128

conservatism 1

conservative 1

context 9, 10, 101, 104, 107, 109, 110, 113-115, 117, 127, 129

contextual 9, 102, 104, 107, 108-110, 113, 114

contextual absolute 108-110, 113, 114, 286

contextuality 109

contradiction 10, 18

convertible money 301, 305

Copernicus 111, 112

creation 252, 268

D

De Morgan, Augustus 89

de Tocqueville, Alexis 307

definition 8, 9, 18, 19, 45, 48, 49, 55, 76, 85, 86, 95, 96, 100-102, 104-107, 109, 111, 115, 116, 118 121, 129, 149, 167, 171, 176, 180, 191, 228, 233, 254, 257, 258, 263, 265

Descartes, R. 57, 217

determinism 280, 281

dialectical 21, 22, 150, 197, 200, 201-11, 213-219, 271

Dialectical Materialism 21, 197, 199, 201, 203, 204, 205, 206, 207, 208, 209, 210, 211, 213, 214, 216, 217, 218, 219

dialectics 97, 202, 209, 211, 244

dualism 44, 51, 98, 164, 203, 204

E

Einstein, Albert 103, 104, 190, 191, 193, 194, 195, 196, 197, 208, 209, 216

Einsteinian 51, 192, 195, 197

empiricism 35, 59

energy puffs 44, 45, 97, 147, 179

Engels, Frederick 22, 150, 209, 210

entity 10, 12, 43, 62, 226, 231, 233

epistemology 77, 103, 113, 159, 196, 197, 199, 207, 251

Euclid 56, 62, 78, 105, 137, 138

Existence 131, 132, 148, 152, 194, 234, 235, 236, 237, 239, 240, 241

existence 26, 27, 37, 38, 44, 50, 53, 60-62, 64, 78, 79, 95, 120-122, 127-141, 143, 145-148, 152-155, 158-161, 167, 168, 171, 172, 174, 177-179, 183, 185, 193, 194, 201-205, 209, 213, 214, 223, 227, 228, 232-242, 247, 248, 251, 252, 254-256, 259, 263, 265, 282, 283, 285, 287, 289, 301

existent 27, 34, 56, 72, 76, 78 80, 85, 93, 100, 101,

115, 133, 139-141, 145
147, 148, 154, 158, 182,
203, 211, 234, 237, 242,
243
existential 47
existentialism 132
extension 56-58, 60-62, 64,
66, 67
extrospection 33, 36

F

fact 42, 43, 44, 47, 49, 52,
55, 58, 132-134, 136-138,
140, 141, 143-146, 151,
153, 161, 163, 166, 167,
169, 172, 201, 202, 204,
212-214, 222, 226, 229
234, 237, 241
242, 244, 245
fact-value distinction 9, 10,
249, 254
Factivity 318
FDR 217, 301, 309, 310
Federal Reserve 296, 303, 304
finite 142, 150, 169, 213,
215, 219
finitude 184, 188, 293
force 106, 107, 120, 121,
125, 158, 203, 274, 298,
313, 314
fractional reserve banking
296, 301, 304, 305
free will 232, 243
Friedman, Milton 295, 296,
317
furniture 81, 92
future 19, 36, 174, 180, 185,
204, 217, 236, 237, 239,
240, 268, 273, 286, 293,
313

G

Galileo, G. 112
Galt, John 3, 6, 11, 188,
248, 251, 252
geometry 34
God 4, 16, 234, 236, 243-
245, 250, 251, 256, 258,
261, 266, 267
gold 291-301, 303-305
Gould, James L. and Grant 31
Government 23, 105
government 105, 106, 107,
153, 217, 225, 226, 289,
291, 294, 298, 300, 301,
305, 308, 310-312, 313,
316
Grant, General and President
Ulysses S. 31
grant 211, 258, 262
Greenspan, Alan 3, 303, 304
gremlins 142

H

Hamilton, Sir William Rowan
33, 98
Hasenöhrl, Friedrich 103
Hazelett, Richard 194
Hazlitt, Henry 290, 317
hearing 42, 118, 121,
206, 282
heat 57, 58, 65, 66,
67, 97, 128, 160, 251, 282
Hegel, G.W. 131, 143,
188, 195, 210, 211, 215
Hegelian 210, 215, 216
Hollinger, Robert 274-276
Hollywood Ten 316
Hume, David 135, 149, 279
Hurst , Martha 151

I

idealism 2, 20, 22, 23, 201, 205, 208, 209

identity 11, 16, 18, 27, 46, 53, 59, 72, 74, 78, 131, 132, 139, 147-162, 164, 167, 169, 171, 174, 183, 187, 194, 210, 213, 216, 220, 228, 234, 241, 242, 251

imagination 5, 35, 37, 84, 128, 129, 238, 239, 244, 302

incommensurable 82, 83, 85, 89, 90, 118, 143, 177, 185, 204, 210, 304

induction 37, 122, 124

infinite 21, 23, 89, 121, 142, 180, 181, 184, 185, 186, 188, 189, 201, 205, 209, 217

infinity 21, 88, 89, 104, 122, 180, 181, 184, 185, 187-189, 213, 217, 219, 230, 251, 281

integration 42, 61, 76, 95, 99, 141, 290

introspection 33, 36, 312

J

James, William 273, 274, 309, 311

Joachim, Harold 143

Joseph, H.W.B. 309, 317

K

Kant, Immanuel 17, 37, 38, 41, 61, 131, 150, 159, 164, 168, 169, 176, 182, 227, 245, 273

Keller, Helen 38

Kepler, Johannes 112

L

Lee, Robert E. 287, 308

length 50, 57, 58, 60, 62, 83-93, 105, 118, 137, 185

Lenin , V.I. 21, 22, 199, 203, 206, 208-215, 217, 271, 282

life 2, 5, 6, 9-12, 14-16, 26, 50, 54, 69, 91, 98, 111, 117, 123, 151, 152, 158, 163, 240, 244, 248-258, 261-263, 265-268, 273, 275, 283, 285, 286, 310, 318

Locke, John 57, 59, 61, 69, 148, 217, 243, 313

Losky, N.O. 200, 201

Lovejoy, Alfed O. 51, 52, 55, 114, 183

M

MacArthur, General Douglas 276, 309

Marx, Karl 22, 23, 209, 215, 216

Marxism 5, 22, 97, 206, 207, 213, 215, 217, 218, 219, 259

Marxism-Leninism 22, 97, 206, 215, 217

Marxist 21, 23, 150, 199, 203, 206, 210, 216, 244, 257, 259, 266, 271, 317 materialism 20, 21, 22, 150, 182, 197, 199, 201, 203-211, 213, 214, 216-219, 271

Materialism and Empirio-Criticism 208

materialist 98, 199, 214, 215

mathematics 18, 29, 34, 75, 76, 86, 89, 92, 93, 97, 142, 143, 305

Matson, Wallace 19, 72

matter 12, 17, 19-23, 31, 44, 48, 53, 77, 78, 82, 84, 87, 94, 96, 98, 103, 110, 123, 124, 125, 140, 151, 152, 154, 159, 161, 178, 179, 182, 183, 186, 188-190, 201, 203, 204, 209, 210, 212-217, 220, 230, 231, 235, 238, 240-243, 244, 247, 250, 254, 255, 263, 277-279, 283, 287, 313

McCarthy, Senator Joseph 280, 309, 317

McCosh, James 140

measurement 72, 75-77, 81-83, 85, 86, 93, 94, 96, 97, 173, 177, 197, 213, 247, 248

melody 34, 37

memory 33-37, 54, 67, 75, 79, 84, 124, 125, 128, 138, 144, 145, 151, 158, 162, 164, 165, 167, 175, 182, 196, 233, 235, 301

metaphysical 19, 47, 76, 79, 92, 93, 101, 102, 104, 108, 123, 129, 130, 138, 144, 148, 149, 175, 184, 187, 205, 226, 230, 281, 282, 284-287

metaphysically 10, 44, 77, 92, 105, 110, 122, 153, 173, 202, 237

metaphysics 19, 20, 23, 39, 97, 103, 156, 188, 196, 199, 258, 271

Mexican 297, 308

Mill, John Stuart 35

mind 4, 14, 17, 18, 19, 20, 22, 26, 31-38, 41, 45, 59, 71, 74, 76, 77, 80, 84, 85, 98, 114, 116, 126, 129-131, 133, 135, 136, 138-140, 145, 159, 164, 165, 169, 178, 179, 187, 196, 203-206, 208, 209, 214, 220, 226, 235, 238, 242, 244, 251, 253, 277, 283, 310, 313

miracles 148

moiré 54, 55, 90

money 8, 13, 14, 258, 259, 263, 266, 288, 289, 291-294, 296, 297, 300-305, 310

monism 20, 22, 204, 213, 282

monist 20, 215

motion 54, 55, 57, 66, 67, 113, 120, 166, 176-179, 181, 186-188, 194, 195, 201, 209-213, 215-217, 230, 231, 251, 271, 298

music 6, 67, 68, 70, 98, 182, 239, 308

N

Natural Number 91

necessity 37, 79, 100, 120-122, 125, 126, 128, 129,

146, 152-158, 160, 168, 169, 187, 237, 272, 279, 281, 286

New Deal 259, 289, 310

Newton, Sir Isaac 112, 217, 245, 305

Nietzsche, Frederick 7, 16, 21

non-existence 10, 12, 140, 143, 234, 236, 237, 239, 241

non-repeatable 230, 231, 233, 242

number 21, 26, 32, 33, 76-78, 87-93, 96, 104, 118, 120-124, 142, 143, 148, 149, 151, 152, 159, 176, 181, 185, 186, 189, 212, 230, 259, 266, 296, 311, 312, 314

O

object 8, 9, 25-27, 30, 36, 45-50, 52, 53, 55, 57, 58, 60, 61, 64, 71, 73, 75, 80, 82, 84, 90, 93, 95, 107, 108, 135, 139, 154, 155, 160, 162, 164, 166, 168, 204, 206, 207, 210, 213, 215, 220, 222-224, 228, 233

objective 4, 5, 17, 21, 38, 48, 51, 52, 54, 55, 57, 58, 80, 108, 129, 160, 162, 199, 201, 206, 207, 213, 214, 235, 241, 242

Objectivism 7, 12, 17, 19, 20, 22, 24, 25, 29, 33, 34, 41, 43, 44, 48-50, 54, 68, 72, 81, 82, 121, 130, 134, 147, 149, 150, 169,

171, 174, 175, 190, 193 197, 199, 204, 205, 207, 214, 217-220, 231, 236, 248, 253, 259, 272, 287

op art 54, 160

Oppenheimer, Robert 208

ordinal 96, 97

organization 30, 224, 225, 226, 227

Orwell, George 2

P

Paley, William 243

particular 11, 15, 26, 28, 29, 38, 50, 71, 76, 78, 80, 81, 85, 95, 96, 100, 105, 114, 125, 133, 137, 140, 146, 154, 155, 157, 171, 173, 183, 190, 191, 222-230, 232, 233, 245

particulars 19, 72, 79, 120, 136, 137, 157, 172, 221-227, 229

past 6, 7, 19, 34-37, 111, 123, 152, 167, 171, 174, 175, 177, 180, 181, 185, 218, 230, 236, 237, 239, 240-242, 273, 286, 287, 305

Peikoff, Leonard 13, 20, 28 31, 37, 43, 44, 46-50, 54, 61, 77, 97, 109, 110-112, 123, 142, 146-149, 153, 154, 157-159, 163, 164, 169, 180, 181, 195, 202, 203, 204, 272, 276

percept 26, 32, 35, 45, 48,

perception 17, 25, 30, 33, 34, 37, 38, 41, 43-45, 51, 53, 58-62, 64, 68,

75, 79, 108, 116, 126,
127, 129, 139, 146, 154,
164, 165, 166, 169-171,
180, 182, 187, 201, 205,
212, 220, 251
petitio principii 179
Planck, Max 103
Plato 17, 200, 242, 245
Poincaré, Henri 103
positivism 4, 264
possibility 14, 36, 111, 112,
123, 129, 138, 149, 153,
171, 186, 189, 191, 211,
220, 230, 237, 252, 267,
277, 278, 284, 286
primacy of consciousness
17, 22, 202
primacy of existence 17, 22,
202
Protagoras 76
Protestant 307, 308
Protestantism 1, 308
Puritans 316
Pythagorean 86, 87, 123

Q

quality 45, 50, 57, 58, 60,
63, 65, 69, 72, 84, 97,
100, 124, 128, 144, 189,
199, 206, 215, 223, 227,
229, 257
quantity 85, 94, 95, 97, 100,
135, 137, 143, 162, 185,
188, 189, 199, 257, 292,
305

R

race 90, 231, 262, 267, 268,
285, 310
racism 3, 290

reason 5, 9, 10, 11, 16, 17,
19, 28, 31, 46, 51, 58,
60, 70, 79, 95, 112, 118,
121, 125, 129, 130, 132,
133, 135, 136, 141, 146,
158, 164, 168, 175, 180,
182, 183, 187, 194, 196,
197, 207, 220, 232, 233,
237, 245, 252, 253, 259,
261, 265, 274, 286, 315
relative 50, 61, 62, 65, 102,
103, 104, 113, 114, 160,
180, 182, 205, 206, 292,
301, 303
relativity 103, 170, 190, 192-
195, 197, 208, 209
RH factor 109, 110
Renouvier, Charles 273, 274,
278
repeatable 230-234, 241, 242,
244, 245
Rienzi 37
Robbins, John W. 80, 114
Roosevelt, Franklin 259
Rosenbaum, Alice 200
Russia 2

S

Schwartz, Anna Jacobson
295, 296
Sciabarra, Chris Matthew
200, 201, 204
Second Amendment 106
second Amendment 106
selfishness 3, 23, 258-262
sensation 21, 25, 35, 36, 41,
42, 50, 127, 128, 164,
168, 171, 201, 206, 210
sensations 24-27, 30, 33, 35,
41, 42, 43, 56, 76, 93,
135, 201, 205, 206, 208,
271

Seurat, Georges 67
Shelley, Percy Bysshe 69
sight 42, 44, 55, 56, 64, 77,
    93, 114, 118, 126, 149,
    165, 2 82
silver 276, 294-301, 305
similarity 71, 72, 77- 80, 82,
    85, 91, 95, 99, 165, 167,
    196, 206, 215-217, 221,
    222, 228, 229, 291
simultaneity 177, 187, 191
smell 28, 43, 48, 282
social contract 225, 226, 266,
    313, 314
socialism 290, 311, 317
Soviet 2, 21, 150, 200, 201,
    217-219, 225, 290, 317
space 21, 38, 39, 45, 55, 64,
    90, 94, 107, 140, 146-
    148, 151, 152, 159, 172,
    173, 176-178, 181-190,
    193, 194, 196, 211-217,
    220, 230, 233, 235, 238,
    240, 243, 245, 247, 251,
    287, 293, 294
Stalin, J.V. 97, 202, 203, 219,
    244, 282
Statement And Inference 122
stereoscopic 38, 77, 114
Story, Justice Joseph 106,
story 90, 93, 128, 166, 200,
    236, 259, 281
subject 39, 45-49, 52, 53, 61,
    102, 106, 108, 111, 116,
    122, 142, 162, 167, 169,
    190, 204, 207, 209, 215,
    220, 225-227, 269, 277,
    278, 280, 300
subjective 36, 37, 48, 53, 68,
    107, 108, 126, 128, 160,

    183, 206, 207, 213, 214,
    224, 234, 236, 241, 242,
    265
syllogism 141, 156, 157, 179
syllogistic 146, 147

T

Taft, Senator Robert A. 309
taste 42, 50, 58, 67, 282
teleological measurement 97,
    247, 248
The Animal Mind 31
the animal mind 32
The Fountainhead 2, 293
The Revolt Against Dualism 51
The Virtue Of Selfishness 3
TIME 36, 173
time 1, 3, 5,-7, 13, 14, 16,
    19, 21, 24, 27, 28, 31,
    33-39, 49, 55, 64, 66, 70,
    71, 73, 74, 76, 77, 104,
    106, 110, 111, 113-116,
    122, 123, 125, 127, 128,
    130, 140, 142-147, 148,
    150-152, 155, 158, 159,
    162, 172, 173-194, 196,
    200, 203, 209-217, 220,
    224, 230, 231, 233, 235,
    236, 238-241, 245, 247,
    249, 250, 251, 260, 262,
    266, 272-276, 279, 285,
    289, 290, 293, 294, 296-
    300,
    302, 305, 307-311
triangle 185
Tripartite System 305
Turner, Dean 194

U

unit 21, 27, 29, 32, 72, 75-77, 79-83, 85-93, 95-97, 99, 100, 114, 118, 119, 143, 147, 154, 175, 177, 185, 190, 219, 291, 292, 295, 305
unity of opposites 203, 215
universal
52, 62, 78, 100, 107, 121, 136, 137, 140, 148, 154, 167, 171, 172, 192, 194, 215, 221, 222, 224-233, 244, 245, 264, 265
UNIVERSALS 101, 221
universals
18, 37, 72, 79, 80, 85, 120, 125, 127, 129, 136, 142, 172, 220-223, 228-233, 242, 244

V

value 8-11, 13, 14, 204, 216, 249, 251-258, 260, 262, 264, 279, 282, 283, 291, 293-295, 299, 300, 301, 315
volition 23
volitional 272, 291

W

Walker, Francis Amasa 298
Wetter, Gustave 21, 214
Wilson, John Cook 37, 61, 102, 122, 160, 223, 228

Z

Zeno 185, 211
zero 92, 140, 142, 143, 152, 178, 210

ORDER FORM

Name _____

Address_____

City/State/Zip_____

Phone_____

Enclosed is my check for $23.95 [$19.95 For THE STANCE OF ATLAS: AN EXAMINATION OF THE PHILOSOPHY OF AYN RAND] and $4 for shipping and handling.

Credit card #_____
Expiration date:_____
    MasterCard__Visa__American Express__

Books to be shipped within 48 hours of order placement (holidays excepted).

HERAKLES PRESS, INC.
P.O. Box 8725
Portland, OR 97201-5421

Toll free 1-888-492-2001